To
Whose ~~Will~~
Love is Timeless.
Thank you for being
a true friend.
Michael Robb

ALCOHOLISM

TREATABLE ILLNESS

J. George Strachan

Orca Book Publishers

Canadian Cataloguing in Publication Data
Strachan, J. George, 1914-
   Alcoholism

   ISBN 0-920501-35-4
   1. Alcoholism. 2. Alcoholism — Treatment.
I. Title
HV5276.S87 1990   362.92'2   C90-091117-4

This book was first published as
Alcoholism: Treatable Illness,
An Honorable Approach to Man's Alcoholism Problem
by Mitchell Press Limited
Vancouver, B.C.   Canada, 1967.

An up-dated Edition was published in April of 1982 by
the Hazelden Foundation, Center, Minnesota.

All names and places in the experiences and case histories
cited have been changed to protect the persons involved.

The Author

Orca Book Publishers Ltd.
P.O. Box 5626, Stn. B,
Victoria, B.C., V8R 6S4

Cover design by Rick Dykun
Typeset by the University of Victoria Students' Society Graphics Shop
Printed in Canada by Hignell Printing Ltd., Winnipeg, Manitoba

To Jane, with love and gratitude
for tolerance and devotion
above the call of wifely duty!

And to R. Brinkley Smithers, staunch friend,
my deep appreciation
for making this work possible.

"There are no hopeless situations;
there are only men
who have grown hopeless about them."

Anonymous

Contents

Preface

by J.A.L. Gilbert, M.D.
F.A.C.P., F.R.C.P.(LOND), F.R.C.P.(E), F.R.C.P.(C)

Dr. Gilbert is Professor of Medicine at the University of Alberta. An internationally recognized expert in the field of medical education, Dr. Gilbert directs research in medical education for the Faculty of Medicine and is in charge of the teaching program in internal medicine at the Royal Alexandra Hospital. He is also Chairman of the Curriculum Advisory Committee for the Faculty of Medicine at the University of Alberta.

He has been active in research programs in the fields of diabetes and alcoholism. Long concerned with the illness alcoholism and the critical role it plays in retarding recovery from other illness, he incorporates lectures about alcoholism in his curriculum for medical students.

Dr. Gilbert came to the University of Alberta from the University of Edinburgh in 1950 and was appointed a full time professor at the University of Alberta in 1957.

Dr. Gilbert has authored numerous papers and contributed to many books. His recent book entitled **Evaluation in Medical Education,** *has received wide acclaim.*

The magnitude of the alcoholism problem is almost incomprehensible; as a single cause of human suffering it probably ranks only behind that of starvation. Apart from Eskimos in their natural habitat, and a few religious sects, man has used alcohol since time immemorial. Nevertheless, only in the past few decades has society begun to appreciate the enormity of the problems caused by the abuse of alcohol and the magnitude of the ensuing social and economic tragedies.

Defining the alcoholic as one who cannot function without the drug, the incidence is conservatively estimated at 1,000,000 in Canada and 10,000,000 in the United States. Alcoholism is a cause of widespread misery, loss of family income, marital heartbreak and conflict. As an adverse factor in recovery from other ills, and as an entree to drug addiction, alcohol plays a paramount role. Moreover, as a disrupting force in the national economy, impairing lay and professional skills, alcohol has few equals. Alcoholism is one of the commonest causes of absenteeism, tardiness, termination, inefficiency, waste, and breakdowns in morale and supervision. The magnitude of both direct and indirect costs makes it nearly impossible to spell out the resulting loss of national revenue or the compounded costs generated among health, welfare, legal, correctional and other institutions. These adverse effects are not balanced by government taxation on beverage alcohol and the benefits allegedly accruing from such revenues.

To evaluate the problem in a single country or community is no less difficult. Since alcoholism remains shrouded by a certain social stigmata, its diagnosis is often over-simplified as a headache and party hangover, or on the other hand, misrepresented as a shortlived socially acceptable organic disease, such as 'flu or migraine. Critical to these attitudes, it is of considerable interest that in spite of man's long craving for and dependence on this drug, until only recently, little has been done in the way of research in depth, either at a psychological or organic level.

The excessive use of alcohol, an expression of self indulgence, resembles the use of food by the obese person, who no less than the alcoholic, is gluttonous, although through a different medium. However, to single out the alcoholic as an isolated expression of over-indulgence is not entirely valid. And, too, although the effect of obesity may be tragic to the patient, it does not generally subject the family to the misery of the alcoholic relative.

Since World War II, and particularly through the pioneer work of those such as the late Dr. E.M. Jellinek and the author, a more humane and intelligent attitude is being adopted both by the public and the concerned professions in the management of alcoholism. Until several decades ago the alcoholic was largely left on his own and only those strongly motivated to stop drinking did so. No longer regarded as beyond the pale of therapy, the alcoholic is now looked on as someone who not only requires treatment, but for whom effective therapy is a probability.

While it is certainly true that the greatest number of recoveries among alcoholics stems from the work of Alcoholics Anonymous, a new team approach involving the co-operative efforts of business, industry, labor, and the personnel management of governmental, civil and military services physicians, psychiatrists, psychologists, social workers, sociologists, the clergy, and the judiciary, is generally contributive to this success rate. Nevertheless, their combined efforts are still not stemming the ever-increasing tide of alcoholism. Much more still needs to be done, especially by the healing professions, if the recovery rate is to approach that of the incidence.

Lack of investigation into the effects of alcohol has been even more marked in the organic than in the psychic field. Thus, only in recent years is the metabolism of this substance being investigated and high level symposia on the basic aspects of its chemical effects studied. It would seem that there are confirmatory data to substantiate the long held clinical view that the alcoholic utilizes this drug more rapidly

2

than temperate users. It might be, also, that the alcoholic has developed some special type of metabolic pathway.

It is often contended that the alcoholic, prior to realizing the depth and profundity of his or her illness, must have fallen into the abyss commonly referred to as "hitting bottom." In the future we should be able to arrest the illness at a much earlier stage. It is the recognition of this early stage of dependency on alcohol that must be the key to effective diagnosis and treatment. Although there can be few people who at least in some measure have not been affected by alcohol, either personally or in a relative or close associate, there remains a tendency to ignore it, reject it, or at least under-estimate the gravity of alcohol dependency.

Solutions to alcoholism can only come about through better education and appreciation of the illness concept. While no single volume can possibly present a total picture, a book such as the present one makes a significant contribution to informing patients, their families, professional contacts and society of the seriousness of the problem and an acceptable method of dealing with it.

Until only recently the bulk of rehabilitation of the alcoholic has been carried out by such lay organizations as Alcoholics Anonymous — the medical profession as a group tending to avoid these patients for several reasons, not the least of which has been their low recovery rate.

It is apparent that organized medicine will have to assume a more active role in this problem, commencing in the medical school. There can be few, if any, medical schools in which time devoted to the teaching of alcoholism is commensurate with its clinical frequency. Similarly in postgraduate courses, the infrequency with which alcoholism is discussed would lead one to conclude that either it is a rare disorder or one for which there is already a cure. One of the methods of dealing with a difficult problem is to reject it or at least to deny its existence. With a few notable exceptions this has been the role of organized medicine in the management of alcoholism. It is a sad commentary indeed for a teaching physician such as myself to acknowledge that in general, the awareness, knowledge and understanding achieved about this illness has stemmed from the efforts of lay organizations and recovered alcoholics. It is time this was changed.

J.A.L. Gilbert, M.D.

Acknowledgements

One cannot accomplish a project like this alone! I am most grateful to Marge Scott, my personal secretary, for her understanding and critical encouragement. A warm thank you to typists Pam Attchison, Nancy Hill, Sylvia Klarenbach, Terry Kurylow, Cheryl Spicer and Helen Buitendyk; and to Stephen Good, whose editing and assembly assistance in this updating was of inestimable value. In spite of long hours and repetitive drafts we are all still speaking.

A sincere acknowledgement to A.A. General Service Office and particularly to the Christopher D. Smithers Foundation for helping me to initiate this book. May *Alcoholism: Treatable Illness* reward their support and faith.

Each reference source, The General Service Office of Alcoholics Anonymous, The National Council on Alcoholism, The Alcohol and Drug Problem Association of North America, The Rutgers Center on Alcohol Studies, and The Christian Science Monitor, was most co-operative. All permissions to quote from their publications, together with those of Al-Anon Family Group Headquarters, Inc.; The Alcoholism and Drug Addiction Research Foundation of Ontario; Doubleday and Company, Inc.; and the Viking Press are sincerely appreciated.

A particular thank you to T.G. Coffey, T.E. Dancey M.D., J.A.L. Gilbert M.D., D.B. Jones, H. Morse and Associates, C.C. O'Brien Ph.D., L. Skogg, J.D. Taylor Ph.D., and W.E. Wilby for their individual contributions; and to Mr. and Mrs. H.T. Mitchell for their personal interest and guidance.

Much of the general content of this book reflects the experience gained with the Milwaukee Information and Referral Center, the former Alcoholism Foundation of Alberta (now the Alberta Alcohol and Drug Abuse Commission), and The Gillain Foundation and Gillain Manor; programs it was my privilege to develop and direct.

Proper acknowledgements to all concerned will hopefully be expressed better by such contribution as this book may make to the field of alcohol studies, and more particularly to the recovery of the alcoholic who still suffers.

Introduction

Alcoholism, the illness stemming from the misuse and overuse of beverage alcohol, is as ancient and modern as man. It is a tragic waste that the human misery of this illness in virtually every culture, with its consistent medical, social, economic and spiritual implications, has gone so long unattended. It took us until well into this century to realize that we were dealing with a treatable medical ailment. While the Depression of the Thirties shook the whole world, that era did see the birth of a new approach to the problems of alcohol per se and, more importantly, recognition of alcoholism in particular as an illness in the clinical sense.

The dramatic advances we have seen in recent decades stem principally from the dedicated leadership of scientists Dr. H.W. Haggard and Dr. E.M. Jellinek, who in the early 1930s founded the Center on Alcohol Studies (then at Yale University and now at Rutgers University), and of men like Bill Wilson and Dr. Bob Smith, the co-founders, in 1935, of the Fellowship of Alcoholics Anonymous.

Though these four pioneers have not survived to see all the promise of the years ahead, their contributions have served to point the way, stimulating treatment, education and research, and inspiring acceptance of alcoholism as a treatable illness.

As the harbinger of much of today's improving philosophy toward addiction per se and alcoholism in particular, they would be gratified with the ever-increasing acceptance and sensible, dignified approach being demonstrated by a growing segment of society.

The now famous words of *Alcoholics Anonymous* have opened the door to hope and brought recovery, sobriety, sanity, happiness, dignity and serenity to many thousands of alcoholics: "Rarely have we seen a person fail who has thoroughly followed our path."[1] A.A., recognized as one of the greatest sociological phenomena of our time, has demonstrated that the alcoholic is not simply a hopeless case. Countless recoveries convincingly attest to the truth of this dictum.

During his productive life, Dr. E.M. Jellinek contributed more knowledge to the understanding of this ailment than all others combined in the history of medicine and social science. Drawn to this service by his concern for the ordinary man, he devoted himself to his work with a zeal and energy none could match. His contributions were

7

Alcoholism: Treatable Illness

both manifold and magnificent, but the one that stands out most clearly for all to see is his interpretation of alcoholism as a treatable, clinical ailment.[2]

Though much has been learned, said and accomplished to encourage more positive action to cope with alcoholism in the years since Jellinek's original work, two serious issues remain to be faced: firstly, the results achieved to date have hardly been spectacular; secondly, it is time to take inventory of our present position and of future directions in the fight against the ravages of this illness; otherwise, we will forget the most important focus for all services in the field — the individual alcoholic.

Everything about alcoholism has *not* yet been said. Much has been implied — but always nicely. The evil in alcohol is not only its misuse and the problem of dependent drinking; it is the rationale that society fosters (a social factor of first magnitude and priority) which bespeaks a willingness, even an anxiety, to gloss over and close our eyes to the human costs of alcoholism and condone the unacceptable behaviour associated with excessive drinking. Problem drinking and alcoholism continue to be neglected, shunned and ignored. The sick alcoholic should not be made to shoulder all the blame for the situation to which he or she is regularly reduced. The rest of us, the so-called healthy ones, must assume much more responsibility.

We are responsible professionally, because most of us shirk our share of the load; and politically, because governments (including those politicians whose personal beliefs favour temperance) find it more expedient to listen to party purse donors, and so to break or defer political promises "to do something." The religious among us are also responsible, because it is still so much easier to condemn self-righteously while hiding under a cloak of prejudice and false morality. Our legal system is responsible, because of its unwillingness to effect change in established systems, despite the fact that illness cannot be a crime, and that treatment is much more effective and economical than fines or incarceration.

Alcoholism agencies are also responsible, because they sometimes fail to step forward at the times when they should stand, without fear, for the principles they claim to represent. The general public too is itself responsible, because there comes a point when, sensitive to the tragedies occurring almost daily around us, we must acknowledge our duty to protect the dignity that is vital for each of us to survive. We as individuals are accountable, in that as members of the public and of special interest groups or agencies, we must take responsibility for creating new attitudes to approach positively the plight of the millions of people who suffer from the illness alcoholism.

While the alcoholic population includes less than five percent who are the known and *recorded* recidivists, among the other ninety percent who are hidden and unrecorded cases, there are an unknown number of sufferers, the depths of whose illness has not been explored. Some of them are on the fringe of losing everything, and how large a segment of the hidden group these alcoholics represent is totally unknown —although it must be enormous.

Among these hidden alcoholic sufferers are to be found physicians, surgeons and nurses who regularly practice their skills while partially anaesthetized by alcohol, many of them operating on reflex abilities alone. There are lawyers, judges and magistrates charged with protecting and rendering weighty decisions on people and matters while their reason is fogged by their dependency on alcohol. There are men of the cloth striving to give spiritual direction and comfort to members of their flock while suffering acutely the anguish of personal alcoholic conflict; there are "Senator Flagstones" in every level of government allegedly representing the interests of the people, but the strengths which made them fit representatives are now diminished by a perpetual hangover state.

There are prominent personages in positions of confidence and national trust, whose alcohol dependency makes them doubtful security risks. There are air and marine pilots and railroad engineers and bus drivers; and there are the tycoons of business, industry, finance and labour, whose presumed good judgment is impaired by alcohol and whose mistakes cost countless millions of dollars and lives, causing innumerable other problems. There are supervisors, foremen and skilled craftsmen whose alcoholism causes waste and damage, adding an expensive load to an already high cost of living and to production problems. There are the wasted lives of leaders, playwrights, artists. The list is virtually endless.

It is no idle jest when we hear someone say, "God takes care of children and inebriates!" He must, or else their problems with security, morale, judgment, efficiency and the like would have caught up with them long since. However, since we all have had a hand in their protection and sheltering, and helped to keep concealed the harsh facts of alcoholism within a society that grows increasingly complex and that more than ever needs clear-mindedness and an honorable approach, perhaps we should expect nothing else.

We must continue to challenge old attitudes and stereotypes which still prevail. Are we really helping when we laugh at, disdain or ignore those who are ill from alcoholism? It is more likely that we are being defensive about our own ignorance and sense of futility. If we are to approach positively this problem with its millions of sufferers, we must establish an aware and understanding climate to make alcoholics willing to seek the help they need. We can best do this by indicating our willingness to recognize, accept and help them recover from their illness with dignity.

One's immediate reaction and reply could well be that there are slow learners in every calling. While this is true, those afflicted in the named groups and vocations have meaningful roles and, though small in numbers, are vitally important to society. In other words, notwithstanding modern egalitarianism, one doctor,

Alcoholism: Treatable Illness

clergyman or lawyer may proportionately represent a lot more to the community than a person from most other vocations — especially if the doctor, clergyman or lawyer attempts to serve the community while suffering "under the influence" of this disease. The potential for harm is proportionately greater because of the nature of the vocation.

So, why are they allowed to go unattended until a serious episode brings about formal complaints? Why are they not approached more positively by their own peers? Old attitudes, based on the false premise of protecting one's own, create serious problems. Like bad habits, old attitudes are not easily changed. All too many current improvements merely reflect an *intellectual recognition* of the magnitude and costs of alcohol and other drug related abuse — the *emotional or gut acceptance* of the resulting medical, legal, social and spiritual concerns continues to lag far behind.

Nevertheless, it is gratifying to record that much progress is being made in business, industry and labour. As prophesied by the late Dr. E.M. Jellinek, **Employment Assistance Programs** will, in our time, lead the way before the medical and social sciences in achieving recovery programs.

Modelled after these effective early intervention counter-measures developed by industry, the professions are implementing in-house efforts such as "Impaired Physicians" and "Impaired Lawyers" programs. A growing number of governments are investing large sums of money as well, and researchers are even talking about prevention as a more effective coping strategy to deal with alcohol and drug dependency.

Unfortunately, much of this support is not well planned or coordinated with existing resources — and it's often more political than resourceful. Despite all of this alleged performance, adequate treatment resources are tragically lacking for the majority of those afflicted, especially among the poor, the young and the senior. For them, alcohol abuse remains the most neglected and ignored issue of our time.

There are still charlatans who prey upon the alcoholic's illness as fair game. Thankfully, the number of these has also decreased somewhat in recent years; but the unethical practices of even a few such have raised barriers of distrust between alcoholics and some members of the professions, effectively deferring or preventing the alcoholic's recovery.

Responsible lay, professional and governmental leaders, the public at large, and we as individuals must appreciate the many adverse influences deterring a realistic understanding of the problems of alcohol and alcoholism. Practising and recovering alcoholics, their families, recovered members of Alcoholics Anonymous and workers in the field all must be equally knowledgeable of the barriers that block positive recognition and response to this medical and social disorder. Individual recovery is not quite enough.

Alcoholism: Treatable Illness covers the spectrum of these problems. It is dedicated to the goal of achieving a common denominator of awareness, knowledge and understanding of alcoholism as a treatable illness. It reviews the nature and magnitude of the illness, the confusion of attitudes that prevail about it, and the range and extent of problems that the use, abuse and misuse of alcohol can create. This book emphasizes the importance of achieving a more realistic and acceptable image of the alcoholic. It outlines the philosophy and techniques essential to the treatment of the individual patient, spouse and family. It describes the role of collaterals regularly exposed to problem drinking situations. The importance of the Fellowship of Alcoholics Anonymous to successful treatment is affirmed.

An earlier book, *Practical Alcoholism Programming*, interprets alcoholism as a public health problem and responsibility of major proportions. To this end, community roles and programming needs are explored. It outlines the prerequisites essential to sound programming and the obstacles and pitfalls to be avoided in planning overall services. The manuscript charts the course of administrative, treatment, educational, research and community services which are essential to a comprehensive and effective *total program*. The relationship of Alcoholics Anonymous to public level programming is fully and impersonally defined, with particular emphasis on the Fellowship's precept, "Cooperation **yes**, but affiliation **no.**"

An appendix section of the book includes a summary of the early history, organizational structure, function and goals of the major organizations active in the field of alcoholism study, control and prevention.

The author, a recovered alcoholic who has spent over forty-five years in the field of alcohol studies, while not against the moderate and controlled use of beverage alcohol, is admittedly against its overuse and misuse, feeling there is a real urgency to do much more for those who incur alcoholism. To the end that more can, should and will be done, this book is directed.

When you and I and the man on the street — as the result of achieved awareness, knowledge and understanding — believe and voice the same acceptance of alcoholism as a treatable illness, both intellectually and emotionally, alcoholism will be on the road to control, and perhaps even eventual prevention.

J. George Strachan

Notes

1. *Alcoholics Anonymous* — Chapter V, "How it Works," (first published in 1939). Reprinted with permission of the Directors of A.A. World Services, Inc.

2. *Alcohol Explored* — by H.W. Haggard and E.M. Jellinek. Copyright 1942 by Doubleday & Company, Inc. — with permission.

Part 1

Nature and Magnitude
of the Illness

1. Identifying the Illness

Marjorie W., a diabetic, no longer suffers from her illness. Today she called to express her happiness on the recovery of her husband from his illness, alcoholism. A continuing aftercare program keeps both of them well, and him happily sober.

In both their cases, an awareness of and a positive approach to a serious health problem brought the desired results: an opportunity for a normal, happy life, instead of sickness and tragedy.

I was thankful for Marjorie's call. It was reassuring, as I had not yet recovered from a disturbing experience of the previous evening.

With decades in the care and management of problem drinking situations, I should be immune to emotionalism and shock. I'm not, and thankfully so, because, as an alcoholic knowing the gratifications of sobriety, I am ever reminded that "there, but for the grace of God, go I."

Early last evening, Bert R. called me to his home. He and his wife Ann both have drinking problems. His is the more serious and long-lived, exaggerated now by remorse and guilt following a two-year period of rewarding sobriety. Ann's is more desperate, however. Begun late in life, her dependence is a refuge from her own other serious emotional problems and her husband's return to drinking. Their children, wise beyond their years in some respects, are distracted and tortured in many others.

After an interminable period of pointless discussion in bringing Ann from apparent oblivion to some degree of consciousness, she agreed to go to the hospital. The children helped her get dressed and pack a bag. This is always an emotional time: "Who will care for my babies? Don't you love or want your mother?" and all the pathetic questions a moment like this calls forth. The children went quietly about their tasks, fetching garments, helping her dress, patiently pleading for each step made — brushing her hair, a touch of lipstick, and "Mother, here's your jacket. Please try to stand." Now to make it to the car.

I had made the necessary hospital arrangements, which is still a most difficult task in all too many areas. Bert, comparatively sober, was scared. His argument —

Alcoholism: Treatable Illness

"We must work together and start over" — had helped convince her to go. Then she changed her mind and played rag doll. The youngest lad, about eight, stepped up and announced, "I'll go, too. Mother will feel better if I go along." He did come along, and she entered the hospital without further incident.

That's the shocker. Youngsters with more compassion, understanding and moral courage than most adults tend to show themselves at times like these. The family has been in turmoil for years, though they number several professional members on both sides. The conditions of both Bert and Ann are known to all their colleagues and associates, who are avoiding them and are in turn avoided. Home, family, profession — all hang on a mere thread. Everyone is keeping things quiet for fear that Bert will be finished professionally. There have been no quietly positive measures taken to protect each from the other, to salvage the family and the children or to preserve the contribution to society this man once made when at the top of his profession.

The initial problem is one of recognition of the condition as the illness alcoholism. It must be **identified** for what it is beneath the trappings of social disgrace it frequently bestows on its victims. The problems with identification are manifold, and can be listed with the excuses that are offered as a means of avoidance of the real issue — after all, "What can one do?" Even some A.A. members glibly pronounce, "He isn't ready — he hasn't been hurt enough yet!" Balderdash! I remember when Bert started over once before from the absolute bottom.

In Ann's case, her psychiatrist feels she is not an alcoholic and is just being "uncooperative"! True, he sees her only when she is sober! He hasn't been to the home to see either or both of them in action, or to count the hidden and empty bottles. He cannot see the need to commit her long enough to remove at least the temptation of alcohol that is too easily accessible, and to help her husband and protect the children. Like the ill-informed A.A. members, this doctor and the family will wait until there is nothing left to work with or to bother about.

Ann's problem has been compounded by pills. Where before her situation was desperate, it's now tragic: medication, "if Mother needs it." Medication, "so Mother won't need to drink." Medication, "so Mother can perk up." Medication, "so Mother can sleep a little." If this sounds frightening, you are sane — it should sound frightening. If it sounds familiar, you may need help — **help identifying the problem**.

This is not a solitary case; it is repeated many times over in any community. Such situations are almost identically the case in more homes or communities than we care to count. While individual circumstances may differ, their patterns are as like as peas in a pod. Many readers may identify the problems somewhere in their own experience.

The illness alcoholism not only affects adversely the individual sufferer; it also encompasses the spouse, children, relatives, employers, employees, clergyman, physician, psychiatrist, and everyone else related to the alcoholic. All public and private health, welfare, protective and rehabilitative agencies of the community, and every level of government are involved in, and reflect the magnitude of, this costly medical, legal, spiritual and social problem.

We must acknowledge that the very nature of and reasons for man's affinity for beverage alcohol cannot help but create problems. If we are going to continue to use and live with beverage alcohol, and evidently we must and are, then we must be prepared to accept our responsibilities by identifying the resultant problems accurately, and by doing something about the tragedy and suffering alcohol brings to those who **should not** use it.

2. Who Are The Alcoholics?

A spritely little grandmother, concerned that her husband had joined his children in a bottle of beer the previous New Year's Eve, came to seek advice. It was the first time she had seen him use an alcohol beverage. Was he an alcoholic? The family had just never had "one of those."

Another woman, well known in the community, was referred by a judge. Her husband had been arrested. In fact, his name had been in the paper twice in one week — once for tearing up the shrubbery and lawn of a neighbour, and the second time for driving into the porch of another. She had a black eye and bruised cheek, which dark glasses and make-up did not hide. She opened the conversation by saying, "I don't really know why I'm here. Of course, Tom drinks, but really not too much and he has fun with it." On being questioned, she revealed that he hardly ate, that his drinking was continuous and his dependence on it complete. However, because he was president of a company and was both affluent and socially prominent, it was beyond her comprehension that he could be an alcoholic!

A doctor friend, whom no one had ever seen drink to excess either publicly or at home, was never without a small medicine bottle of beverage alcohol. He had them in his car, his medical bag, at the office, everywhere. He simply wet his tongue every so often, "for his nerves." When hospitalized, he went through a serious period of withdrawal.

A woman, regarded as one of the more well-dressed of her social group, similarly gave no indication of problem drinking behaviour. At one time she had enjoyed a considerable income of her own. Her husband began to notice the absence of a growing number of prized possessions from the home: antique plates, miniatures, furs and other things.

He investigated, and quite by accident, he unearthed a large supply of empty bottles. He learned, to his dismay, that she could not dress, fry an egg or do anything without having just a "tiny sip" of beverage alcohol first. She was completely dependent and required extensive medical care when she finally agreed to a program of recovery.

In another case, a businessman was hospitalized for an ailment. The family had a large pre-war supply of bonded whiskey which his wife decided to sell to a

18

friend since neither she nor her sick husband were drinking. The purchaser's good fortune was short-lived: every bottle in the several cases had been emptied, refilled with tea and returned to the case! In the hospital, the sick husband was found to have an advanced case of alcoholism.

I remember being asked to visit a clergyman in the hospital. He had purportedly suffered a heart attack during a funeral and fallen by the grave. When he subsequently went into D.T.'s ("delirium tremens"), his alcoholism was brought to light.

These examples serve to remind us that our stereotypes about alcoholics and alcohol abuse have been obstacles to proper action long enough. Even those seemingly knowledgeable about alcoholism may subconsciously reveal their contempt for the alcoholic. Without realizing the damage they may be doing, they pass their feelings on to those about them. This is especially tragic when exhibited by individuals involved in the counselling of alcoholic patients.

It is time to discard the stereotyped caricature of all alcoholics as skid row derelicts. We have continued to hold up this symbol as the tragic end result of alcoholism, and thus have maintained the ignorant misconceptions and prejudices of the past. Any attempt to approach the ill alcoholic or to motivate those around the patient to seek assistance can be negated by this caricature of the "drunk" as seen by society. From a treatment standpoint, such an image does not offer much hope in encouraging patients or their families to seek the help needed, or to influence to good purpose those responsible for administering health programs.

In reality, the skid row alcoholic represents only a small percentage of our alcoholic population. The majority of dependent drinkers have never encountered the law or known institutions, jails, unemployment or the other experiences with which the stereotyped alcoholic is supposedly familiar.

Most alcoholics (probably 90% or more) comprise a representative cross-section of people from every walk of life. Available studies indicate that of the eleven million or more alcoholics on the North American continent, the average alcoholic is about forty years of age, is (or has been) married to a spouse, is in a good job, owns a home and car, is presently married and has two or three children. There is one alcoholic woman to every two or three males. These studies certainly disprove the concept of the alcoholic as a stereotyped derelict.

It is now also recognized that every sick and practising alcoholic directly affects an average minimum of five other persons — spouse, children, parents, sisters, brothers, employers, employees, personal and working associates — or at least another five million people in Canada and fifty million in the United States. Because of this, the cost in human tragedies and monetary losses is inestimable.

Though many alcoholics (and their family members) remain hidden and protected from the adversities of their dependency, advances in treatment, education and research are bringing them to light. In my experience, I have known them to come from every vocation and profession and from every socioeconomic level, as well as from the recidivists of society. Alcoholism, as with any other illness, is no respecter of race, creed or position. *I know of no one group that includes more cases than any other group.*

One's mental image of the alcoholic may not have the emotional appeal of a polio-crippled child. Yet both ailments can handicap their victims, to say the least.

When we see the alcoholic as a person beset with life's pressures, with a life as real, complex, mysterious, miraculous and precious as our own, whether as our neighbour, doctor, lawyer or clergyman, or even our own self, spouse or family member — as a person dependent upon alcohol who should not use it — then we begin to have a clearer image of who the alcoholic is. The knowledge that alcoholism is a treatable illness may then be perceived by us with a sense of relief and hope.

3. A Complexity Of Attitudes

The apathy shown by society as a whole to the problems of alcohol per se, and to the illness alcoholism in particular, is an issue of great importance that demands a priority of attention. While intellectually there is a beginning response to the seriousness of this medical and social disorder, its impact on society is still only superficial. There is no real emotional acceptance or understanding in depth of the enormity of the matter. The confusion and ambivalence of our collective attitudes is a major reason behind society's apathy.

Attitudes of ignorance and prejudice, influenced by misinformation, moralism, hypocrisy and emotionalism, have kept the real issues hidden. Attitudes influence every factor reviewed in this book. The relationship of these attitudes to alcoholism must be recognized if we are to achieve a positive approach to the control and prevention of the illness, and, more particularly, of the kind of climate necessary to attract patients, their families, and those close to them, to willingly seek and accept treatment.

Let me explain what I mean. Over the years, I have attended innumerable conferences on the problems of alcohol and alcoholism, in several countries. It is always interesting to note that, while most participants use beverage alcohol moderately, some do use excessive amounts. The traditional practice of "relaxing" applies as well to alcohol discussion gatherings. Presumably everyone attending is sympathetic to the goals of the particular association of the moment — otherwise, they wouldn't be there. The problems discussed, however, do not seem to apply personally to all of those participating. The alcohol or alcoholism problems under study and discussion are always applicable to other people.

An aloofness or rejection of any personal involvement is the reason for much of this existing confusion of attitudes and for our lack of an emotional interest in coping with the problems of alcohol and alcoholism. This attitude of evasiveness is reflected in the defensive reluctance that keeps individual alcoholics, and those close to them, from admitting the need for help. It is deterring the development of an emotionally charged collective spirit of action to deal with these issues.

A laugh-it-off attitude is often manifested when the subject of alcoholism is opened for public discussion. The speaker may be introduced facetiously or with tasteless jokes. It is always interesting to open an alcoholism discussion by requesting the participants to reveal frankly their feelings on the topic. Some enlightening viewpoints can emerge. One will sense the discomfort and personal resentment and prejudice in many of those participating. In others, clearly related to an alcohol problem situation, one can glimpse bitterness and frustration. If given an alternative, many would not attend.

As we learn to appreciate the depth of these very personal emotional feelings about alcohol and alcoholism, we may understand better the conflicts that exist in every segment of society — the tug-of-war between those with beliefs of abstinence and those wishing to prove their right to drink, and the influence of our varied opinions on the alcoholic.

Let us examine the attitudes of some of the groups responsible for moulding much of that opinion which you and I hold.

Religious Groups

While a number of religions use alcohol ritually and condone its moderate social use, there are others who have moved from a moderate or temperate attitude to one of professed total abstinence. The latter, tied to rigid moralistic precepts, label any alcohol use sinful. Nevertheless, most denominations, even those preaching total abstinence, realize that numbers of their congregations use beverage alcohol. Thus their own positions and philosophy regarding drinking can be beset by conflicting ideologies. These differences are more apparent between the younger and older clergy within a given denomination. With such variances, religion does not always have a positive and common denominator of understanding.

Recognizing this lack of internal objectivity, most church denominations have openly assessed their position. With a growing awareness of and more positive response to the moral differences involved in moderate drinking, drunkenness and involuntary dependency, today we see members of the clergy becoming increasingly knowledgeable. Finding past practices wanting, they are taking a more realistic and responsible approach to their role in the recovery of alcoholics and their families. Additionally, aware and knowledgeable clergy are becoming a much more meaningful force in coping with the many other serious problems of alcohol in their communities. This must ultimately produce a far-reaching and positive effect. And for the guilt-ridden alcoholic, another cooperative and understanding ally is on the recovery team. Enlightened clergymen who improve their own attitudes cannot help but bring greater understanding to their membership.

Drys

The old conflict still goes on between the wets and the drys. Each side continues to be more concerned with proving *who is right*, while ignoring *what is right*. The dry organizations have differences of philosophy and practice within their own ranks. There are those who advocate complete abstinence, and others who advocate temperance in its true sense. While some stand firmly by their principles, others, taking advantage of current trends, have gone so far as to change their names to incorporate research and educational labels without sound bases for such changes. This is unfortunate, as there is no reason for these organizations to resort to subterfuge. They can and should cooperate with and utilize the resources of available professional facilities to substantiate their efforts. In this way they can play a more meaningful role, maintain a responsible position in the field, and not compromise principles or subject themselves to ridicule.

Temperance organizations have an important function in the field of alcohol studies. While their militant viewpoint is perhaps not widely supported, they do bring to the field a policing influence and service not otherwise available. Frequently the drys impose meaningful pressures against government only to find the reaction of both government and the public at large not as positive or wholesome as it could be.

When these organizations resolve internal confusions and conflicts, and take a more realistic course, their efforts will be more effective. There are a goodly number of workers from these associations who have always made vital and meaningful contributions to the progress of alcohol studies.

Wets

Historically, the breweries and wineries have professed, and largely advocated, moderation. They have generally been cooperative in supporting developments in this field. Unfortunately, some producers of distilled alcohol tend to take the position that the whole alcohol problem or issue is somewhat overblown. Resenting implications of being labelled by the "sins" of their products, they present a rigid and unswerving "hands-off" attitude.

Nevertheless, there are sound reasons for the industry to promote and support effective efforts to cope with the problems it helps to create. The industry's very existence could depend upon it if the unfavourable public image that alcohol problems create is not to destroy it. This is especially so if it is brought to light that the social and economic advantages to beverage alcohol are seriously outweighed by the human suffering and economic costs caused by the improper use of this beverage.

The distilled beverage industry militantly opposes the direct allocation of tax funds to deal with the problems of alcohol. They urge that funds allocated to rehabilitative services be appropriated from the general funds so that they may not be tarred with the "evils" of the industry. If it is a legitimate business, why be concerned with such implications? I know several beverage industry members who

Alcoholism: Treatable Illness

take a very positive approach to the treatment of their own problem drinking employees. Why not be sympathetic to the whole spectrum of need?

The beverage alcohol industry represents one of the strongest, wealthiest and most influential bodies, with a prime concern for promoting the sale and use of its products; but it must learn to appreciate the need for overall improved attitudes. As the tug-of-war, of which they are part, begins to abate, they can learn to be more amenable and cooperative in helping establish a common ground to better approach the issues which the abuse and misuse of their products creates. In my own experience, those programs which I administered received exemplary support from most wet interests, without bias or restriction, because we sought and achieved common grounds of discussion and cooperative effort.

Government

A lawyer running for the state legislature in one of the last citadels of Prohibition in the United States was put on the spot by the local newspaper editor, who demanded to know how he stood on the question of whiskey. The old lawyer replied by saying, "Sir, you ask how I stand on the question of whiskey. I had not intended to discuss this controversial subject in view of the fact it is so fraught with controversy. You ask how I stand on whiskey. Well, sir, here is my stand:

"If, when you say whiskey, you mean the devil's brew, the poison scourge, the bloody monster that defiles innocence, dethrones reason, creates misery and despair, yes, literally takes the bread out of the mouths of babes, if you mean that vile drink which topples the Christian man and woman from the pinnacle of gracious, righteous living into the bottomless pit of shame and despair, helplessness and hopelessness — then sir, I am against it with every fiber of my body.

"But if, when you say whiskey, you mean the oil of conversation, the philosophic drink that is consumed when good fellows get together, which puts a song in their hearts, laughter on their lips, and a smile of contentment in their eyes, if you mean Christmas cheer, if you mean that stimulating drink which puts the spring in an old man's step of a frosty morning, if you mean that drink which permits a man to magnify his joys and happiness and to forget, if only for a moment, life's tragedies and sorrows, if you mean that drink which pours into our Treasury untold millions with which to provide tender care for our little crippled children, our aged and infirm and to build schools, hospitals and roads — then sir, I am for it with all my heart.

"There, sir, is my stand — from it I will not retract; I will not compromise. There is my stand."

Governments charged with the obligation of facing up to these issues are confronted by a real dilemma. On the one hand, they are naturally prone to grasp and use the ever-increasing revenues from the sale of alcohol beverages. The manufacture, sale, distribution and other assorted enterprises represent one of the major gross revenues to the economy of any governed area. Conversely, governments are faced with immense problems of health care, welfare, rehabilitation, policing, and penal and other like services in the abuse and misuse of alcohol. Governments must also deal with the pressures of all opinionated interests for and against the use of beverage alcohol, within their own parties and in the opposition, from church and reform groups, from agencies interested in alcoholism rehabilitation, from dry and wet vested interests, health and welfare organizations and the public at large. Pity the administrator, with strong opinions of his own, who must somehow navigate a middle course!

Disappointingly enough, some governmental bodies allow themselves to be influenced into giving only lip service to effective remedies. Reluctant to acknowledge the magnitude of the alcohol problem, they demonstrate a defensiveness to these issues that has retarded the effective investigation and action these problems demand. The success of programs is dependent upon the attitudes and degree of interest evinced by each changing group of officials. This has been reflected in fluctuating budgets, lip service, and the lack of a positive attitude and policy.

Confusion in government attitude initiates entirely new conflicts. A government may make substantial grants to alcoholism programs but contradict its own policy by continuing to terminate problem drinking employees without due referral for help. Not infrequently, a government will fail to change the statutes controlling welfare and rehabilitation policies in problem drinking situations, and will do nothing about the proper admission of patients for treatment to hospitals and institutions; nor will a government make sufficient effort to resolve recurrent problems in courts and protective agencies.

Lacking comprehensive and positive policies to approach problem drinking situations, they continue the mistaken attitudes and practices of the past. Such ambivalence plagues the field from every angle and adversely affects the development of a constructive approach to alcoholism. Governments, by virtue of their mandates, controls and moneys, must provide the direction and support so urgently needed in all areas of service. Their leadership and example in achieving sound working attitudes should and must provide the impetus so vital to all other segments of society.

Medical and Social Sciences

A study done several decades ago reported that fewer than sixty percent of physicians surveyed could (or would) treat alcoholics, and that over ninety percent of public and private hospitals refused to admit alcoholic patients. The few admitted were generally entered for "other reasons," and their alcoholism was handled with incompetence and indifference. Those hospitalized in mental institutions received little more than custodial care. *This is still the case in too many areas.*

The multiplicity of regulations covering admissions to hospitals and

Alcoholism: Treatable Illness

institutions in the same city, county, province or state is beyond comprehension. The attitude expressed by each facility reflects the opinion and often the prejudice of the individual in charge.

Penologists, criminologists and professional administrators in the field of rehabilitation are similarly swayed by personal feelings. The programs they administer project their attitudes — and those in their charge are dealt with accordingly.

If medicine, the social sciences, insurance interests and most other sources of contact involved indicate this total rejection, how can one expect the alcoholic or the family and associates of that patient to do otherwise? The role that doctors, hospitals, clinics, institutions, agencies and all related professional personnel can and should play within their own communities is one of immeasurable influence. Their positive response to the problems of alcohol and more especially to alcoholism, **as a treatable illness**, is vital to those attitudes essential to eventual control and prevention.

A doctor, the senior staff member of a large hospital, had received repeated in-patient treatment for gastritis, tension, exhaustion and the like. Finally, his physician, on re-admitting him to hospital, recorded chronic alcoholism as the reason for hospitalization. The staff openly and properly treated his illness as alcoholism. Once over the initial shock, the patient made the diagnosis unanimous, thus taking an active part in his own treatment and recovery. He never relapsed, and eventually became the Medical Officer of that hospital.

Divergent opinions in medicine, psychiatry and the social sciences have seriously hindered the development of common attitudes by presenting misconceptions and conflicting viewpoints within their disciplines. These problems are greatly exaggerated when related to the attitudes of alcoholic patients, their families, and the general public.

The Teaching Profession

Recently, a visiting professor to an adult extension course on psychology created a furore in his class during a discussion on alcoholism. He opened his remarks by announcing in an offhand manner that the subject was one that should be touched on to put it in its proper place, but it was not too important since "drunks" represented a pretty hopeless, weak-willed and no-good lot. He dumped all problem drinking categories and the several alcoholisms into one pot — drunkenness. He went on to say that alcoholics were for the most part homosexuals. He expressed the opinion that so-called rehabilitation programs currently under development were molly-coddling the issue.

In the class were several nurses, social science workers and doctors, a few of whom were sober alcoholics; others had spouses with extensive periods of sobriety and recovery. A social worker with a master's degree, the wife of a prominent professional man with some fifteen years of sobriety, was aghast and took exception to his remarks, though without revealing her relationship to the illness.

The resentment and frustration of the several students closely related to alcoholism recovery were quite understandable. Their orientation to the illness had taken place in a community which had enjoyed considerable effective lay and professional educational programming. No longer embarrassed by the illness alcoholism, they were gratified with their own good fortune. They had learned to cope with their problems and accepted alcoholism in its proper light — as a treatable illness. Their real concern was the damage such prejudiced teaching does to others desperately needing the same informed direction they had received. While most of the states and provinces are expected by law or tradition to deal with the problems of alcohol, the subject is generally evaded, or loosely fitted into broad areas of health and social studies. Here again, the attitude and quality of the teaching is entirely dependent upon the teachers. Naturally it is coloured by their personal feelings on the subject. Teaching may take the form of intensive moralism, or the subject may be glossed over as unimportant.

A serious issue arises in seeking qualified workers to fill administrative, educational, treatment and research vacancies in the growing number of alcoholism and other drug dependency recovery resources and facilities. It is certainly not easy for an otherwise qualified person with academic credentials and experience in other medical or social sciences to admit to a lack of knowledge or abilities in the care and control of alcoholism and other addictions. To be open-minded enough to be willing to seek the basic orientation essential to the demands of work in this field is certainly one significant sign of a true professional. Fortunately, in recent years a number of training and staff development programs have sprung up among universities, among treatment centers and within the development programs of those provincial and state agencies or universities with an eye to the future.

Until every learning and teaching mainstream shares the responsibility of advancing awareness and understanding, that task essentially falls upon the alcoholism agencies now in operation. Priority must be given to the development of adequate and meaningful materials within the curricula of the teaching faculties, with emphasis on teaching the present teachers. Much more must be taught to the professionals who must regularly cope with problem drinking situations.

Beginning with the School on Alcohol Studies, originally at Yale University and now at Rutgers University under the direction of the Center of Alcohol Studies, other similar schools have mushroomed across the continent. They are helping to assume the responsibility of providing direction to all of the disciplines and to those individuals interested in serving this field. Stimulated by the leadership of dedicated professionals within successful treatment programs, urged on by voluntary

Alcoholism: Treatable Illness

organizations such as the National Council on Alcoholism and its local affiliates, and assisted in some instances by seed grants from the Butler Foundation, the Christopher D. Smithers Foundation and other sympathetic foundations, major universities have initiated accredited courses and faculty programs designed to correct voids in proper orientation to alcoholism and addiction among the health professions and field personnel. It is to be hoped that others will soon follow and that eventually all medical and social science graduates will have the benefit of pragmatic in-service training in qualified treatment and training centers.

The Legal Profession

A judge was censured by his superiors for having criticized a man appearing before him. He publicly "took strips off this man's hide" for half an hour in the courtroom. The plaintiff was one of those caught in alcoholism's revolving door. The judge was known by reputation to be an excessive and dependent drinker. Now following personal recovery in A.A. he is a sober, responsible, just and understanding person, admired and respected by all who know or come before him.

It is a unique but well established fact that many of our contemporary advances in coping better with the legal, medical and social issues of alcoholism were spearheaded by lawyers and judges. Many members of the judiciary, dismayed to see friends and colleagues within the legal profession appear before them, sought ways and means to initiate rehabilitation programs. Many judges are the non-alcoholic and recovered alcoholic "fathers" of local groups of the Fellowship of Alcoholics Anonymous.

However, not too many years ago, those active with the law held a biased and usually punitive attitude toward problem drinkers. Historically, whether at the level of an attorney protecting the interests of a family or within the courts, lawyers and judges dealt only with the end of the road decisions for alcoholics. Their attitude was generally one of disposing of these hopeless and frustrating situations with the greatest possible speed and the least possible personal involvement. Today, both in practice and through the support of decriminalizing legislation, members of the legal profession are assuming a new status as co-workers with medicine and the social sciences. Understanding lawyers are currently instigating tremendous social changes to better the alcoholic's lot. The effective results being achieved by some members of the judiciary in resolving marital conflicts, in re-educating drinking drivers, and in rehabilitating offenders whose major problems are related to dependency on alcohol are stimulating others within their profession to participate in this new outlook and movement.

The legal profession, by coordinating its skills and experience with organized medicine and the social sciences, is helping to achieve solutions to those of society's medical and social ills of which alcoholism is a major part. While in the past alcoholics from every station in life had feared contact with this profession, today the enlightened attitude of a growing number of members of the judiciary and the bar has forestalled the downward path of many alcoholics otherwise slated for isolation, skid row, institutionalization or death. Like other professions, however, the collective attitude of this group remains dependent upon the outlook and attitude of the individual, whether that attitude is biased and destructive, or enlightened and constructive.

Business, Industry and Labour

The management levels of business, industry and labour, with so much at stake, were pioneers in learning to deal with employees' dependency problems. Recognizing that alcoholism is a serious management and production problem affecting the most senior and skilful employees, we can now say that programs for employed personnel probably lead all other methods in effectively combatting the problem of alcohol dependency. In cooperation with available local resources, and by combining constructive attitudes with practical and humanitarian remedies, Employee Assistance Program services are achieving dramatic results. With the management of business or industry and labour and the personnel of medical and social departments working together as a team, sound policies and procedures have been established and have proven beyond a doubt the merit of these Employee Assistance Programs.

These joint efforts are giving leadership to the entire field. Similar programs have been and are being instigated within government, civil and military services. Though one still hears the retort, "We fire them all," it is recognized that this can never be the case. The educational, rehabilitative and training procedures resulting from the experience of these programs have brought economic, personnel and production benefits of immeasurable proportions. As the experience of one industry's Employee Assistance Program brushes off on another, impetus is given to the development of similar services in an ever increasing number of companies. In like fashion, labour movements are establishing national policies and procedures within their own groups to facilitate and expedite such services; they are also developing training and orientation programs for their own counsellors.

The leadership, progressive attitudes and productive results emanating from **Employee Recovery Programs** should do much to encourage greater interest and involvement from the medical and social science practitioners and their professional schools.

The General Public

To appreciate the many conflicting attitudes that still exist, one need only assemble a representative cross-section of the public. Most individuals, represented

Alcoholism: Treatable Illness

because of the concerns peculiar to each in approaching the subject, are governed by personal biases. For example, imagine that we are organizing a "Community Advisory Committee on Alcoholism." Included among the members (who will ultimately perform a teaching function in the community) might be a judge, a doctor, a clergyman, a social worker, a volunteer community worker, a farmer and an industrialist.

The judge's primary concern is a means to eliminate all those faces that regularly appear in the Monday morning line-up of drunks. The doctor is concerned with having someone take off his or her hands those incorrigibles who call in the middle of the night, never follow directions or pay their bills. The clergyman, while trying to bring some spiritual strength to those who seek his help, finds himself completely incapable of giving answers to either the family or the patient on the basis of a spiritual approach alone. The social science worker, having little or no background knowledge about the illness, might be concerned only with the payment of welfare and the recurring problems of unemployment caused by alcoholism. The industrialist may have a simple answer — he or she fires them all, still knowing that this isn't quite right, either. All too many well-intentioned community volunteers, engaged in many community activities, still retain the traditional concept of alcoholism as a matter of will power or as a moral issue. The farmer with a strong principle of abstinence feels that prohibition is the only answer. A representative of the beverage industry might well be defensive about his or her product. Each member of the committee, unable or unwilling to recognize and respect the prerogatives and needs of the other members, will only reflect and emphasize his or her own personal interests.

Add to this a distortion of past prejudices, a confusion of religious, ethnic and social backgrounds, coloured perhaps by a tragic personal involvement with an alcoholic, and you have a potentially explosive combination. The whole group is unaware of the fact that the problems with which they are concerned represent only a small segment of the total issue. They are not aware of any of the other types of hidden problems. The abstinent farmer perhaps does not realize that most of his choice grains may be going to a distillery or brewery. The industrialist is not aware, when terminating the new employee for excessive absenteeism, that an old and trusted associate is a hidden alcoholic of long standing who has been covering up with an alleged bad heart or a chronic case of ulcers.

This then is the dilemma facing the chairman of that committee. Certainly, it suggests a teaching of these teachers first; the goal is the achievement of a common appreciation of each other's problems and the realization that there are definitive and vital differences between drinking, drunkenness and alcoholism. Excessive drinking is not necessarily alcoholism. Not all of the people depending upon missions and hostels drink of necessity. All crime is not necessarily an offshoot of drinking. There are even varying degrees and kinds of alcoholisms. These are some key issues; and, extending the problems of this committee over a whole area or a whole nation, one can appreciate better the concern facing educators in dealing with such confusion and conflict of interest.

To achieve a common attitude. it is essential that these areas of individual conflict and often misplaced sincerity of purpose be defined and clarified to enable all to appreciate and agree upon common interpretation and goals. This is vital to achieving cooperation from those whose support is sought for services in this field.

Official Alcoholism Resources

The attitude of each of these preceding groups duly influences the efforts of those establishing alcoholism programs, information and referral centers, clinics, and any agency conducting rehabilitation, education and research services. These outside attitudes filter through each of the personnel related to the programs and have a direct bearing on the policies established by the programs themselves.

Because of seemingly conflicting interests many official alcoholism agencies have established policies prohibiting the acceptance of financial support from so-called vested interests, particularly the beverage alcohol interests. I submit that this deters the breaking down of old taboos, while keeping alive the unhealthy connotation attached to the use of beverage alcohol and to its producers. Such rejection was not entirely without reason, as regrettably some support given in the past had strings attached which adversely affected the integrity and usefulness of the contributions. Restrictions on either side are unwarranted.

Why should agencies dependent on outside contributions be denied any potential avenues of support for the educational programs and the research studies and investigations so vitally needed by everyone? And why should alleged non-controversial service bodies be involved in setting up new plateaus of prejudice and discord?

Government-sponsored alcoholism programs can also become involved in budget and power struggles. There is conflict as to who and which department should control programming. This is a growing concern, as the field has become more respectable and remunerative and so attracts greater interest among workers. These programs fall into another trap as well; rather than pursue a policy of training people up to open positions and attracting new personnel, they compete with one another. In these circumstances, new programs are unable to qualify for the manpower each desperately needs.

In the early days of programming most agencies were warned against becoming involved with the broad spectrum of alcohol problems. They were advised to stay within the alcoholism field. This is not possible. Studies pertaining to one area of concern are related to problems of another area. Attitudes delaying an approach to alcoholism also seriously impede the control and prevention of other alcohol problems.

It is essential, therefore, that those charged with the administration and support of alcoholism agencies and concerned with related alcohol problems remove themselves from such conflicts in order to ensure that they do not get bogged down in the morass of dissident attitudes which pervades the field. Official agencies must take the lead in creating positive attitudes and in breaking down old barriers of ignorance and prejudice. Each group is really dependent on the other. I submit that alcoholism programs must assume the responsibility of alleviating problems of inter-agency communication and cooperation which, because of controversy and emotion, are crippling efforts in this public health area. Only in this way will it be possible to recognize and respect the prerogatives of each agency and to hammer out mutually agreeable and attainable goals.

Public Attitudes Toward Drinking

Drinking habits, tastes and attitudes toward drinking have gone through a dramatic period of change since the Second World War. These changes would seem to be universal and of considerable concern to all nations — so much so that many countries have moved to achieve national controls in an effort to curb the apparent abuse that is on the upswing. For generations, not much was written about the "drink habit." Today, the attitudes and activities of every nation concerning alcoholism and alcohol abuse are daily in the news not as temperance complaints, but rather as matters of governmental concern, legally, medically, socially and spiritually. This is also true at the level of subnational government units, as recent provincial and state government programming in North America and elsewhere illustrates.

Virtually all immigrant populations, regardless of the alcoholism rates that may be ascribed to them in their countries of origin, generally meld into the average ration of the North American scene by the third generation. They tend to relinquish their national orthodoxy, assume (North) American customs and generally begin to act in accordance with the expectations of our society. Obviously, there are those ethnic groups who retain strong national ties and traditionally maintain aspects of their culture which may relate to drinking. Many Poles, Ukrainians and Germans, among others, continue to practice the same rigorous drinking habits they have always known; the Jews, Muslims and Chinese still generally respect their cultural or religious restrictions. But though drinkers in these groups have traditionally tended in the main to be non-problem drinkers, there are signs of an increasing number of individuals from these cultures developing serious problems. The result is that even groups which have resisted assimilation into our cultural pattern in other ways are beginning to drink beverage alcohol as we do, developing dependency problems fitting into the North American pattern.

While it is reported that there is some decrease in the North American rate of consumption of beverage alcohol on a per capita basis, this does not mean that there is a decrease in the total volume consumed. Along with increases in population, a greater number and percentage of those of drinking age are using beverage alcohol. The economy is richer, incomes are higher and a more affluent society tends to consume more alcohol. There are more parties and outside activities of all kinds, hence the occasions to drink become more frequent. Sources of distribution and consumption are much more widespread than before prohibition. The general use of alcohol beverages is therefore much more public, prevalent and uninhibited.

Given the changing role of women in business, industry, government and family life in the wake of the quiet (and sometimes not so quiet) revolution of the women's movement — an ongoing phenomenon, and rightly so — more women are drinking today, and they are drinking openly, to the extent that the distinction between male and female problem drinkers which used to exist in the minds of the sober is fast disappearing. Alone, in groups, or with male companions, women imbibe as men do. It would probably be fair to say that the number of female problem drinkers has increased dramatically with the entry of women into the marketplace on equal footing with men — not because they are more susceptible, but because societal pressure, which for centuries restricted women's activities in all aspects of life and also created a particular social and cultural stigma against alcohol abuse by women, has changed. The stigma no longer carries special burdens for women, or at least the burden is less. This coupled with the factors of accessibility and social acceptability, has exposed more women to the risks of problem drinking than would have been the case even ten or twenty years ago.

Among young adults generally, there has always been a desire to emulate their elders. While the concept of alcohol-free parties is now experiencing a resurgence, an appalling number of young people are becoming problem drinkers before they even leave their teens behind. In all truth, we cannot refer any longer to "young adults." In years past, few young people would have taken the risks associated with getting drunk for a good time; now, particularly in economically disadvantaged inner city environments, children as young as ten or eleven are being identified as problem drinkers and/or abusers of other substances.

There was a time when the trend in outside-the-home drinking seemed to be veering toward hard liquors, and increases in home consumption appeared to favour beers and wines. Efforts were made to teach users about the various types and "proper uses" of wines, and over the years it has become very "in" to be knowledgeable about wines and vintages. Because of the new pressures and changes within our culture in the past twenty-five years, it is no longer quite so easy to focus on increases in consumption of specific types of beverage alcohol, particularly where young people are concerned. The problems of abuse and misuse are

Alcoholism: Treatable Illness

becoming so acute and so widespread that the distinctions between the types of beverage alcohol are beginning to disappear, at least with respect to the social, economic, human and political costs of that abuse/misuse. From the legal perspective, the regulations governing the consumption of beverage alcohol and infractions against its misuse — even though they are changing regularly nowadays in response to the public's increasing awareness and sensitivity to the issues — are based on practices, controls and attitudes of slower-paced generations left behind long ago.

Drinking and driving is a major issue and a problem confounding governments, experts, protective agencies and the public. It is clearly beyond the scope of this book to examine all the ramifications of alcohol abuse in this area; but we can say that until relatively recently, mounting accident costs and death rates seemed to appal nobody other than the families of the dead and injured, the insurance industry and the police. Slogans meant little to the average social or problem drinker. They were meant for those "who can't hold their liquor." To some, even today, an inability to "handle one's liquor" is perceived as a lack of maturity or a personality weakness!

Happily, there are changes taking place in this area at least. Provincial and state governments have reacted by altering motor vehicle legislation; criminal law has been altered specifically to cover a broader range of driving offenses where alcohol is concerned. Mobile breath-testing units and increased police investments in terms of manpower and vigilance seem to be reaping rewards in terms of apprehending drinking drivers and getting them off the roads. In many cases, we can probably assume that fear of legal penalties and social stigma associated with them is beginning to be effective in terms of scaring off the roads at least some drivers who would otherwise have attempted to drive while under the influence.

This is, however, not sufficient to change the public's view of the role of alcohol. More beverages are being imported to meet the tastes of a more sophisticated generation of drinkers. There are beverage alcohols for every taste and budget. Business luncheons and dinners, conferences, home entertaining and the like all provide reasons or excuses for indulging in the use, abuse or misuse of alcohol. Drinking has attained its own mark of sophistication in some socioeconomic strata and is, in some respects, a status symbol of considerable importance. Brands used vary with the place in which the beverage is consumed, with whom one is drinking, and with the nature of the occasion. It is considered acceptable and appropriate to thank a business colleague for a small service rendered by presenting a bottle of fine aged Scotch, or to give liquor as a Christmas present. For the people to whom this scenario is familiar, the use of alcohol may represent an aspect of their stature and an accepted way of life.

On the other hand, the people in these socioeconomic strata do not readily permit the same status to apply to the drinking of other groups. Neither the tipsy labourer nor the poorly groomed drunken native Indian (a stereotype frequently used by those who view themselves as non-problem drinkers) is welcome at the upscale lounge. There are levels of drinking groups, of kinds of beverages consumed, and of places for each drinking subculture. Attitudes of discrimination are easily noted, and the discrimination is practised with firmness and little exception. The young urban professional drinks a particular brand, with particular people, and in particular places. Downward mobility through the levels of drinking is possible (and for all too many people, even probable); but upward mobility through the ranks of drinkers is virtually impossible!

The places where drinking is advertised or occurs vary in kind and appeal, but there are sufficient to serve any level or inclination of society. There are the desolate and drab bars in old hotels and dreary skid row taverns; there are average cocktail lounges and bars; there are fashionable lounges with dress codes, and beautiful restaurants for romantic, candlelight dinners. There is, of course, an increasing move toward the luxurious and glamorous; and in many places the attractions consist of performers or even staff, some of whom serve the drinks in scant attire or no attire at all. There is, in fact, such a range that an evening's entertainment may well consist of a "pub crawl" from one drinking establishment to another. The risk of becoming intoxicated increases dramatically.

How can the industry miss? Every gimmick is on parade to add to the *glamour* and *importance* of drinking. Such settings make drinking per se open to attack by moralists. With the broadening of drinking occasions and patterns and the decreasing minimum age of drinkers who consume illegally, the relationship to crime, delinquency, divorce, drunken driving and all the other disorders of alcohol abuse has become less easy to disregard. A vehicle may be faulty mechanically, but if the driver has ingested alcohol at the time of an accident there is usually no argument over the cause. However, while we may blame the accident on drinking, shouldn't our real concern be the public's apathy toward alcohol abuse generally?

Individual Attitudes

The array of attitudes reviewed has a terrific impact on the individual attempting to assess his or her personal drinking behaviour. Let me give you an example. Several years ago, I addressed a senior service club luncheon. Though the presentation was well received, no one there gave any indication of a personal relationship with problem drinking. A few club members did call later seeking advice on how to approach an 'employee,' a 'relative' or a 'friend.'

A number of years later, I addressed the same group. In the intervening period

Alcoholism: Treatable Illness

the community had been exposed to extensive education, professional orientation studies and investigations. An excellent treatment program had been developed, which saw the recovery of hundreds of patients from all levels of that community. Following the second talk, a number of members openly asked questions about their own kind of drinking, spoke of alcoholism within their own families, and expressed frank concern about personal problem drinking. On this occasion the subject was discussed "before God and everybody." It was as open and forthright as one could wish for without any indicated embarrassment to anyone. This is attitude change. This is the climate of operation conducive to attracting patients to seek the help they need, or to bring to families and the collaterals of alcoholics guidance without stigma, fear or delay.

The individual's ability to accept help and to overcome his or her own attitudes of resentment, defensiveness and reticence is dependent on the attitudes of one's associates. One cannot deal with the alcoholic patient without keeping this factor constantly in mind.

Those who have had the courage and resolute integrity to overcome the obstacle of adverse attitudes have enjoyed dramatic results. Even those with conflicting interests have learned that by eliminating fruitless controversy and prejudice, they could work together to achieve common goals. After all, on the one hand, practising alcoholics must certainly be recognized as the worst possible advertisement for the use of beverage alcohol, while a recovered alcoholic can become a meaningful and contributing member of society.

The learning process of every individual is directly affected by family, religion, ethnic and social groups, vocational position and the like. A person moves from one setting to another, each emphasizing new opinions and pressures. Everyone, therefore, is more or less subjected to a barrage of attitudes from birth. When we try to cope with the illness alcoholism, we find that such pressures are magnified many times over by the various groups whose attitudes we have just explored.

The reader may now appreciate why attitudes demand a priority of attention. This is not to belittle current programming. Rather it is to point up the vital need to achieve a willingness to honestly assess the complexity and magnitude of these problems.

Each group, on achieving an enlightened attitude, becomes an aware, knowledgeable and positive influence in the treatment of alcoholics. The explicit role of these groups as meaningful collaterals is further interpreted in a later chapter.

4. The Alcohol Language

Labels

Alcoholism, perhaps more than any other illness, has been bedevilled by labels and a confusion of definitions that make it difficult for a reader new to the subject to know what we are talking about. Administrators, agency workers and related professionals often seem to contradict and deny one another. If this is confusing to the "pros" in the field, one can imagine how frustrating it must be to the patient, the family and other collaterals of the alcoholic. And, since the patient is the single most important factor to consider, we should discuss his or her need for clarity and understanding first.

The alcoholics' fear of labels is well founded, inasmuch as historically they have been tagged with countless disparaging terms. He or she has been pointed to with scorn, shame and ridicule. Family, friends and professional advisors have traditionally added to the patient's fears, guilt and concern by suggesting that all alcoholics are immoral, immature, mentally disturbed, pathological, incompetent, irresponsible. perverse, weak-willed, no-good drunks — you name it.

Patients and their families, when seeking guidance, are often repulsed by the new labels incorrectly and regularly applied to their affliction. Already fearful of the progression of the dependency, perhaps even concerned about personal sanity, the alcoholic properly refutes the implications of these labels. Often, to avoid the concomitant negative inferences, the alcoholic finds it easier and less threatening to continue drinking and denying.

In diagnosing the illness (too often described as symptomatic of an emotional disorder), professionals refer to alcoholism as acute, addictive, symptomatic, chronic, compulsive, poison-related, psychotic, or resulting from deliberately irresponsible or self-inflicted behaviour. With such unsound (albeit well-intentioned) comment from so many professionals who should be acting as knowledgeable and aware friends, who needs enemies?

While it is well known that the alcoholic is usually the last one to appreciate the progression of the illness, a distorted picture of alcoholism, tarred with labels, only dissuades the patient and his or her family from seeking treatment. A further

Alcoholism: Treatable Illness

concern in failing to obtain treatment for one's alcoholism is that other illnesses from which the alcoholic may suffer remain undiagnosed and untreated.

Consider the increasingly enlightened approach to mental illness. More progress has been made in achieving public recognition and acceptance of this national health problem since the terms "crazy," "insane," "nuts" and other similar expressions have been replaced by the simple phrase "mental illness."

Alcohol Language

The language is severely complicated by a confusion of interpretations reflecting personal attitudes and use. To appreciate more fully the problems that alcohol language presents, let's discuss some of its facets. One must remember that drinking as such means different things to various segments of society, individually and collectively. To one person, it may mean the use of beverage alcohol; to another, it may mean the use of any beverage. To some ethnic groups, the use of wines or light alcohol beverages is synonymous with the use of milk, water, tea or coffee, while to others it is completely taboo. To some groups which support temperance, not to drink means not to use spirituous or hard liquors, while to others it means complete abstinence from anything containing alcohol. At a luncheon in Europe which included people from various temperance groups, I was the only one *not* drinking. All others enjoyed ales or wines.

Drinking, drunkenness and alcoholism to many are completely synonymous, with no degree of difference whatsoever. To some, the words "drinker" or "imbiber" connote one who drinks excessively or in a "sinful" or "socially unacceptable" manner. Thus it follows that problems of excessive drinking, obnoxious and disorderly or incorrigible behaviour, impaired or intoxicated driving and all other disorders in the abuse and misuse of alcohol are linked with alcoholism by the "evilness" attached to drinking beverage alcohol. Even temperate, social users of beverage alcohol are inclined to classify excessive and alcoholic users in the same category, *while in fact many alcoholics may drink far less than so-called social users — and may never even have been visibly "under the influence" or "drunk."*

Drunkenness has its own galaxy of expressions — tight, high, soused, plastered, stoned, lit up, and the like — each again being interpreted individually. As noted, there are many interpretations for the illness alcoholism itself.

One will sometimes hear old-time members of Alcoholics Anonymous refer to "a true alcoholic." In the early days of the Fellowship, this term was applied to those people who to the old membership apparently were afflicted with the one malady — alcoholism. These alcoholics were presumably free from other emotional problems or addictions, particularly the conjunctive use of other mood-altering drugs. This interpretation served as the basis for incorrect diagnoses, adverse treatment, and failure to reach many of those people seeking help.

38

The expression "problem drinker" came into use to connote one whose kind of drinking created less serious problems for the individual and to differentiate this type of user from the stereotyped alcoholic who was viewed as a derelict, bum or "fallen" man or woman. Industry latched on to this less stigmatic interpretation as better befitting the employee. Many early stage patients definitely feel that they are not "bad enough yet" (rather than "not sick enough") to go to Alcoholics Anonymous or to stop drinking.

The use of the word alcohol-*ic* with beverages is in itself really incorrect, because beverage alcohol does not necessarily promote an alcohol-*ic* state in all people. Nevertheless, all beverages containing alcohol are usually referred to in this way. The term *alcoholic* should be freed from other synonymous use and stand alone to denote its sense, definition and relationship to the sufferer from the illness alcoholism.

To try to define the term *drunk* in its many and diversified uses is nearly impossible. This vulgar, facetious, scornful and shameful application usually expresses the intensity and personal prejudices of the person using this word.

While the members of Alcoholics Anonymous use the term "drunk" freely among themselves, seemingly without implication, they react rather violently to being labelled "drunks" by outsiders.

Homeless men or women, as transients in missions, Salvation Army hostels and the like are considered to be drunks by most of the population. Few realize that perhaps only fifty percent of these people use beverage alcohol. In fact, the number may be even smaller, given the growing number of homeless individuals who in recent years have had to rely on the missions and hostels for assistance, and who have been forced into this position by economic or personal circumstances unrelated to alcohol abuse or misuse.

Recovery from alcoholism carries its own language. A.A. members use the expression "being dry," which is certainly contrary to the activities of "drys" as we know them. Many people will talk about ex-alcoholics, reformed alcoholics and the like; and despite the laudatory tone intended, such expressions place an incorrect connotation on alcoholism recovery.

Because of the adverse inferences that the word *alcoholic* itself carries, it is not easily accepted by many. Workers in the field have long sought a term that carries less stigma, because there are still those alcoholism sufferers who simply cannot believe the illness could ever touch them.

Definitions

Two definitions most quoted are those of the World Health Organization and the American Medical Association.

The World Health Organization defines alcoholism as:

"Any form of drinking which in its extent goes beyond the traditional and customary dietary use or the ordinary compliances with the social drinking customs of the whole community concerned, irrespective of the etiological factors leading to such a behavior and irrespective also of the extent to which such etiological factors are dependent upon hereditary, constitutional or acquired physiopathological and metabolic influences."

The American Medical Association's definition is:

"Alcoholism is a disease which is characterized by a compulsive drinking of alcohol in some form. It is an addiction to alcohol. The drinking of alcohol produces continuing or repeated problems in the patient's life."

Mark Keller in his *Selected Vocabulary* includes the following definitions:

Alcoholism: A chronic disease, or disorder of behavior, characterized by the repeated drinking of alcohol(ic) beverages to an extent that exceeds customary dietary use or ordinary compliance with the social drinking customs of the community, and that interferes with the drinker's health, interpersonal relations or economic functioning.

Alcohol Addiction: An overwhelming desire, need, impulse or compulsion to drink alcohol and to obtain alcohol(ic) beverages by any means, with psychological and possibly physiological dependence on alcohol, marked by a tendency to be unable to stop when drinking is begun. Distinguished from drug addictions in which there is, in addition, a tendency to increase the dose and in which physiological dependence is much more probable.

Blackout: Amnesia for the events of any part of a drinking episode, without loss of consciousness.

Alcoholism with Complications: Alcoholism marked by a defect of health consequent to excessive drinking.

Loss of Control Over Drinking: The inability, whether on some or on all occasions, to stop voluntarily when some alcohol(ic) beverage is ingested. Said to be characteristic of alcohol addiction and distinguished from deterioration of motor coordination or of social propriety under the influence of alcohol.

Problem Drinker: A person who drinks alcohol(ic) beverages to an extent or in a way that causes private or public harm.

Symptomatic Alcoholism: Drinking, usually excessive, as a means of handling overt tensions and unconscious problems, or as a symptom of a mental disorder.

Moderate Drinking: The drinking of alcohol(ic) beverages in such amounts and frequencies as to comply with the dietary or customary usages of the community, without involvement in pathological behavior or consequences.

Temperance: Moderation.

Abstinence: Total abstinence; refraining completely from drinking any alcohol(ic) beverage.

Alcohol: Ethyl alcohol (ethanol, $CH(3)CH(2)OH$) when the type is not specified; a colorless, volatile, slightly aromatic, flammable liquid, one of the products of vinous fermentation. Distinguished from alcohol(ic) beverages, of which it is the characteristic and essential ingredient and from other alcohols, as isopropyl, methyl, etc.

Hangover: The immediate pathophysiological or pathopsychological after-effects of drinking, usually of large amounts, other than the effects of the presence of alcohol.

Drug Addiction: An overwhelming desire, need or compulsion to take a drug and to obtain it by any means, with a tendency to increase the dose and with psychological or physiological dependence on the drug. Distinguished from alcohol addiction, in which there is no tendency to increase the dose and physiological dependence is relatively questionable.[1]

The development of this list of definitions represents a meaningful contribution to resolving alcoholism terms and their interpretations. The variance which exists within these definitions allows perhaps too much leeway of individual interpretation. Most recovered alcoholics would disagree with Mr. Keller in his closing reference to alcohol addiction as compared with drug addiction, since they do increase the dose.

Alcoholics Anonymous saw fit to define alcoholism as "*an increasing physical sensitivity to alcohol — an allergy — coupled with a mental obsession so powerful that no amount of human willpower may break it*" (emphasis added). Alcoholics approaching A.A. found this definition to be less offensive and more acceptable than the labels by which their illness had previously been known.

Some "professionals" continue to interpret alcoholism through only one of its components. A number feel that alcoholism is caused by a physiological disturbance, as an organic, glandular, or deficiency disorder; others define alcoholism as a psychological symptom of an underlying emotional problem or as

Alcoholism: Treatable Illness

maladjusted behavior. And of course, there are those who still look upon alcoholism as a matter of morals and willpower. This presupposes the use of alcohol to be the sole cause of alcoholism. It is not that simple.

Though these matters will be dealt with at greater length in chapters on treatment, I must emphasize here that alcoholism is but one of the problems in the use of alcohol. There are also many kinds of alcoholisms which require individual diagnosis and specific treatment techniques. *Alcoholism can be approached more positively when it is defined as an* **illness**, *consisting of physical, emotional, social and spiritual components, the interrelationship of which cannot be ignored.*

Terms used by the author in this book are listed and defined as follows:

Alcohol Beverage: The expression alcohol beverage, as earlier noted in the alcohol language, is used interchangeably with beverage alcohol to denote any beverage containing alcohol.

Alcoholism or Dependency on Alcohol: When one's use of beverage alcohol evidences a progressive loss of the ability to drink according to *personal intent*, progressively interferes with one's normal relationships at home, at work, in matters of budget, and in one's other interpersonal relationships, and/ or is in fact different from or unacceptable to the rest of those persons with whom one functions (lives, works and normally socializes), then some form of the illness alcoholism or dependency on alcohol is indicated.

Drinker and Drinking: The words "drinker" and "drinking" are used to denote the drinking of beverage alcohol.

Worker: The term "worker" is used to denote the personnel of alcoholism programs or other agencies related to such programming, to preclude the necessity of spelling out each worker's lay or professional role and discipline.

Collateral: This expression denotes the primary associates, other than the immediate family, related to the recovery of the alcoholic or patient, and is used to preclude the need of spelling out employer, pastoral counsellor, doctor and other such individuals.

Counsellor: The term counsellor is used to denote anyone, lay or professional, providing guidance to the patient, family or collaterals. Counsellors may therefore range from professional workers in the field, to doctors, clergymen, members of Alcoholics Anonymous, industrial personnel, and the like, serving in a counselling role.

Referral: The term "referral" is used to denote the motivating source by which or from whom a patient, spouse or collateral is to be referred for assistance.

While emphasis will be given to the many kinds of alcoholisms, for the writer's present purpose it will suffice to pool the several types under the single term alcoholism. This approach is not to be considered as an overall simplification of the matter. The many complexities and the extent and range each single problem area presents are well understood.

The reader will recognize the continuing emphasis placed on a recognition and acceptance of alcoholism as a treatable illness. To me, the illness concept better reflects the manner in which this sickness afflicts its sufferers, physically, emotionally, socially and spiritually. It does not raise arguments of etiology, symptom or moral judgment as does the term "disease." Many read into the term "disease" the need for a specific cause. Also the expression "disease" to some evidences a repulsive connotation as something contagious. There are no problems of connotation, response or acceptability to the term "illness." If the matter of semantics has proved so helpful to the whole field of mental health, is it not then timely that the same principle be applied to this ailment? In so doing, we will begin to resolve problems of labels, language and definitions and eliminate the unkind attitudes oppressing the treatment of alcoholism, while providing interpretations acceptable to those seeking help in recovering from or dealing with the treatable illness — alcoholism.

Notes

1. *The Alcohol Language: Keller & Seeley — with a Selected Vocabulary* (Brookside Monograph No. 2), Alcoholism Research Foundation (now The Alcoholism and Drug Addiction Research Foundation) 1958 and 1963, University of Toronto Press — with permission. Note that in quoting from this work, the author has taken the liberty of deliberately separating the "*ic*" from the expressions "alcoholic beverages" used by Keller in order to emphasize the author's suggested interpretation of this expression, i.e. beverage alcohol.

5. Relationship to Other Ills

In recent years a growing number of effective studies confirm that chronic drinking deters and eventually nullifies the finest medical care in treating other sicknesses.

The "practising alcoholic" simply does not take adequate care of his or her well-being physically, emotionally, socially or spiritually. Neither can the alcohol-dependent patient properly follow the simplest convalescent instructions. When new problems of neglect and poor personal habits — lack of sleep, improper diet and the like — are added to existing sickness or disease, one cannot anticipate much in the way of sound recovery. While alcohol may not always cause deterioration of bodily organs, it can and does serve as a serious irritant. The aftermath of malnutrition and dehydration are bound to take their toll, in spite of the iron constitution many alcoholics seem to possess. To ignore or shy away from the added problems which misuse of alcohol creates in such situations, is to blind ourselves to the total recovery needs of the patient.

In the past, investigation by researchers revealed evidence that alcoholism was a primary cause for the non-recovery and repeated re-admission of tuberculosis patients. It probably still is, though to a far lesser extent because of the great strides that have been made in the last thirty or so years in the fight to eradicate tuberculosis. Today, as in the past, chronic drinking seriously impedes the care of heart disease, diabetes, cirrhosis, asthma, epilepsy, ulcers and other physical ills. Where emotional problems are concerned, excessive or addictive drinking masks the patient's real needs, making it almost impossible to deal with the other disorders which may be present. When alcohol is added to or mixed with medication (whether prescribed or over-the-counter) the results can be devastating, particularly given the proliferation of both patent medicines and the constantly growing collection of "miracle" prescription drugs which are often prescribed in combinations producing numerous unpleasant side effects.

Records on patients in custodial and veterans' homes, mental institutions and the like indicate that the revolving door process of admissions and re-admissions is caused in far too many instances by alcohol problems, not infrequently combined with other addiction or substance abuse problems. A study of the outpatient

44

services of a large general and teaching hospital indicated that over 25 percent of their patients had an alcohol-related problem in the patient or spouse.

In surgery, even very simple operations can be complicated and made serious by alcoholism. A surgeon friend had the unique experience of having a patient, following minor surgery, go into DTs, run from his bed and jump down the laundry chute. Fortunately, he landed on a pile of laundry below! Another friend died as the result of damage she inflicted on herself by leaving her bed to get a badly needed drink from a bottle she had stashed away in her luggage. Similarly, dentists who used to use gas and now use other chemicals as anaesthetics for the extraction of teeth and such have had equally frightening experiences with alcoholic patients. Though whiskey may have served as a painkiller in years gone by, alcohol does not mix with anaesthetics used by modern medicine and dentistry. Proper tests are well warranted whenever the excessive use of beverage alcohol is indicated, for the protection of both the patient and the practitioner.

Hospitals in which overall therapy has been instigated, including the diagnosis and comprehensive treatment of alcoholism, have had splendid recovery results. It is certainly sounder and more practical to initiate such treatment while the patient is under care for other ills. And it may well be the first time that the patient has ever received a positive and forthright diagnosis of the *illness* alcoholism, without preaching or disdain. This opens the door to the proper treatment of all the patient's ills, assuring total recovery.

Alcoholism often covers up the symptoms of other prevailing problems, and the drinking problem keeps the sufferer from seeking help. I remember a patient coming back to see me after attaining several months of sobriety. After greeting me, he said, "I've never been better off in my life. My wife kisses me goodbye when I leave and when I return. The kids think I'm it! I just got a raise and promotion and am nearly out of debt — but I feel awful, somehow."

The man did not wish to question his good fortune or to complain, but he did want help. I asked when he had last seen a doctor for a thorough checkup, and learned that he hadn't seen one in years. He resented them. One had called him a drunken bum and had thrown him out of his office; another wouldn't come when he was sure he was dying. Still another had cost him his driver's licence (he felt) by giving him mood-altering drugs — and on it went.

Finally I said, "You know that may all be so — but you were so well pickled for fifteen years no one could check you properly. You should see your physician now, and then make a habit of seeing him regularly. Tell him all about the alcoholism *and your recovery*, and remember, request a thorough examination."

Well, he did just that. He had a perforated ulcer, which could have killed him. It was remedied, and now he and his family swear by the physician who helped him.

In another instance, a former patient called his A.A. sponsor at midnight in a state of anguish and panic. While he was watching TV, some little men had come

Alcoholism: Treatable Illness

into the room after him! It was not unlike an episode of DTs he had known, though at the time of this incident, he'd had three years of sobriety. He was hospitalized at once, and it was learned that he had received psychiatric care as a young man. He voluntarily entered an institution and after several months returned to his family and position, a well man in every way. In the years since, he has never had a recurrence of any problem. The new insight, together with excellent and knowledgeable care, made him whole again.

These stories serve to illustrate that communication with a physician is a two-way street, particularly where alcohol problems are concerned. While these incidents were more common in the past, and while there has been marked progress in the attitude of the medical profession as a group toward alcoholics and their medical problems, attitudinal bias does still unfortunately exist, though it is perhaps less overt and less clearly demonstrated on a regular basis.

Effective alcoholism clinics, as a result of the thorough examinations they require, frequently find other patient ills which can then be referred for treatment in their own right. The alcoholic's behavior may have a disastrous effect on spouse and children, who may seek treatment for personal disorders when actually the problem lies with the alcoholic spouse or parent. Frequently, they find that their own problems stem from living with problem drinking in an intolerable situation.

I remember an executive's concern over his secretary of many years, who started "going to pieces." Previously, she had capably managed both his personal and business affairs as his administrative assistant. Just prior to granting her sick leave, he learned her husband was a serious alcoholic. She worried constantly that he might pawn their possessions, burn the house down, beat the children or do any of the thousand and one other "bad" things that he could do when he was drinking. By helping to obtain treatment for the woman's husband, the executive not only retained his perfect secretary, but helped to rehabilitate the whole family.

Tragic experiences have proven that not all of those people incarcerated as alleged drunks are necessarily inebriates. In the course of one week (some years ago), a jail in a large metropolitan city had seven prisoners die in their cells; all had been jailed under older and more repressive legislation as "common drunks." Only one of these people was an alcoholic, and he died during the DTs before help was made available. One died as a result of epileptic seizures; one in a diabetic coma; two because of serious concussions and other physical injuries; one, through drinking excessively, died of pneumonia he contracted in his weakened condition; and one, a depressive with a known record of care in a mental institution, committed suicide. The police in that jail, charged with the care and responsibility of these inmates, lacked the knowledge to deal effectively with such problems. The fact that the episode occurred during the Christmas season perhaps gave impetus to the investigation demanded. The result was a complete change in policy and procedure for all prisoners brought in, or found to be, in an unconscious state. Immediate alcohol tests and diagnosis by a competent physician prevented this loss of life from recurring.

Often patients are handled with similar inadequacy in emergency of general hospitals. If they are admitted and treated for excessive drinking, all too often they are released without voluntary or forced referral to proper treatment resources. Proper referral and follow-up would initiate a meaningful approach to their problems and reduce the necessity and cost of repetitive care, at least for some. To arrest and hospitalize, to sentence repeatedly and jail, and then simply to release such cases is archaic, inhuman and costly. A growing number of hospital policy makers are beginning to realize that the vast majority of these cases are not criminals or degenerates, but sick people who require treatment and rehabilitation, and at the worst, simple custodial care.

Many problem drinkers seek medical or other help early in the development of their illness. To thoughtlessly or deliberately gloss over the apparent alcoholism or such other hidden ailments as are indicated is most unethical. To ignore the desperate needs of sick people because of their "weakness for drink" is barbaric. To sentence repetitively the alcoholic to jails and institutions without any effort at rehabilitation, or to fail to provide a total treatment program for others institutionalized in mental, veterans' or chronic sufferers' hospitals is a tragic and costly waste. Nevertheless, this is still being done for far too many of the alcoholics seen in courts (in some jurisdictions), hospitals and institutions.

Social and spiritual contacts demand the same intensity and quality of care in helping the alcoholic adjust to the reality of living. The alcoholic cannot be treated in segments; treatment must speak to the whole person, in a whole family and complete community. The alcoholic's problem drinking has a very real effect on his or her social and spiritual relationships, the depth of which effect is clearly evidenced in the remorse and guilt each alcoholic knows. It is a hell and loneliness beyond description. While we will review these factors in a later chapter, we must call attention to the severity of these ills in relationship to others. Their recognition and treatment is indeed vital to the well-being of the whole person. This concept is accepted as fact in relationship to man's other physical and emotional problems. It must apply as acutely to the illness alcoholism.

6. Legalistic Confusions and Remedial Measures

A friend was arrested for drunk driving. Unable to obtain a cab, he had decided to venture home alone in his car. His errant driving was under surveillance for several miles by a patrol car. When stopped, his reaction to the tests conducted confirmed his impairment. In court the police acknowledged his gentlemanly and cooperative attitude; nevertheless, he was fined and his licence was suspended for six months.

Though he realized his guilt and appreciated receiving only a fine on a reduced charge, he was not without resentment. After all, he had known several years of sobriety and had no previous arrests. Nevertheless, he had no choice but to accept the situation. A costly lesson, but a good one for him.

Some other friends, while stopped at a red light early one Sunday morning, had their car rammed from behind by a man driving home from an all night party. Though they were not injured seriously, their car suffered considerable damage. The case went to court, and at the hearing it was demonstrated that the driver had been seriously intoxicated. He received a fine for careless driving.

In another instance, a man who was stopped for driving too slowly (he was doing about five miles an hour with a flat tire) was found to be intoxicated. After being in jail overnight, he was taken to court while still hung over. Without friends or attorney, he made no defense and pleaded guilty. He lost his license for a year and was sent to jail for ten days, before anyone knew what it was all about or could properly arrange legal counsel. It was his first arrest on any charge.

All three arrests occurred within a few weeks of each other and in the same city. While all three occurred several years ago, they serve to illustrate the inconsistent judgments which were the rule rather than the exception until very recently. They reflected the infirmity of purpose which has for so many years characterized every statute in which the abuse of alcohol plays a part. Though they might not have thought so at the time, the three culprits in these examples got off very easily when we consider the penalties which might have been imposed today in many jurisdictions.

Things have been slow to change in this respect. However, in the last few years, public outrage and the visibility of special interest groups representing those who have been victims of alcohol abuse by drivers have increased greatly. The activities of organizations such as *M.A.D.D.* ("Mothers Against Drunk Drivers"), together with strong lobbying by police and other law enforcement officials in all jurisdictions in Canada and the United States, are forcing a marked change in legislative planning and policy, and concomitant changes in enforcement procedures. Penalties range from 24-hour roadside license suspensions to stiff fines and the loss of license for a whole year for first offenders at one end of the spectrum, right to lengthy prison sentences for crimes such as "vehicular homicide" and criminal negligence causing death or serious injury. The law has changed its approach to the issue of intent in many cases, so that it has become somewhat more difficult for an intoxicated accused to point to his state of drunkenness as a means of suggesting that he could not have formed the intent to commit a particular offense. In other words, he might have been too drunk to be aware of everything he was doing, but he clearly knew when he took his first drink of the day that there was a chance he could become intoxicated and pose a threat to persons other than himself. Drunken recklessness is no longer the excuse it was twenty or thirty years ago, and the public will no longer accept the kind of patronizing condonation which all too often used to characterize court decisions.

Despite this progress, laws and regulations dealing with problem drinking behaviour, as related to health, welfare, rehabilitative and policing services, are still largely antiquated, confusing and contradictory. They add to the magnitude of the alcohol problem by tolerating or encouraging inconsistencies in philosophy, policy and practice in dealing with problem drinkers. Looking across the many jurisdictions which are capable of enacting laws or regulations which touch upon the subject of alcohol and its use or misuse, we can see that the existing "potpourri" of statutes governing alcohol infractions mirrors the intensity of prejudice carried over even from the Prohibition Era. There are still places where the use of beverage alcohol is tacitly or expressly assumed to be both sinful and dangerous, and therefore undesirable and deserving of a prohibitive approach. As we are unlikely to return to Prohibition, we should properly expect existing legislation in many areas in Canada and the United States to be revised and standardized in its approach to the use and abuse of beverage alcohol.

A special area of concern is that which exists in the matter of legal drinking ages. To add to the confusion of "local option and age control," there are further variations by ages governing the kinds of alcohol beverages that may be consumed. Variances in lawful drinking between 18 and 21 years have been found between cities and counties, and even within the same state or province! Neighbouring jurisdictions have a host of differences in laws dealing with similar content, causing no end of controversial problems. Add to this a scattering of "dry" communities, a hodge-podge variation of drinking hours and liquor licensing restrictions and

Alcoholism: Treatable Illness

requirements, differences between jurisdictional controls among the protective agencies of local police, sheriffs, deputies, state patrols, mounties, judges or other forces charged with the responsibility of upholding the laws, and one appreciates how difficult it becomes to enforce and respect these laws.

Laws concerned with drunken, impaired and careless driving, or with driving under the influence, are often subject to the same vagaries of local interpretation. Frequently, an individual in Canada can contravene both the Criminal Code (a federal statute), and a provincial Motor Vehicle Act (to say nothing of municipal bylaws which indirectly address the conduct of drinking individuals). There are innumerable variations in fines and sentences. Sentences are mandatory in some areas, whereas in a neighbouring community a light fine might be meted out for the same offense. It seems that almost all of these statutes are dependent upon the interpretation and charity of the individual judge concerned. One judge might be known by reputation to be pretty tough against some forms of misbehaviour, while another may enjoy a reputation for leniency. Solomon at his best would have given up in despair. And of course, the United States has a problem that Canada does not, simply because of the character of its constitution. In Canada, judges are appointed, and criminal law is a matter of federal jurisdiction (so criminal statutes apply nationwide); in the Unites States, judges are elected and are therefore by definition of one partisan leaning or another, and criminal law is, with numerous exceptions, a matter of state jurisdiction. Imagine trying to enforce fifty sets of criminal statutes in such a way that one's constitutionally guaranteed freedoms and legal obligations are treated with true equality.

It is an enigma of our presumed social advancement that we have not been able to address this legalistic confusion, given its sheer vastness as a facet of the alcohol problem. It seems we are deliberately trying to foul the matter up so as to make it impossible to deal with the situation, or to attain any uniformity of controls.

Welfare statutes still exist in some jurisdictions which demand that before a destitute family may receive aid, the responsible member must agree to a separation if the spouse has a drinking problem. This often creates a state of hypocrisy for both the recipients of the aid and the workers responsible for assessing the situation. Other regulations may compel the spouse to charge the problem-drinking member with common drunkenness, neglect, disorderly conduct, desertion, or another serious infraction. If the charges are not justified, it promotes further discord, adding new problems to existing ones.

To test the potential of rehabilitation versus old procedures in relation to these statutes, informal surveys and demonstration projects initiated as far back as 1949 in the welfare and probation departments of a metropolitan county area demonstrated the effectiveness of early intervention. At the outset both departments acknowledged that about 15 percent of their case loads involved problem-drinking situations. Both groups were then exposed to an intensive orientation on alcoholism. Staff were assured that they would not be jeopardizing themselves or their clients in the program to be adopted.

It was agreed to authorize the welfare workers to grant necessary aid in cases of indicated alcoholism without resorting to the charges mentioned earlier. However, to qualify, both the alcoholic and spouse were obliged to accept referrals to an alcoholism clinic. Aid was also to be continued when indicated during the treatment period. An occupational counsellor was incorporated into the program. Every service was managed on a forthright and positive basis.

In addition to cooperating with welfare personnel, the probation staff were drawn into another role. A policy and procedure was established whereby court cases involving problem-drinking situations were evaluated to determine potential and appropriate rehabilitative measures. These procedures, separate from and in addition to routine pre-sentence investigations, have been and are being introduced into many correctional systems.

Many offenders charged with offences related to drinking, bad cheques, neglect, disorderly conduct and drunken driving are accepting such rehabilitation when so offered. Some sentenced persons continue working days and serve out their time in custody at night and over weekends. They are permitted to attend treatment appointments and A.A. groups. The courts, sparked by cooperative judges, arrange for private interviews in selected cases. Thus, the application of rehabilitative procedures results in recoveries, rather than in repetitive incarceration.

The fact that such measures are becoming commonplace today speaks to the efficacy of these measures, relative to the strategies they replace such as work release, community service and mandatory counselling for alcohol/substance abuse and related offences. Judges, parole officers and probation officers played a significant part initially and during the follow-up in the social rehabilitation of offenders who had tangled with the law in earlier rehabilitative efforts. When properly oriented, their role in rehabilitating alcoholics is even more vital today. It is possible for these officers, within the restrictions of their departmental regulations, to work closely with all of the aforementioned agencies. In many such instances they are preventing the alcoholic from becoming another revolving door victim.

In the initial surveys and demonstrations, several very gratifying goals were achieved. The percentage of recoveries in both departments was much higher than anticipated. All personnel learned to deal with problem-drinking in a positive manner, and not to hide or ignore the illness. Of greater significance, a rehabilitative approach was taken to the problems of the whole person and family by including the spouse and family throughout.

These efforts have other noteworthy results. They encourage welfare and other related departments to appoint full time counsellors on alcohol and other drug-

Alcoholism: Treatable Illness

related problems. Departmental personnel in ever increasing numbers are being sent to schools on alcohol studies to further staff development and training. Despite these measures, the acknowledged related problem drinking case load rose to 55 percent. Why?

In the first place, staff are no longer fearful of being caught giving aid to drunks; and secondly, they have learned to recognize, count and properly cope with these situations.

As a result, too, of the efforts in the mid and late 1960s by Judge Eugene Mangum in Phoenix, Arizona, and this writer in Edmonton, Alberta, two pilot programs — DWI (Driving While Intoxicated) and IDP (Impaired Driver Programs) were implemented and saw the development of new counter measures to combat the ever growing problem of drinking drivers. As noted earlier, this is another area of consideration for total community involvement to cope more effectively with one of alcohol's most costly and adverse problems.

More persons have been killed and maimed by drinking drivers than in the last war. While the costs to the economy continue in the billions, it remains one concern which everyone seems to view as if he or she were somehow exempt from the tragic possibilities of impaired driving. It also continues to be one of the most complex and frustrating issues faced by the protective systems of North American society.

Though programming personnel are in most instances full-time paid workers, the original pilot programs were initiated with volunteer representatives from the courts, police, prosecutors and probation officers, automotive and safe driving associations, universities, insurance companies, helping agencies, personnel from alcoholism educational and treatment programs, relevant governmental departments (Highways, Attorney General, Health and Safety) and members of Alcoholics Anonymous. Administrative and clerical help were minimal. Established courtrooms were used as regular class and meeting facilities. Audio-visual equipment, films and slides were made available by local resources and libraries.

Client referrals came from the courts as convicted drinking-driving offenders. One mechanism still employed is the placement of convicted DWI or IDP offenders on probation — resulting in an 'order' to attend the driver program. Another avenue of referral is still the suspension of sentence, pending the offender's attendance and participation. While this explanation is an oversimplification, it does suggest some of the sources of referral and some of the procedures followed.

The programs developed consist of a series of lectures and discussions on alcohol; its effect on drivers; the laws governing drinking and driving; the use of films showing actual drinking and driving accidents and experiences; a description of corrective services available for poor drivers and/or alcoholics, etc. Usually the program includes a series of four or five lectures, one each week. Earlier programs were an overnight success and were immediately monitored and supported by automobile associations and safety groups. The rest is history. There are many sober people and reunited families who owe it all to the "loving coercion" of an enforced court referral program.

What is particularly relevant in the context of this book is the startling but very real revelation that of all drivers convicted for drinking-driving offences, as many as 30 to 45 percent may be chronic alcoholics. The program, therefore, is for many the first intervention in their progression of dependency and their first real exposure to possible recovery.

Attorneys who early in the program thought to prevent their clients' involvement later encouraged and even urged their participation. Clients sought to have family and friends attend. Schools requested similar presentations. Judges and police were amazed at the numbers of former attendees who would stop them on the street or come to their offices to express their appreciation for being referred to the program, and often for their sobriety.

These demonstration efforts proved that, given direction, many (if not most) alcoholic situations can be resolved with immeasurable savings, both to the community and to those helped. A small percentage of recovered and self-sustaining families can easily offset the costs and additional services required. Of course, the success of these procedures demands a close working relationship among welfare agencies, courts, probation personnel, correctional institutions, family service bureaus, the alcoholism resources of the community and those of Alcoholics Anonymous and the Al-Anon Family Groups. To be effective, all resources must be oriented to a common understanding and acceptance of these problems of alcohol as being treatable.

It is encouraging to see more and improved examples of these approaches to the alcoholic as a treatable person (i.e., as a *patient*) being implemented in a growing number of communities, with equally productive results. Nevertheless, it still involves a slow and painstaking process of education and lobbying to get such efforts under way. There never seems to be enough money or personnel to do an adequate job, even though expenditures continue to mount through inflation and through the inertia of government (which is notoriously slow to change its ways — other than in the lip-service department).

Naturally, there are problems to guard against in establishing the sorts of rehabilitation programs which are modelled on these original pilot programs. In some communities in which such advanced measures are being promoted, a serious new problem has occurred. Alcoholism and other drug dependencies or misuse are being used as an excuse for crime, accidents, marital discord and other acts of deviant or socially unacceptable behaviour. *Alcoholism dependency must not be used as a shield to condone the consequences of wrong-doing.* I alluded to this earlier when I noted the courts' changing attitude toward questions of intent to

Alcoholism: Treatable Illness

commit an offence in circumstances where the accused's thinking processes were impaired by alcohol.

There are obviously alcoholics and addicts who commit crimes. They must be helped to deal with their problems; but if they have committed crimes, they must first be dealt with as offenders under the law. Guilty individuals, while incarcerated, may then be effectively reached and rehabilitated for their whole problem, as has certainly been proven through those penitentiary programs now in force, with the aid of Alcoholics Anonymous.

In some instances, there are regulations operative in hospitals and institutions which are as binding and as detrimental to effective intervention as the most airtight legislative provision. The multiplicity of written and unwritten (attitudinal) regulations governing hospital admissions is one of the most serious detriments to the treatment of the illness alcoholism. This, in spite of statements of long standing by the House of Delegates of the American Medical Association and the Board of Trustees of the American Hospital Association, accepting alcoholism as a serious health problem and sickness. Both acknowledged that alcoholism can be, and often is, a medical emergency and that the alcoholic should not be denied treatment or admission to hospital when so indicated. The U.S. Department of Health and Human Services has taken a very strong position in supporting this principle.

Regardless of this leadership and of the progress which has been made in the past decade, admissions to public or private hospitals, mental institutions, veterans' homes and the like are for the most part regulated by the attitudes of those in charge and so vary accordingly from institution to institution. This is an obstacle of major proportions in achieving the recognition and treatment some patients require. Of even greater import is the fact that such policies maintain the prejudices and false image of the alcoholic among the medical personnel of these institutions, while instilling these precepts in the minds of new generations. If the medical profession raises blocks of this immensity, how can we expect other social sciences within health, welfare and protective agencies to do otherwise?

The abuse and misuse of alcohol reflected in problems of drunkenness and obnoxious, incorrigible and even criminal behaviour, when compounded by poly-drug use, have so cluttered the issue that to attain an enlightened approach to alcoholism, we must tread a slow and careful path, using all the tolerance and understanding we can muster.

All governments, beginning at the federal level, must take a hard and searching look at the antiquated jungle of laws that govern problems of alcohol. It won't be easy — but neither was it easy to solve the incredible intricacies of science leading strolls on the moon or space shuttle technology. Manpower, money, need and demand gave those developments to the world.

Quite a few years back, the governor of a midwestern state was credited with saying, "The greatest advancement of our age is the treatment rather than the incarceration of the alcoholic." It is stimulating to note also that in the mid-1960s, and again in the mid-1980s, high court decisions in the United States determined that chronic alcoholics cannot be stamped as criminals if their drunkenness is the involuntary result of illness. If there is a toughening of the laws today, it comes from a desire to rehabilitate and to minimize danger to the public, rather than to punish or to criminally sanction alcoholics for their drunken behaviour. While intoxication may or may not assist a defence in a given situation (depending on the "voluntariness" of it and its relationship to the illness alcoholism), we may have reached a turning point emotionally as well as intellectually in public acceptance of alcoholism as a treatable illness.

7. *The Revolving Door of Waste*

The difference between rehabilitation and treatment is essentially one of semantics. Both terms revolve about and apply to the care and restoration of sick people. Despite this, society as a whole infers a secondary meaning for each expression that sets the two apart.

The process of rehabilitation seems to imply welfare, meals or lodgings, remedial custodial care, probation or parole, and the renovation of the physically or socially handicapped individual into a better adjusted person. Treatment conjures up references to the healing sciences, and to medication, cures and psychotherapy. These services are in fact synonymous and apply to all persons, and especially to the alcoholic, whether he or she has a silken pillow for a spinning head or a cement curb stone to cushion a pounding hangover.

These individuals — the "high bottom" alcoholic and the apparent derelict — are both sick people requiring treatment and rehabilitation in the fullest sense of each word. Though the skid row group is very much in the minority (perhaps as little as 5 percent of the alcoholic population), it is the most recognized, known and countable group, and so it has been the focus for many statistical reports. An alcoholic in this group may be counted one hundred times in a single year, as a repeater. The judges know these unfortunates by their nicknames. Work houses and prison farms regularly have them picked up when their skills are needed. They are always available — until they die. One thousand arrests and court appearances may thus represent only 20 percent of that number in actual individuals. Few are ever looked upon as really human beings any more. They are the town drunks of every community, our image or stereotype of alcoholism and the alcoholic.

The families of those at the bottom of the scale fare little better. They are the innocent sufferers caught up in a vicious and tragic cycle of dependency and inhumanity which has roots in and is exacerbated by the nature of our culture and our social patterns. Handicapped by the labels applied to their alcoholic spouse or parent, they magnify the impact of social ignorance and increase the costs of our prejudices and inertia a thousand fold. Given the seriousness of this situation, we need to examine this "bottom" group more closely.

Every time an alcoholic person enters or re-enters the legal system for a drink-related problem, the cost is underwritten by the taxpayer. We additionally pay for the person's board and keep if he or she is put in jail or in some other institution at the behest of the court. In many instances, we also assume the burden of caring for and maintaining any dependents involved. This overhead is further compounded by the payment of unemployment, health and welfare benefits and similar costs. These directly and indirectly increase the price of goods and services to the consumer, and our tax bill. Such expenditures are also reflected in increased veterans' pensions and admissions to veterans' homes and chronic care hospitals.

The revolving door process is repeated again and again through the police, courts, probation, jails, hospitals and other institutions. In some instances, these procedures are even called "rehabilitation." However, this term is nothing more than a lip-service cover-up for the inadequacies of most present systems in dealing with the whole issue. Were we to expend the same effort, time and monies to make available the personnel necessary to develop more positive rehabilitative measures, the results might be fantastic indeed.

A medical officer of one particular institution, in discussing this archaic treadmill of waste, once advised me that his facility was repetitively institutionalizing a growing number of chronic drinking patients, and that in his opinion, they represented perhaps as high as 50 percent of the institutional case load. He could remember when there were very few such cases — at least on paper. As it became acceptable to include alcoholic problems in the statistics, without repercussion and censorship, the numbers began to rise. Similarly, as the community at large began to perceive a need for treatment versus incarceration, more admissions were made under the classification of problem drinking and alcoholism.

This individual felt it was time that we became cognizant of the wasteful process of admission, custodial care and release without provision of a more effective program of treatment. Fresh air, food, rest, work and some A.A. are not quite enough! While many respond to the A.A. philosophy, when it is available, others require sound professional therapy to achieve recognition, admission and care.

The quality of both professional and A.A. care, and the results obtained, are dependent upon the empathy, ability, interest and continuity of personnel. Thus it is vital that all who are concerned with "rehabilitation" maintain a cooperative and well integrated total treatment effort, if the remaining framework of the barbaric system of admission, release and readmission is to be eliminated.

An alcoholic, on the verge of DTs, voluntarily entered a mental institution where he had been a patient several times before. On readmission, he was placed in a locked cell and kept in the nude with nothing more than a mattress on the floor. He received no care of any kind. At the end of five days, being able to sign himself out, he left. Having had a similar experience many years ago, I appreciate well his

Alcoholism: Treatable Illness

resentment. In all these years, there has been far too little change or improvement in the care provided in far too many jurisdictions. The principle behind the old way seems to be, "This will teach him or her a lesson."

Similarly ineffective procedures are still used in many health, welfare and prison institutions, though in very recent years the rate of progress has accelerated dramatically. Rehabilitative measures can be designed for each and every type of unit with effective results. Funds are being expended, the personnel and facilities are there — if only truly sufficient resources can be directed to achieving rehabilitative goals, as opposed to continuing mere custodial care.

There comes to mind an institution on which millions were expended, as a separate and distinct rehabilitative facility for alcoholics. Initial planning lacked the calibre of personnel and programming required to pursue a constructive course. Its only claim to fame was the quality and quantity of vegetables its garden grew. As a pilot effort, this establishment attracted people from all over the world. They went away confused and disenchanted, for the program emphasis seemed to be on the vegetables! In spite of itself, this facility, through the help of A.A., provided help for many. New officials, aware of and sympathetic to the potential of the institution, planned and instituted a meaningful rehabilitation service. Subsequently integrated with the overall program in its region, it provided a demonstration effort second to none.

It has been argued that proper programming would demand capital allowances and operational funds beyond attainment. This is absurd. Greater capital allowances are being provided every year to add to the building of institutions, simply to house more people. The revolving door process expands and multiplies at a phenomenal rate. Repetitive incarceration and institutionalization have never cured any of these problems. And today the increasing numbers of homeless people are a blight on our society.

While costs must be justified, we should be willing to measure the social and humanitarian gains potentially available, without placing dollars ahead of people. It is time for us to redirect the application of funds now being allocated and reapply the skills of the qualified personnel at hand. Sufficient knowledge has been and is being accrued, and is, in fact, being used in some areas to provide an intensive and productive regime of programming to better cope with the issue.

What of the majority of alcoholics — the "hidden" group that accounts for perhaps 90 to 95 percent of the alcoholic population? These people, too, reach a treadmill process and period in their problem-drinking lives. The alcoholic goes from doctor to psychiatrist, clinic to hospital, private sanatorium to institution, pastor to chaplain, position to job, and so on. The alcoholic may try the geographical cure, moving from one community, or even one country, to another. Man and woman alike, the alcoholic may involve spouse and family. Tragically, some will move into the visible alcoholic minority group — and become "nothings" too.

This group also projects its costly burden onto the taxpayers. This group is responsible for poor management, waste and error, employee replacement, premature retirement and early pension, absenteeism and poor morale, professional misconduct, family neglect and poor parenthood, and all the other costly wastes of the minority group, compounded many times over. Again we pay that bill, directly and indirectly, in increased consumer costs and taxes. Pity the poor alcoholic indeed, who self-righteously announces, "I am only hurting myself," and "My drinking costs nothing to anyone."

The real tragedy is that this group has every right to expect and demand more — at least while they can still pay for it. Their "revolving door" could more easily become an open door to recovery, if those about them would become understanding of their illness. I have known patient after patient to say, "Why didn't my doctor tell me it was alcoholism and show me a way out?" Individually and collectively, we all have that responsibility — and some a little more than others.

Every alcoholic should receive the most that treatment and rehabilitation conjunctively may offer. The illness alcoholism demands the focus and attention of all the resources of medical science, physically, emotionally and spiritually. They require and should receive every possible aid in their social rehabilitation. And this applies to patients and to all those around them — men and women, old and young alike.

Perhaps we cannot reach all of the last-stage alcoholics, but they do deserve our attention and compassion. What we do with the hidden majority group will lessen the numbers reaching the end of the line. The revolving door process and its ongoing tomorrows may only be eliminated through the control and prevention programs we are motivated to implement today in both segments of the problem drinking population.

I continue to emphasize the illness alcoholism over other dependencies because in our fear of and concern about other drug issues, there is a growing tendency to neglect, even to ignore, alcoholics as our number one problem. It must ever be recognized that there are probably more alcoholics than dependents on all other drugs combined. This new phase in society's rejection is further exacerbated by current attempts to minimize, even deny, the concept of alcoholism as a disease.

8. Range and Extent

Much has been accomplished in the past half century in achieving a greater awareness of and improved attitude changes toward the dependent use of beverage alcohol. Nevertheless, society generally is still less than willing to recognize and respond positively to the magnitude of the issues and costs involved. Even temperate social users and non-users seem prone to ignore the critical role the excessive use and misuse of beverage alcohol plays in everyday life, in the economy and in personal well-being.

Most alcoholics claim only to be hurting themselves, without harm or cost to others. They remain completely indifferent to, and subjectively defensive about, the scope of the problems of dependency and their horrendous costs to the alcoholics themselves, their families and associates, and society *per se*. Nor are individual cases scared by the serious personal effects of their illness.

By some strange paradox, alcoholics and their families alike imagine themselves to be very much alone and singularly different from other imbibers of beverage alcohol. This myth is belied, first by the fact that the majority of people do use beverage alcohol, and second by the staggering numbers of their kind who, unbeknownst to them, also fall prey to the illness alcoholism!

Only when tuberculosis, polio and cancer were finally accepted as national public health problems did it become possible to measure both incidence and cost with accuracy. Similarly, as the acceptance of alcoholism increases, it will be possible to more accurately assess the numbers of afflicted and the costs involved.

Precaution must be taken to guard against unwarranted estimates because of an apparent upsurge in the misuse of beverage alcohol, particularly (and tragically) where adolescents and the elderly are concerned. Increases may in part be attributable to such relative factors as: normal population growth; a more tolerant public attitude toward drinking generally, and even toward excessive drinking; increased drinking among women and younger people; an affluent economy; less restrictive policies permitting more frequent occasions, more places and longer hours in which to drink, and more liberal promotion of beverage alcohol. Many of today's drinking practices were once seriously frowned upon or considered taboo.

In addition to the many new forms of outlets — grocery and drug stores, transportation facilities and the like — even illicit or "bootleg" outlets remain a serious concern in certain regions.

All of these factors permit a more favourable climate in which to drink, while glamorizing the use of alcohol beverages as a necessary and important part of life. These influences manifest themselves in the earlier trend to lower the legal drinking age and in the pressures to reduce existing drinking restrictions even further. Conversely, as greater awareness and knowledge of these social problems surface, pressure is exerted to raise drinking ages, narrow the numbers of facilities available, increase the prices of beverage alcohol, and establish more controls over its use. Despite all the compilations of data (and though there have been some indications of decreasing consumption in certain segments of the population), one fact is irrefutable: *when there are more "users" of beverage alcohol, there will inevitably be more "abusers" and more "alcoholics."* As one result, more women and more young adults and teens will be afflicted with alcohol dependency.

One must appreciate that definitive studies on consumption and incidence, magnitude, range and extent, and on the economic costs of dependency on alcohol and other related drugs, are simply not easily attained — especially with respect to more local data on our home communities. We often lack the broad spectrum of current data that is required, and those investigations in hand can be dated, incomplete, and overly conservative. This situation is further compounded by the multiplicity of attitudes described earlier and the social changes presently occurring related to the use and misuse of beverage alcohol. Nevertheless, it is important to be aware of the astounding costs associated with the abuse of beverage alcohol and the illness alcoholism.

Without becoming overly involved in detail, let us examine a sampling from several landmark investigations. In doing so, we must be cautious. These studies date from the early '80s. Since that time, some advances have indeed been made. While there is growing evidence of increasing intellectual awareness and acceptance of the magnitude and incidence of problem drinking, there is little emotional 'push' to better cope with the many problem areas which are still inadequately addressed.

The materials to be considered are listed below. We have taken the liberty of paraphrasing where necessary for purposes of clarity and accessibility, and we have made alterations where necessary in order to help the reader grasp current applications. The information and data considered in the remainder of this chapter is drawn from or based on one or more of these sources, unless otherwise noted.

1. The Fourth Special Report to the U.S. Congress on *Alcohol and Health* — from the Secretary of Health and Human Services. U.S. Department of Health and Human Services — Public Health Service — Alcohol, Drug Abuse and Mental Health Administration — National Institute on Alcohol Abuse and Alcoholism — Rockville, Maryland 20857 (1980).

Alcoholism: Treatable Illness

2. The Institute of Medicine — Report of a Study on Alcoholism, Alcohol Abuse and Related Problems, Opportunities for Research. Division of Health Promotion and Disease Prevention — National Academy Press, Washington, D.C. (1980). A study prepared as a resource paper for the Committee (Institute of Medicine) by Leonard G. Schifrin, Ph.D., Catherine E. Hartsog, and Deborah H. Brand, Department of Economics, College of William and Mary, Williamsburg, Va.

3. Canada — Special Report on Alcohol Statistics. Health and Welfare, Canada — Statistics Canada, Ottawa, Ontario (1981).

4. Preventing Alcoholism — Primary Prevention (1981). The Christopher D. Smithers Foundation, Inc., Mill Neck, N.Y.

5. Other miscellaneous materials, including various "Fact Sheets" prepared by the National Council on Alcoholism.

Consumption Trends

Following earlier patterns evolving since World War II and as demonstrated by studies between the years 1970 and 1979, North Americans consumed increasing amounts of beverage alcohol. Apparent consumption in the United States rose to 2.7 gallons (American) and in Canada to 2.6 gallons (Imperial) of absolute alcohol per person, per year. While the rates seemingly levelled off in 1978-79, the consumptions noted represent an approximate increase of one-third in national per capita use.

The absolute alcohol use was distributed as follows:

BEVERAGE ALCOHOL	UNITED STATES	CANADA
Beer	49%	22%
Distilled Liquors	39%	52%
Wine	12%	26%
	100%	100%

In the United States: During the 1970s, apparent consumption of ethanol continued to rise, but the rate of increase slowed considerably. By 1978, apparent consumption had risen to more than 2.7 gallons of ethanol per person per year. Approximately one-third of the self-reported adult population of the United States continue to classify themselves as "abstainers"; one-third as "light drinkers"; and one-third as "moderate" (24%) or "heavier" (9%).

In the heavier drinking category, males (14%) outnumber females (4%). While 25% of males reported abstaining from alcohol, 40% of females reported abstaining.

Beer accounts for 49% of the ethanol consumed by Americans; wine accounts for 12%; and distilled spirits for 39%.

Heavier drinking appears to peak at ages 21-34 for males (19%), at ages 35-49 for females (8%), and to decline thereafter for both sexes.

Blacks of both sexes reported relatively high rates of abstention. However, among black adults who drink, the proportions of self-reported heavier drinkers are similar to those for most other groups. Hispanic groups of both sexes, but especially males, reported relatively high rates of heavier drinking.

While the frequency and quantity of adolescent drinking does not appear to have changed much since the 1974 national survey, the proportion of 10th-12th graders who reported ever having consumed alcohol is very high — 87%.

In the 1978 survey, a substantial number of youths reported drinking fairly large amounts of alcohol by age 15. Heavier and moderate/heavier drinking appears to increase to age 17 and then level off.

In Canada: The total abstainers are indicated to be approximately 25%, with about 20% for males and 30% for females. Canadian drinking consumptions also reveal several important trends:

Canadians have not only been using a greater amount of alcohol but have also been consuming more drinks of higher alcohol content.

In the high-range consuming provinces of the Yukon, Northwest Territories, and British Columbia consumption declined, but rose in Alberta. Increasing consumption was more widespread in the middle-range consuming provinces of Prince Edward Island, Saskatchewan and Ontario.

Though wine had the smallest share of the absolute alcohol market, its share is increasing steadily and consistently across all of Canada. Again, more drinking by women and by younger people, and lifestyle factors — affluence, increased drinking with meals and more frequent occasions to drink — are indicative of even greater and faster increases in consumption of wine and spirits.

The Canadian male drinking population was on average about 10% larger than the female drinking population.

The sharpest increase in usage occurs between the lower and upper teens for both males and females, with the current rise being steeper for females than for males.

Older age groups, 40 and over, had a progressively lower proportion of users than younger age groups 20 to 39. For males the proportion of users averaged nearly 88% for ages 20 to 39, declining to 69% by age 60 and over. For females, users declined from 80% for ages 20 to 39, to 49% for those age 60 and over. Thus the largest differences in usage between the sexes occur between older males and older females.

Alcoholism: Treatable Illness

Incidence

Based on current adult populations above age 20 it is estimated conservatively that there are 11,000,000 alcoholics in North America, over 10,000,000 in the United States and approaching 1,000,000 in Canada.

Though the Jellinek formula continues to provide a working basis for estimating incidence, the late Dr. Jellinek in his own last analysis cautioned that this basic formula is probably much too conservative for most areas. While national approximations are those usually reported, in order to have any impact or meaning, *each community, through legitimate research procedures, should determine its own drinking patterns, problems, incidence, costs and needs.*

Initial statistical investigations on incidence were predicated on those alcohol users of the then legal ages of 20 years and over. *Today we know that as many as 80% of the young adults in high school, ages 15 and over (and all too many below that age), have tasted or are regular users of some form of beverage alcohol.* Contemporary studies therefore must be based on scrutiny of populations with a minimum age *at least* as low as fourteen.

Though some consumption figures are currently reported to be decreasing, there was a significant increase in the numbers of people ingesting beverage alcohol, with a greater number of men, a steadily increasing number of women, and a greater number of both at younger ages. There is no doubt that there is a dramatic lessening in the differences between the numbers of females and males who, in using beverage alcohol, become alcoholics.

Prior to the 1960s it was estimated that one person in fifteen of those using beverage alcohol would become an alcoholic; *today, one in nine or ten imbibers will develop alcohol dependency.*

In the early 1970s it was determined that one of every six to eight alcoholics could be a woman; *today, that ratio is reduced to one woman to two or three men.* It is claimed by some researchers that the ratio is now even; and by a few, that there are already more women than men alcoholics in some areas.

It is also now known that women, because of physical and emotional differences, can become dependent upon alcohol in a third of the time it takes for the average man to do so.

A further serious factor which has emerged from care centers is the fact that many women admitted to treatment are found to be suffering from dual addiction. Over and above alcohol dependency, many women have innocently become addicted to prescribed medications (especially sedatives and tranquillizers like valium). The growing number of young adults also so dependent is alarming and reaching epidemic proportions.

In the 1960s, the average alcoholic was estimated to be in his or her early fifties; in the 1970s the mid-forties; and now in the late 1980s, we find the average alcoholic to be in his or her mid-thirties. He or she is usually employed in a good vocation or profession, has a home and family, or is the spouse of a person in such a situation.

While there are an estimated 11,000,000 North Americans who are alcoholics among the adult population, there are another approximately 3,500,000 young adults or youths suffering from problems related to alcohol use, overuse and abuse. Many of those in this younger group are already advanced alcoholics, and others incipient alcoholics.

I submit that there are more cases of alcoholism than we dare recognize. Proportions such as these figures represent warrant the most intensive investigation and attention possible. In measuring the total numbers of those affected by the illness alcoholism, three additional groups should be included.

The first group concerns all those persons who are directly or indirectly adversely affected by the alcoholic patient. It is estimated that the alcoholic seriously affects a minimum of five to six other people — spouse, other family members, employees, associates and collaterals. Thus, conservatively speaking, another 55,000,000 people are involved. Therefore, the alcoholics' defensive argument that they only hurt themselves is contradicted by the emotional, social and economic disturbances in their families, and (as will be discussed later) requires as much attention as does the alcoholics' illness. A problem drinker in a position of responsibility affects the morale, stability, performance, productivity and well-being of all close associates. This disturbance radiates out to anyone who has a relationship with that individual.

The second group which must also be considered consists of those problem drinkers whose drinking is rapidly progressing into alcoholism. There are many incipient and early-stage dependent users who will assuredly progress into the more chronic phase of the illness unless their dependency is arrested. It is with this group that earlier awareness, knowledge, education and intervention can perhaps achieve effective results prior to the full onslaught of the illness. Similarly included in this category are those who have just begun the revolving door process through agencies, the courts and hospitals. One can appreciate that this is a vital concern in measuring both the overall incidence and the costs of alcoholism.

A third group demanding much more immediate investigation and attention is the growing number of alcohol and drug dependent retirees. All too many retired persons today are already — or will soon be — very serious dependency cases. Their increasing use of beverage alcohol, often compounded by the overuse and/or misuse of prescribed medications, is becoming an ever more serious problem in popular retirement areas. While many of these elderly sufferers regress and develop even more deeply hidden problems, society seems only too willing to ignore their plight. Only in the last while has this problem of the elderly begun to surface, and its incidence and magnitude been recognized.

Alcoholism: Treatable Illness

Remember, by far the majority of alcoholics are not the stereotyped image of the skid row derelict. Over 95% of the alcohol dependent population are a cross-section from every walk of life, of every age, race and creed. Less than 5 percent are the so-called "recidivists." There is reason to believe that employees in professional and managerial positions have the highest consumption of alcohol of all groups and also the highest incidence of alcoholism.

In summary, there are an estimated 11,000,000 alcoholics in North America. They directly and adversely affect an additional 55,000,000 individuals. Putting the matter plainly, if:

(a) a conservative one in ten adults who imbibe beverage alcohol incurs alcoholism;

(b) a minimal 6 percent of all employees are alcoholics;

(c) only 25 percent of persons seeking assistance through health, rehabilitation, protective and institutional services; or

(d) only 25 percent of those involved in divorce or juvenile delinquency, spouse or child abuse

are directly or indirectly implicated in problem drinking situations, then alcoholism does easily rank as the first single most serious and costly medical, legal and social problem of our time — *before* heart disease, mental illness or cancer.

Magnitude of Economic Costs

To the individual alcoholic and the family, all of this data may seem to be trivial and unimportant to his or her needs; it may even be resented or discounted, until through recovery and sobriety the alcoholic becomes an active part of the solution and no longer a continuing part of the problem.

Like "Topsy," the economic costs and human misery associated with alcohol abuse and the illness alcoholism have continued to mount. With each facet of the many legal, medical and social issues involved remaining for the most part unchecked, and the enormity of their costs going unrecognized or ignored, the problems of alcohol and alcoholism are compounded at a fantastic rate. Society's seeming indifference for so many years can perhaps be seen as an indication of the hopelessness we have assumed in the matter.

Any attempt to measure actual and related economic costs attributable to the abuse and dependent use of alcohol is faced with serious obstacles. Most of the pertinent information available deals primarily with that minority group, the recidivists, who represent at most a bare 10 percent of the problem drinking population. Because of regular contact with health, welfare, preventive and other agencies these known alcoholics are statistically reportable. Bear in mind, however, that the majority of alcoholics are *hidden* people whose problems are not public statistics, and who at least in the earlier stages of their illness, are not generally known to or recognized by others. Even during the latter phases in the progression of dependency, the spouse, other close family members and associates deny, protect and cover for the patient. Such denial, deterring recovery, further complicates the attainment of factual data that we need to combat properly the problems of alcohol abuse and misuse *per se*.

In the mid-1940s, B.Y. Landis did a study entitled "Some Economics of Alcohol and Certain Expenditures on Account of Inebriety."[1] Nothing of that scope and calibre had previously or has since ever been done — it was a comprehensive and really thorough investigation into the economic and social costs of the problems of alcohol misuse and overuse, and the illness alcoholism. The study concerned itself with expenditures related to the problems of alcohol in the United States, and to the then 2,400,000 "excessive" drinkers as estimated by the late Drs. Haggard and Jellinek of the Center of Alcohol Studies — then at Yale University.

The Landis investigation, based on a bibliography of eighty-seven titles, covered: costs of problem drinkers in state and private hospitals, veteran and mental institutions; costs associated with accidents of intoxicated drivers (fatal accidents even in 1940 were found to be twice as great a source of death among chronic alcoholics as among the general population); estimates on the maintenance of drunkenness offenders in jails; costs associated with crime; potential wage losses; costs of family assistance; and other areas of expenditure.

In 1945, a study by the National Council on Alcoholism found that while there were about three times more alcoholics than the diagnosed total cases of tuberculosis, cancer and infantile paralysis *combined*, only half a million dollars was expended on the treatment of alcoholism, compared with over one hundred fifty million dollars for the other aforementioned ills. Though the numbers of alcoholics have tripled and though tuberculosis and infantile paralysis have been all but vanquished in North America, expenditures on the care, control and prevention of alcohol problems and alcoholism are proportionately still only a fraction of the money spent on other public health problems (many of which are, statistically, far less severe).

As time has passed, costs have skyrocketed. According to government reports in the late '70s and early '80s, the direct measurable cost of alcohol abuse and alcoholism to the economy of the United States had by that time grown to an incredible $53 billion a year. The corresponding costs associated with other drug abuse at that time were estimated at $13 billion.[2]

A major survey and comparison of the economic costs of alcohol and alcohol abuse in the United States, as undertaken in 1974 and again in 1977 by the National Institute on Alcohol Abuse and Alcoholism (NIAAA). revealed the following costs of alcoholism and alcohol abuse.

Alcoholism: Treatable Illness

1971 Costs in 1975 dollars	Components	1975 Costs in 1975 dollars
11.8 billion	Lost Production	19.6 billion
11.0 billion	Health Care	12.8 billion
8.6 billion	Motor Vehicle Accidents	5.1 billion
1.2 billion	Social Responses	2.7 billion
0.5 billion	Criminal Justice	2.1 billion
—	Fire Losses	0.6 billion
33.1 billion		42.9 billion

This report, as with other studies, affirms that:

(1) alcoholism and alcohol abuse impose very large costs on society, and

(2) that research in this area is seriously underfunded when weighted against those costs and when compared to the social-cost-research-effort ratios for other major health disorders.

The study emphasized, as have others, that in all probability the figures and data quoted were conservative understatements. It also pointed up the vital need for further investigation with this timely comment:

. . . because the costs of alcoholism and alcohol abuse exceed those of most other major disorders, and because the research effort is much smaller, there is a prima facie case for believing that expanded research effort in regard to alcoholism may well offer society relatively high returns.

While the legal, medical and social components of all economic costs to society are virtually indivisible, let us review several individual cost factors considered in these studies:

Health complications related to alcohol abuse include cirrhosis of the liver, some cancers, gastritis, hepatitis, heart disease, and malnutrition, plus all those others that go unrecognized and uncounted.

Approximately one-half of all highway fatalities, and as high as one-third of all injuries from auto accidents are related to alcohol use, as are a substantial number of fatalities in industrial accidents, drownings, fires, falls and suicides. Each year 205,000 individuals prematurely die from these alcohol-related factors in the United States.

Although research has indicated a significant association between alcohol and violent crimes (homicide and assault) it is not possible to specify alcohol abuse as the causal, or even contributing factor behind any specific proportion of crime. The only crimes included in this analysis are homicide, rape, and aggravated assault; there are no figures covering robberies, vandalism or the many unreported crimes that could also be related to alcohol.

If, therefore, an accurate compilation had been possible at the time, the figure would have been much more than the $2.1 billion included. If, too, all other categories could similarly have been more accurately assessed, the report estimated that the 1975 total economic costs of the illness alcoholism and of alcohol abuse could have been as high as $60 billion.

Given the exponential growth rate of all related costs, what increments there have been in programs, services, research and educational efforts to combat the problems of alcohol misuse and alcohol dependency have not even kept up with inflation, assuming that since 1981 the rates of misuse, abuse and dependency have remained constant. But we know these rates have not remained constant; rather, they seem to have increased dramatically. When one considers new programming from this perspective, can it seriously be suggested that enough new programming has been developed, or that existing programming has been properly augmented and adequately funded?

Some years ago, when the public's initial vociferous reaction to drug abuse — particularly abuse among young people, many of whom were thought to be using alcohol and the so-called "soft" drugs — lessened, the financing of programs regressed. Alcohol and alcoholism efforts, perhaps tied too closely to the broader anti-"drug" crusade, also suffered. Though alcoholism was and is our leading drug problem (though perhaps no longer our most visible or high profile drug issue), alcohol abuse and dependency services, being at the bottom of the health service totem pole regardless of their importance, were among the first to be reduced.

I have said repeatedly that steps — albeit faltering steps in some cases — are now being taken by government and the private sector to make up the ground previously lost. This is an uphill struggle, since the circumstances which led to a lax attitude about alcohol problems seem to have led also to bureaucratic myopia and to a kind of political and social paralysis in the face of more current problems. This applies not only with alcohol, but also with cocaine, heroin, PCP and the "designer" drugs of the last decade, and with the economic, social and human costs of the trade in such proscribed substances.

While we are intellectually beginning to accept the ramifications of alcohol abuse and the concept of alcoholism as a 'treatable illness,' we are still reluctant to move to an emotional acceptance of it as a medical (as well as legal and social) affliction. We have not, in other words, removed the understandable but really undeserved pejorative connotations to which discussions of alcoholism and alcoholics lend themselves. As a result, meaningful teaching "about alcoholism" is still not routinely required in all the professional learning mainstreams of medicine,

Alcoholism: Treatable Illness

law and the social sciences. Perhaps it is for these reasons that such a small percentage of the victims of alcoholism voluntarily seek help. In the words of Dr. Bert L. Vallee:

> . . . Alcoholism as an illness, rarely exists as a distinct entity, without a variety of other concomitant disorders. For example, we now know the relationships between cirrhosis and chronic alcohol ingestion. I think we should keep in mind the many factors other than ingestion of large quantities of beverage alcohol that may correlate with a specific index of metabolism or behavior. For example, alcoholics, as we all know, suffer from a variety of disease entities, hepatic, renal, cardiovascular, etc. These variables have to be examined in detail when we are studying biological fluids, particularly in a clinical population. An alcoholic is usually a very sick individual in terms of derangement in many organic systems which may not be specifically related to those factors which originally initiated his drinking.[3]

As one who has laboured in the field of alcohol studies for more than forty years, I can certainly agree that if all the dollars lost, wasted, misspent and duplicated in business and industry, in health, welfare and educational services, in the protective agencies of courts, jails and police, and in other corrective institutions were combined, the total would be astronomical.

In no way could these horrendous economic costs compare with the misery, pain and heartbreak resulting from the illness alcoholism. Truly, as stated in Dr. Alan Gilbert's preface to this volume:

> The magnitude of the alcoholism problem is almost incomprehensible; as a single cost of human suffering it probably ranks only behind that of starvation.

Consider these social costs, relative to the times in which they were estimated:
Alcoholism ranks with cancer, heart disease, and stroke as a major ailment.
Alcoholism reduces the life expectancy of its victims by approximately twelve years.
Alcoholism destroys the marriages and jobs of three-fourths of its victims.
Alcoholism affects one of every ten drinkers of beverage alcohol.
Suicide rates among alcoholics are 55 times that of the rest of the population; 60% of all murders, 50% of all car accidents (27,000 deaths per year in the U.S.), 40% of all pedestrian fatalities, 50% of all family court problems, 33% of all arrests for public drunkenness, and 38% of all child abuse cases are alcohol-related.
In business and industry the estimated annual costs are 19.6 billion dollars for loss of time, illnesses, waste and spoilage, morale breakdown, accident and health benefits, disability and other factors. The estimated cost per year for employed alcoholics is $2,000.

And these:

Bio-Medical Consequence of Alcohol Abuse: Longstanding use of substantial amounts of alcohol has been found in a large proportion of patients with unexplained heart muscle disease.

Brief drinking sprees in apparently healthy individuals can result in premature heartbeats or total loss of rhythmic beating in the upper chambers.

Epidemiologic studies show that in all races and both sexes, regular consumption of large amounts of alcohol is associated with a substantially higher prevalence of high blood pressure.

Several studies have shown a statistically significant inverse correlation between alcohol use and susceptibility to heart attack from coronary atherosclerosis. But it is not firmly established that alcohol in small amounts protects against coronary atherosclerosis.

Alcohol is associated with stroke, phlebitis, and varicose veins and also may be involved in an unusual form of angina pectoris (chest pain) called Prinzmetal Variant Angina, which is widely believed to be due to spasms in large coronary arteries.

Numerous studies have shown that acutely or chronically administered alcohol results in lowered testosterone levels in the males of all species. The reduced testosterone level causes sexual impotence, loss of libido, breast enlargement, loss of facial hair, and testicular atrophy in many male alcoholics.

Loss of brain cells is one of the major consequences of alcoholism. In any given sample of alcoholics, the proportion of individuals with brain atrophy ranges from 50% to 100%, depending on the selectivity of the alcoholism treatment program from which the sample is drawn. New evidence suggests that heavy social drinking also results in brain atrophy.

Heavy alcohol consumption has been related to an increased risk of cancer at various sites in the human body, especially the mouth, pharynx, larynx, and esophagus. Cancer risk is further increased for heavy drinkers who also use tobacco.

The positive association between liver cancer and alcohol consumption is related to cirrhosis; very often the cancer is preceded or accompanied by cirrhosis or hepatitis and infection.

A rapidly growing body of literature provides evidence that abusive drinking during pregnancy is potentially detrimental to the development of the human fetus. Effects may range from mild physical and behavioral deficits to the fetal alcohol syndrome (FAS). The major features of FAS are mental retardation, poor motor development, extreme growth deficiency before birth and throughout childhood, and a characteristic cluster of facial abnormalities.

Alcohol consumption during lactation and the consequent effects on nursing

Alcoholism: Treatable Illness

infants is also an area of concern. Alcohol readily enters the breast milk, thereby providing alcohol to the nursing infant.

Social Implications of Alcohol Abuse: As many as 50% of those who died in falling accidents had been drinking.

Approximately one-half of adult fire deaths involve alcohol. Alcoholics were found to be 10 times more likely to die in fires compared with the general population.

Alcohol plays a significant role in drownings. One study reported that 68% of the drowning victims had been drinking and another study reported that 50% of such victims had been drinking.

Among Native Americans, 5 of the 10 major causes of death are alcohol-related: accidents, cirrhosis of the liver, alcoholism, suicide, and homicide. Among ethnic groups, Native Americans appear to have the highest prevalence of drinking problems.

Employed women have a higher rate of alcoholism and employed married women have significantly higher rates of both problem drinking and heavier drinking than either single working women or housewives. Women appear to drink more in the company of men than in the company of other women. A woman's risk for alcohol-related problems is increased by living with a heavy drinker.

Women are at high risk of abusing other drugs. Approximately one-third of recovered alcoholic women reported that they had abused prescription drugs, too.

Children of alcoholic parents have been underserved and underresearched [sic]. Clinical efforts with children of alcoholics suggest that sensitively designed programs can achieve positive results.

Problem drinking among adolescents appears to be associated with pessimism, unhappiness, boredom, aggressiveness, frustration, impulsiveness, distrust, cynicism, irresponsibility, inflexibility, and dissatisfaction. Correlations exist between adolescent problem drinking and antisocial or delinquent behavior. Heavier consumption has been linked to precocious sexual behavior, poor school performance, problem behavior in the classroom, number of absences from school, problems within the family, other drug use, and higher dropout rates.

Treatment, Social and Recovery Trends:

Societal attitudes have been the most formidable barrier to successful intervention. However, recent observations suggest that meaningful attitude changes have and are occurring, and the stigma associated with alcoholism and problem drinking has and is being reduced.

Occupational programming is the most well-developed and extensively implemented intervention approach. In 1950, there were approximately 50 occupational alcoholism programs; by 1980 the number of programs had increased to 4,400; today there are perhaps 7500 in North America alone.

In the private sector, approximately 25% of representative organizations had occupational alcoholism programs in 1972. In 1979, 56% of the organizations had implemented programs. Today, we may be reaching 70%.

Management and union support for occupational alcoholism programs has increased steadily since 1976. In 1979 the percentage of executives reporting lack of management support fell to less than 0.5%, while perceptions of union support have increased to 70%.

Corporate social responsibility remains the single most important reason given for program adoption. Those most often referred to programs for help were at the rank and file, middle management, and staff employee levels; those least often referred were at the clerical and top management levels.

The number of public sector occupational alcoholism programs has increased steadily. Since 1972, when there were very few programs, nearly half of all United States federal installations have implemented programs. These federal installations with programs employ over 80% of all federal employees.

Approximately 100,000 federal government employees have been referred to, or sought, treatment since such services were first offered in 1972.

Success rates for occupational programs are quite high (75-85%) and indicate the great promise of early intervention with younger, less impaired persons who have shorter treatment histories and greater social stability.

Drinking-driving programs are an important context for early intervention. Large numbers of persons enter formal alcoholism treatment as a consequence of early intervention resulting from an arrest for driving while intoxicated and referral to a drinking driver program.

The number of persons receiving treatment for alcoholism and problem drinking has continued to increase. However, approximately 85% of the population of alcoholics and problem drinkers are not receiving formal treatment services. In NIAAA-funded programs in the United States, over 75% of the services received by alcoholics and problem drinkers are outpatient services.

Alcoholism treatment has been shown to be effective, particularly for socially stable, middle class alcoholics. Studies of treatment effectiveness for this group, which constitutes the majority of alcoholics in the United States, have yielded improvement rates ranging from 30% to 92%. For socially stable alcoholics, sustained abstention rates of approximately 60% have been reported at 18 month follow-up.

For socially unstable alcoholics of lower socioeconomic standing, it is difficult to

Alcoholism: Treatable Illness

evaluate the effectiveness of alcoholism treatment *per se*; as high as 10% to 15% may find recovery. However, additional resources for this group, substantial extra treatment supports (outpatient and family care, halfway homes) concerning primary survival needs, education and training, and return to the opportunity structure of society are necessary if changes acquired through treatment are to be maintained.

Depending upon psychological status, medical condition, and a host of sociocultural, familial, and situational factors, patients may be served appropriately in hospital-based inpatient programs, nonhospital-based free standing alcoholism treatment facilities, or outpatient clinics. Research continues on the effectiveness of different treatment contexts and lengths of stay for particular patients. Depending upon a number of factors, safe detoxification may take place in either a medical or a social setting and the management of withdrawal may involve medical or psychosocial procedures or a combination of the two. While it is difficult to estimate precisely the numbers of persons who could be detoxified safely in a social setting rather than a medical setting, recent research and experience suggest that these numbers may be substantial.

Though the effectiveness of 'Family Treatment' is well recognized and is increasing, it is still absent from all too many programs. In 1978, in NIAAA-funded programs, only 9% of the patients were involved in family treatment.

Efforts to understand the changing population of the public inebriate and to provide for the needs of the homeless and skid row alcoholic continue. The public inebriate population is heterogeneous with regard to social class, sex, primary diagnosis; only a portion of this population fits the stereotype of skid row alcoholism. Skid row alcoholics are also heterogeneous and include a number of identifiable subgroups. Greater understanding of the skid row subgroups has been achieved. Attention to the design of ideal service delivery systems, multimodal treatment and rehabilitative programming, appropriate expectations, and commitment to provision of adequate resources are likely to result in realistically positive achievements with these groups.

In 1978 NIAAA's eighteen funded specialized problem-drinking-driver programs served 15,798 persons. Twenty-eight percent of all intakes to treatment were the result of an arrest for driving while intoxicated.

The Veterans Administration (VA) is the largest provider of direct treatment services to alcoholic patients. In fiscal year 1979 the 100 VA Alcoholism Dependence Treatment Programs served almost 50,000 patients.

The U.S. government offers approximately 50 health insurance plans most of which include alcoholism benefits. Aetna Life and Casualty Company and NIAAA are currently involved in a joint project to provide systematic cost and utilization data with regard to a newly expanded Aetna alcoholism benefit for 300,000 federal employees.

The NIAAA has continued to work with public and private insurers to encourage expanded alcoholism benefits and, in particular instances, has joined demonstration projects involving insurance carriers.

The NIAAA has provided leadership in the form of technical assistance materials: model cost-accounting manuals, a model alcohol insurance benefit package, a health insurance resource kit, and development of a set of treatment standards in cooperation with the Joint Commission on Accreditation of Hospitals.

About 85% of the seventy Blue Cross plans nationwide now recognize alcoholism as a covered condition and provide benefits that are generally comparable with those other covered diagnoses.

Medicare categorized alcoholism and drug abuse within psychiatric or mental health services; coverage for these problems is less than that available for physical illness.

A 1978 NIAAA-funded study found that the majority of State Medicaid plans are silent on the issue of coverage for alcoholism treatment services.

The NIAAA has recently joined with the Health Care Financing Administration in designing a four-year $1 million demonstration project to expand alcoholism benefits under Medicare and Medicaid in five regions of the United States.

Under title XVI of the 1973 Amendments to the Social Security Act, Supplemental Security Income (SSI) benefits are available to alcoholics in treatment as disabled persons.

Available alcoholism benefits under CHAMPUS are brief hospital care for detoxification, inpatient rehabilitation, and outpatient psychiatric care. Consideration is being given to further expansion of alcoholism benefits.

In 1980 the Alcoholism Services Development Program was implemented. The purpose of this program is to demonstrate that systematic planning by state and local governments, communities, service providers, and consumers can result in more responsive and efficient service systems, eventually decreasing reliance upon Federal funds.

Efforts are under way to increase alcoholism-specific curriculums in various professional schools and to expand training opportunities in alcoholism to physicians, psychologists, nurses, social workers, and others whose disciplines bring them into contact with alcoholic patients or clients.

In 1979, American funds for federal projects devoted solely to the treatment of alcoholism and alcohol abuse amounted to approximately $180 million.

Alcoholism: Treatable Illness

The NIAAA was responsible for 30% of all federal expenditures for treatment services in 1979, with expenditures of $84 million.

A large source of public funding for all alcoholism services is taxes raised by the states. In fiscal year 1979, the states expended about $203 million or 25% of the total funds available. Local revenues contributed roughly $74 million for alcoholism services in fiscal year 1979.

In Canada, while "numbers" because of the population difference are smaller (approximately 10% of the U.S. figures), the percentages are remarkably similar concerning incidence, costs, medical, social, treatment and recovery trends.

The Canadian study, in the survey, included among alcohol-related problems those which are both directly related to alcohol abuse and those which are indirectly related, listing them as follows:

Directly related to alcohol:

(a)mortality: cirrhosis, alcohol poisoning, alcoholic psychosis, alcoholism, motor vehicle accidents.

(b)social and physical problems: impaired driving, traffic violations and drunkenness offenses.

Indirectly related to alcohol:

(a)Coronary and respiratory diseases, suicides.

(b)Crimes against persons, child abuse, marital disruption, occupational alcoholism.

In examining the Canadian mortality statistics, we can see the report estimated that alcohol use was *directly* implicated, in 1978, in 2,520 deaths. *Indirect* alcohol-related deaths amounted to 5,668 deaths from such events as motor vehicle accidents, falls, fires, drowning, homicides and suicides. Additional deaths, in which alcohol may be a factor, including medically diagnosed categories as coronary and respiratory diseases, and various types of cancers, amounted to 1,142 deaths.[4]

These alcohol-related fatalities in 1978, estimated at over 18,000 deaths, indicated that *one out of every eleven Canadians died from an alcohol-related condition*, whether directly (one in sixty) or indirectly (one in ten).

Dr. Vince Tookenay, Director of Native Health Policy with the Canadian federal department, at a midwest regional meeting of the Canadian Addiction Foundation, reported that "Alcoholism and drug abuse cost Canadian taxpayers about $150 million a year. Nor does this figure include alcohol problems among Canada's estimated one million Metis and nonstatus Indians." Tookenay, born on an Ontario reserve, said alcoholism is also partly responsible for the high number of native children in care homes, five times the national average. Alcohol is involved in sixty to seventy percent of these cases, costing the Canadian government over $160 million a year. Nine percent of the native population is in correctional institutions, compared to three and one-half percent of the rest of the population.

Dorothy Betz, a member of the Canadian National Parole Board, told the conference:

"In all the years I've been interviewing people . . . I have yet to talk to an individual who had not been drinking. From shoplifting to murder, everyone was under the influence, usually alcohol."

The per capita disparities for the care, control and prevention of alcoholism are self-evident. Though costs and numbers have ballooned, these differences are essentially the same today.

At the same time, expenditures in treatment, education and research as projected for the 1980s, percentage-wise and per capita, remained as consistently low as they were in the 1940s. In a large measure too, the same barriers continue to exist in dealing adequately with this social, legal and medical concern, even though the National Council on Alcoholism recently estimated that today "every tenth (and perhaps now every ninth or eighth) North American has an addicted wife, husband, brother, sister, mother, father or child!"

Such staggering costs make the gross revenues from the manufacture, sale and distribution of beverage alcohol, together with allied enterprises, look insignificant by comparison.

These few references, dated, nebulous and incomplete as they are, at least provide some idea of the dollars and human costs involved. However, regardless of the costs incurred, humanitarian implications and responsibilities continue to be de-emphasized. One must also appreciate why those concerned with the production and sale of beverage alcohol — whether legitimately or otherwise — do so zealously protect the revenue from their operations. This, in the final analysis, may represent the greatest single deterrent to more positive action for the eventual control and prevention of alcohol abuse and alcoholism.

The one force that will generate the necessary changes in attitudes and in constructive action is that of recovering alcoholics. Through their sobriety and as living examples of what recovery achieves, they will, by the very immensity of their own numbers, change things.

To better appreciate some of the wastes involved in the practices of the past, it is perhaps pertinent to call attention to the savings accrued by those who have recognized such spiralling costs.

In 1948, when the Fellowship of Alcoholics Anonymous had only 60,000 recovered members, it was estimated that they were returning 150 million dollars in goods and services to society. Since that time their membership has increased over twenty fold to over 1 million members with over 3 billion dollars (*in 1940 dollars*) returned to society.

Alcoholism: Treatable Illness

Having become aware of their losses, business, industry and labour have taken a leading part in reversing old patterns. While there is no means of accurately evaluating nationally lost man hours and wages, expenditures covering premature retirement and termination, the training of replacement personnel, spoilage and waste, sick leave, insurance and unemployment benefits, and the cost of many other related problems of morale, the figures reported are stupendous. Business, industry and labour have the most to gain by positive programming to cope with the current estimated losses of millions of man hours annually due to employee problem drinking situations.

None of the estimates of dollar costs can possibly reflect the incalculable losses and suffering the problems of alcohol create. The unhappiness, despair, broken hearts, disintegration of family life, delinquency, suicide, poverty, disease, insanity and death that result are a blight that infects every level of modern society. All of history warns that controls are essential. This glamorous and remunerative coin has its grim side which cannot and will not be kept face down.

Notes

1. The Quarterly Journal of Studies on Alcohol, Volume 6, Number 1, June 1945. With permission.

2. Part of a Statement of Concern from A.D.P.A. — The Alcohol and Drug Problems Association of North America. April 1981. (Professional).

3. Dr. Bert L. Vallee, Department of Medicine, Harvard Medical School. Excerpt from a Presentation to a Symposium on the Biochemical and Nutritional Aspects of Alcoholism, as reported in "*Preventing Alcoholism.*"

4. There remains the tendency to protect the feelings of family and the dignity of the deceased by not including in medical reports or death certificates the alcoholism or acute alcoholic state of the patient which precipitated the coronary or stroke, or the lack of personal care in accidents. Similarly omitted are references to the alcohol problem in the context of other ills, as in the case of the drinking diabetic.

9. Awareness — Knowledge — Understanding

The ingredients essential to alcoholism are actually within man's own self. Add the alcohol, and it acts as a catalyst, causing a series of reactions potentially leading to disaster. The problem cannot be blamed on alcohol alone, though many do just that.

We all resist change so we find it hard to overcome attitudes and habits we have long followed. Whether they are sane or sound doesn't seem to matter until we are faced with the need to change in order to survive. Thus some of us are forced to realize that people plus alcohol equals problems.

That's what happened to me. While I knew the fun and conviviality of social drinking, as an alcoholic I also learned the heartache and despair that alcoholism can bring, personally and to those about me. In my case, the loss and costs were enormous, and the damage to my family tragic.

To me, acceptance of alcoholism as a treatable illness is not a public crusade against alcohol *per se*; it is a matter of personal survival, for myself and other alcoholics. Recovery from alcoholism doesn't leave me bitter or make me a loser, casting aspersions or spitting sour grapes at the world. My personal life demands association with social drinkers a good deal of the time. Most of my family and friends use beverage alcohol. Alcoholism is my illness, not theirs. Though I suffered and lost some things, blew one silver spoon career, knew institutional care and the depths of human suffering, this gives me neither the right nor the inclination to wish the same on anyone else. I have gained and recovered much more than I lost. These things I would share.

Having more experience than most in the treatment of alcoholism, if I criticize I must also accept the responsibility to offer a solution. This I am trying to do. But we must also attempt to learn something about alcohol itself: the chemical that sets up one kind of reaction for most people and lights the fuse of the affliction alcoholism for others.

Part II:

The Illness Concept

10. Beverage Alcohol: What It Is & What It Does

What is Alcohol?

It is relevant to their well-being for all drinkers to know what alcohol is and to realize what it actually does to those who use it. While there are numerous kinds of alcohol, our only concern is ethyl alcohol, or "ethanol."[1] An almost odourless and colorless liquid with a strong burning taste, it is the one used in approved alcohol beverages.

Nature produces alcohol through the process of fermentation. Yeast, a form of mold present in the air everywhere, when given warmth and moisture, converts the sugar of fruits, vegetables or grains into alcohol and carbon dioxide, which evaporates. An example of this action is to be found in baking bread. The yeast used forms alcohol, the carbon dioxide causes the bread to rise, and the heat expels the alcohol. Our bodies perform similar functions in digesting foods.

In nature the process of fermentation continues until the alcohol concentration reaches about 14%, unless it is stopped earlier by heat or other chemicals. At about that percentage, the yeast no longer functions; this is the peak of its natural fermentation. The concentration of alcohol in beverages may be increased by fortifying them with pure alcohol, manufactured through distillation. Though fermented drinks have been in use since man's earliest history, the process of distillation came about at some later date. The Chinese made distilled rice drinks prior to the Christian era. Arabs travelling from the Orient brought the process to Europe.

Alcohol has a lower boiling point than water. During distillation, substances containing alcohol are heated, and the alcohol forms into a vapour which is then converted into a purer alcohol fluid by cooling. This process produces distilled spirits having a much higher alcohol concentration. While too strong to use as a pure chemical, it readily mixes with water, fruit juices or sodas, and so may be prepared in a variety of ways.

Alcoholism: Treatable Illness

Kinds of Beverage Alcohol

Alcohol beverages are generally grouped into three categories: wine, beer and distilled spirits.

Wine

Wine was likely man's first alcohol beverage. It may be prepared by simply leaving a fruit juice containing sugar exposed to the air in a warm place. The juice attracts yeast, which multiplies and works on the sugar to change all or part of the solution to alcohol. While usually associated with the fermented juice of grapes, wine can also be made from the juice of other fruits, grains, flowers, sap of trees, and honey. Though it naturally attains only about fourteen percent pure alcohol, it is sometimes fortified to a stronger percentage. Table wines which do not keep after being opened are about twelve percent alcohol. Dessert wines are fortified to eighteen percent alcohol and will keep. Wine has been and is used ritually by many religions; medicinally, as a tonic, and as a beverage by some peoples in place of water, milk, tea or coffee. It has long been associated with many cultures, and over the centuries, families and communities have made certain wines famous by their special processing and by the quality of the substances used. People have regularly used quotations from the Bible both for and against the use of wine to justify their own attitudes about drinking.

Beer

Beer is made from malted and fermented cereal. The starch of the cereal is converted into sugar during the malting process. With the addition of yeast, fermentation takes place. The resultant alcohol cereal broth or mash contains anywhere from three to six percent pure alcohol. Beer is flavoured with hops or other bitters to give it its distinctive flavour. The addition of hops distinguishes beer from ale, but beer is the generic name for all malt alcohol beverages, ale, porter and the like. Ale is regarded as a lighter beverage.

Ale and beer drinking have also been associated throughout history with festivals, rituals and cultural practices. This is perhaps tragically evident today to anyone who watches television with any regularity. Beer is fast becoming regarded as an essential prerequisite to positive and pleasurable social gatherings, particularly where young adults are concerned. There is no doubt that elements of sexuality, confidence, intimacy, relaxation and athletic prowess are cleverly blended in beer commercials so that they will become inextricably entangled in the minds of the viewing/consuming public. There is clear danger in this.

Distilled Spirits

The category known as distilled spirits or liquor includes brandy, gin, rum, vodka and the whiskies — bourbon, rye, scotch and others. These manufactured beverages contain a much higher concentration of alcohol than beer or wine, usually reaching forty to fifty percent. These higher concentrations are achieved by distillation and subsequent infusion or fortification of the beverage with additional pure alcohol. Distilled spirits are a popular form of beverage alcohol; their popularity is due in part to their ability to mix easily and to be made into many sophisticated and more potent drinks. Liqueurs, such as the various brandies, are generally a strong alcohol beverage sweetened and flavoured with aromatic substances.

Proof

This is a term used to denote the percentage of pure alcohol contained in beverages. Before instruments and chemicals were available to measure the alcohol content, gunpowder was saturated with the beverage. If it burned on lighting, this was "proof" that the beverage contained the proper minimum of alcohol required. Confusion again reigns in factors of proof measurement of beverage alcohol because the term has undergone modification with time and place. United States standards interpret "100 proof spirits" to mean an absolute alcohol volume of fifty percent. British and Canadian standards define "100 proof spirits" to mean a beverage containing 57.1% of absolute alcohol by volume.

The alcohol content of wines and liqueurs is measured or "proofed" in the same manner as distilled spirits. However, brewed beverages, beer, ale, stout, and the like, are measured in terms of the percentage of alcohol present by weight rather than volume. Therefore, to compare beer with wine or liquor, it is necessary to convert the weight expressed to percentage of alcohol by volume, and finally to the proof indicated. For example, if something is 8% proof, this is equal to 4% by weight or 5% by volume, or 10 proof U.S. So, it takes a mathematician to determine the percentage of alcohol present among the various kinds of beverages, and in each of their divergent proofs.

Physical Properties

While "eau de vie" and other beverage alcohol names are referred to as "water or blood of life," this interpretation is contrary to the dietary and malnutrition problems that arise from the excessive use of any beverage alcohol, if used to the exclusion of proper food. Though beers and wines retain some of the minerals and vitamins originally present in the substances from which they were made, *distilled spirits do not contain or retain any of these elements.* Though wine and beer may have some food value, replacement of food by distilled spirits creates serious vitamin and mineral deficiencies. Alcohol provides sugar energy but contains none

Alcoholism: Treatable Illness

of the essential or nerve energy foods. Preoccupation with drinking can cause one to neglect the intake of food.

Alcohol in the Body

Through absorption into the blood and water, alcohol is distributed uniformly throughout the body. On ingestion alcohol remains in the stomach where a small percentage is absorbed into the blood. It then passes into the small intestine and is absorbed rapidly and completely into the blood and body. Unlike food, it does not have to be digested before the body uses it. Some people have a built-in defence against alcohol. For physical or emotional reasons the stomach outlet muscle (pyloric valve) will not release the alcohol from the stomach, retarding its absorption. Vomiting may result. As these people get sick when they drink, their discomfort prevents continued or excessive drinking or any likelihood of incurring alcoholism.

The presence of food in the stomach, especially fatty foods, protein and milk, delays absorption; consequently, the immediate effects of alcohol are delayed also. A drink before dinner may have more effect than several after dinner. Like amounts of distilled spirits have more effect than similar amounts of beer or light wines. Gaseous drinks with extra carbon dioxide, such as champagne, are absorbed more quickly and are said to "go to one's head."

Most of the alcohol ingested is eliminated by the process of **oxidation**, which liberates the energy of the alcohol as heat. Oxidation begins in the liver and continues in the blood and muscle tissues of the body. It varies with individuals, depending upon the health, size and efficiency of the liver. If the functioning of that organ is impaired, adverse conditions develop. A small amount of alcohol is also eliminated through perspiration, urine, breath and vomit.

Absolute alcohol is eliminated from the blood at 0.002 oz per hour, per pound of body weight. Therefore, in one hour a person weighing 100 pounds eliminates 0.20 ounces; one of 150 pounds, 0.30 ounces; and one of 200 pounds, 0.40 ounces. Though the amount of food consumed materially affects this rate, the only function that coffee, exercise, baths and such perform is to give the individual time away from drinking. They have no effect on the rate of oxidation of the alcohol.

In measuring blood alcohol concentration it is necessary to consider the type and quantity of alcohol beverage consumed, body weight, the period of time taken to ingest the beverage, and the kind and amount of food eaten. Body weight is a major factor since about seventy percent of our body weight consists of water. Therefore, heavier persons more readily dilute like amounts of alcohol than do drinkers of lesser weight. The length of time that elapses after drinking, before measuring takes place, is also a factor. Alcohol concentration is at its peak just about one and one-half hours after drinking, and continues to lessen as time goes by.

Effects of Alcohol on Behaviour

Although beverage alcohol is often referred to as a stimulant, it is in fact an anaesthetic similar to ether or chloroform. Its first and primary effect is that of a depressant of the nervous system. The effects of alcohol are reflected in those parts of the body usually under our direct and conscious control. These disturbances may appear in the slurring of speech, staggering and apparent inebriacy, depending upon the concentration of alcohol in the blood as it surrounds the brain.

At a concentration of 0.05% of alcohol in the blood, functions of the uppermost levels of the central nervous system are affected. This is the part of the brain (the cortex) that controls inhibitions, judgment and self-control. At a concentration of 0.10%, the lower or motor areas of the brain are affected, and thus the drinker may stagger, have difficulty dressing, fumble his keys, and be unable to speak coherently. Even small amounts of alcohol reduce sensitivity and do not promote stimulation.

At a concentration of 0.2%, the mid-brain, which controls emotional expression, is affected. The drinker may then need help to walk or dress, be easily angered. become hilarious or develop a crying jag. At 0.3% the lower portion of the brain, controlling the more primitive areas, is affected. Sensory perception is depressed further. The drinker may not know what he or she sees or hears and may be unaware of what is going on about him or her. At 0.4 to 0.5%, this area becomes completely depressed. The drinker is now stupefied or anaesthetized.

At 0.6% alcohol concentration, the base of the brain, which controls the heartbeat and breathing, is affected. When brain signals to these organs cease, death follows; however, this rarely occurs simply because the drinker "passes out" before ingesting such a fatal amount. As the alcohol is oxidized the drinker gradually returns to sobriety. Clearly, the most distressing effect of alcohol is that which it has on the functioning of the brain.

A small amount of alcohol will increase the flow of juices in the stomach, which when activated are experienced as a feeling of hunger. Thus, small amounts of alcohol can serve as appetizers. Nevertheless, concentrated solutions of alcohol can seriously irritate tissue. Excessive drinkers may develop chronic inflammation of the lining of the stomach — a condition known as gastritis. Alcohol may cause loss of control in the kidneys. There is no evidence that alcohol causes chronic damage in all drinkers. It does not damage sex glands, nor does it stimulate sexual activity. This is a psychological reaction resulting from reduced inhibitions, judgment and self-control.

An excessive use of alcohol may seriously affect the liver which, by becoming distended and hardened, could malfunction. Abstinence from alcohol usually rectifies the condition incurred. Alcohol may also seriously irritate the nerves in the mouth, throat and gullet. This causes the heart to palpitate, and so to increase the

Alcoholism: Treatable Illness

flow of blood through surface blood vessels, as indicated by flushing and sweating, red nose and bloodshot eyes.

The tolerance alcoholics seemingly develop to excessive use and amounts of alcohol is in effect a "learned process" of how to control and adjust to the alcohol ingested. This explains why some social drinkers become hilarious and noisy, demonstrative or argumentative, while regular heavy users may not. Tests indicate that both groups are similarly affected by alcohol. While experienced drinkers learn what to expect and how to react, the reaction of all drinkers varies with their body weight, their physical and emotional state, the kind and amount of alcohol ingested, and the time of ingestion.

The hangover state may be caused by a combination of many factors. A light social drinker, perhaps unaware of what to expect from over-indulgence, is usually sick, fatigued, and somewhat guilty. He or she has eaten and smoked too much, drunk too much of perhaps several kinds of alcohol beverages and their mixes, and had little rest. Suggested cures are of no avail. Coffee, calisthenics and the like only help to relieve the shame of his or her behaviour. The alcoholic's hangover, with its bitter remorse, shakes, sweats, butterflies, and with every nerve raw and on edge, is a much different thing. He or she may resort to the "hair of the dog that bit him or her" — another drink — and so postpone the resultant hangover. In both types of drinker, the physical and psychological effects of alcohol cannot be separated.

Alcohol causes little difference in the bodily functions controlled by the lower brain center, but wide differences in the functions controlled by the higher brain center. Therefore, individual differences in behaviour under heavy intoxication are negligible, whereas wide differences occur in people only mildly intoxicated.

Most people who drink do so in moderation. While they do not exhibit overt behaviour symptoms, they are all affected to some degree. This may be evidenced in a release of anxiety, a lighter mood, and a relaxed feeling of ease. Though even minimal amounts of alcohol impair judgment, speech, action, vision and coordination, initially some drinkers may react better after a minimal drink or two. The drinker may become very vocal but without much thought to what he or she says.

While the drinker may be able to perform normal and routine activities without trouble, the execution of unfamiliar or complex ones could be difficult. The ability to respond properly to emergencies is seriously affected. Those things learned over many years become reflex and habit, whereas those which are incompletely or only recently learned can, with the infusion of alcohol, be set aside more readily. As emotions and actions respond in unison to the dominating effects of alcohol, they cannot arbitrarily be separated. This is particularly important to driving a car. The greater feeling of confidence and ease which alcohol creates, causing a reduction of judgment, tension and anxiety, may thus lead the drinker to actions which would not otherwise be condoned. If a person's reaction time is perhaps slowed by forty percent through having consumed a large quantity of alcohol, that person's ability to operate a car is seriously affected.

The acquired controls we master are learned functions; they are not inherited. They are qualities of self-discipline which enable us to live comfortably and happily in a given society. These are evidenced by our feelings and attitudes toward ourselves and all of those about us; by our reactions to authority and criticism; by our mode of expressing hostility, and by the way we may give or take in our relationships with others. This learning process may be very painful for some. As alcohol dulls learned functions or relieves pain, it is in this area that the use of alcohol, though a social condiment for most, may become a disastrous drug for others.

The controls we each may possess and evidence vary from occasion to occasion. While most people travel an even curve, there are those who reach high and low points, which alcohol accentuates. Alcohol will have only a moderate effect on those having established and well-learned controls. While such drinkers may feel more at ease because of reduced tensions and anxieties, only a slight change occurs in their normal forms of expression to others.

Those having difficulty in achieving or learning controls will not function as well. When alcohol is introduced, their inhibitions are set aside and their behaviour is less orderly or disciplined. They may become loud, overconfident, and much less anxious about deviant behaviour. They may become aggressive and express themselves quite vigorously. These persons may become physically abusive to spouses, children or others. When sober again, even minimal controls, learned or acquired, reassert themselves and they have no way of understanding or explaining their behaviour. They see other people drink and safely handle the stuff — so why can't they?

The overcontrolled person, being too set and inhibited, is unable to express adequately any kind of feelings. Alcohol assists this person in self-expression and in functioning with less embarrassment or tension toward others. It may provide a newfound elixir for such a drinker, and thus it becomes much more meaningful and important to him or her. Revelling in this newfound release, the imbiber may very easily and quite subconsciously become overly dependent on what alcohol can do for him or her. At this point, that drinker does not realize that it may take more of this elixir to maintain this new and more comfortable state, and so he or she involuntarily moves into another dependency over which he or she has no control.

As the alcoholic's dependency on alcohol progresses, his or her personality changes, and the phases of alcoholism begin to unfold.

Notes

1. All subsequent references to alcohol will denote the use of "ethyl alcohol," as against methyl or other alcohols. Methyl alcohol, used in rubbing extracts and related products, is extremely toxic and should never be used as a beverage.

11. Social Versus Problem Drinking

Abstainers

About twenty-five percent of the total population of Canada, and in the United States about twenty-nine percent, are *abstainers*. While some voice their feelings through temperance and abstinence groups, many never interfere with the drinking population. They abstain from drinking in the main, because they do not believe it is ethical or morally right to drink.

People also abstain for other reasons. Some simply react adversely to alcohol and so do not invite any discomfort or sickness by trying to drink. Doctors advise some people not to use beverage alcohol. There are those whose budgets will not permit them to drink. If their economic conditions change, they could move into one of the drinking groups. Then, of course, there are the "problem drinkers" who have learned the hard way that they should not drink, and so they abstain. A few people, recognizing their dependency for what it is, quit of their own volition very early. Others have important goals and will not permit problem drinking to interfere. Once these are achieved they may attempt social drinking. Finally, there are those who did incur alcoholism and who of necessity sought and found sobriety.

Social Drinkers

An estimated seventy-five percent of the Canadian population (and seventy-one percent of the American population) twenty years and over do use beverage alcohol. While the percentage of users is higher in Canada than in the United States, the incidence of alcoholism incurred in the United States is double that of Canada. However, drinking patterns and habits in both countries are becoming more closely aligned as time goes on.

Social drinkers may be defined as those persons who drink for socially accepted purposes and to the degree their group permits and accepts. Among the terms used to describe social drinkers' use of beverage alcohol would be found: occasional, ceremonial, dietary, "knowledgeable" (in the sense of the wine fancier or connoisseur), medicinal, compliant, socially facilitating and exuberant. To persons in this category, beverage alcohol is normally secondary to the function or the occasion for the drinking; it is a symptom of the culture, and is representative of the particular group.

While the form and even the amount of alcohol consumed will vary according to the conventions or the culture of the group concerned, the drinking pattern will in a sense remain quite restrictive. This could also permit an individual to drink alone. For example, one might drink beer or wine with meals, because it is the custom of the culture or group to do so. This is an accepted practice within the culture and is *not* a symptom of any inner conflict or need. Most drinkers remain within these accepted conventions.

Social drinkers may be divided into three broad groups: infrequent drinkers, frequent or regular users, and constant heavy users of beverage alcohol.

Infrequent Drinkers

The infrequent users of beverage alcohol are those who do occasionally take a drink, but perhaps irregularly and only on odd occasions. This group would evidence complete control of their intake, perhaps never having more than one drink and at most two. On some occasions, members of this group would refuse a drink without any qualms. On rare occasions a few might drink enough to enjoy a "happy glow," but will never become intoxicated (as that term is generally understood).

Among this group will also be found individuals who claim they never drink, but who do on occasion sip or drink a mild beverage as a toast to the bride, or at some special occasion or anniversary. This is a form of ceremonial use which they clearly do not consider drinking.

While these types of drinkers do not consider themselves to be prudish or against drinking, they fit into the moderate or temperate category. In view of today's changing drinking habits and customs it would be difficult to estimate accurately the numbers of users to be found in this drinking group. Individual shifts in position, social status and the like might cause some members to move to the next group, and of course, vice versa.

Frequent Drinkers

The largest number of alcohol users are frequent drinkers. They regularly use beverage alcohol on every social occasion at which it is served. Most will quite probably maintain a supply of some form of beverage alcohol at home.

While a number of these men and women might occasionally become "high" or mildly intoxicated (under 0.1% blood alcohol concentration), they seldom get drunk. Some will have occasions on which getting mildly high is perhaps acceptable: New Year's Eve, weddings and the like. They may drink more heavily on weekends. They are regular users with "learned skills" of control, necessary to the drinking group to which they belong. They entertain and are entertained frequently. *Drinking according to intent*, most would frown upon anyone within this group who frequently got drunk or lost control. These people will regularly drink and drive and feel little compunction about it. Those who go beyond these rather well established limits simply "graduate" into the next group.

Constant Heavy Users

Constant heavy users compose the next group. Included are those who drink daily, heavily on regular occasions, and who frequently become intoxicated. They might regularly drink at lunch, attend cocktail parties, drink with dinner, and in the evening. Some might drink heavily on weekends and frequently become intoxicated.

Within this group of constant users are subgroup clusters of *"irresponsible drinkers."* Their drinking behaviour does not conform with even the traditional social drinking rules ascribed to the overall constant heavy user group. They will seek out occasions and functions for the definite purpose of getting intoxicated. On occasion some of these "irresponsible drinkers" may choose to limit their drinking, and seemingly they can do so without difficulty. Most will take measures to prevent excessive drinking from seriously interfering with the performance of their vocations. Nevertheless, the irresponsibility of their kind of drinking does affect their domestic and interpersonal relationships with others. These drinkers "stick together" for protection from outside criticism.

The majority of those members of the total population who will incur the illness alcoholism will, for the most part, come from the overall constant heavy user group. Many, however, even though their drinking is excessive, will retain complete control and will not become dependent upon or addicted to alcohol.

The excessive use of alcohol by some of this group may cause them to be ignored or rejected by even their own drinking group. Their drinking behaviour may be impossible; still, they are not necessarily alcoholics. Many such heavy drinkers know no other relaxation or interest — they do not enjoy a football game, a symphony, a good play, or any of the normal social functions enjoyed by most people. Their rejection by drinking associates may cause them to go down the social scale, but as long as they retain control to stop when they have to, they are not compulsive drinkers. The "illness concept" is not applicable to their pattern of drinking.

Among excessive drinkers, in both steady and irregular brackets, would be found those who compensate for social inadequacies: the person who goes unrecognized, drinks and is a tyrant at home, or who gets drunk and becomes a big shot and spender, and such others. There are those users whose occupations seemingly demand continuous and constant heavy drinking: salespersons, advertising and public relations reps and the like. They may drink less with a change of occupation, unless they have become completely dependent. Some excessive drinkers are part of hard drinking recreational and ceremonial patterns. These may be cultural, fraternal, community or national customs: for example, the Polish, Ukrainian and German people are reputed to be heavy drinkers who celebrate and "play" exuberantly; Irish sons are often said to follow in the path of Irish fathers and to learn to drink accordingly.

To social drinkers, beverage alcohol may represent a way of life and is symbolic of social customs related to national practices, conviviality, relaxation and friendship. The chemical properties of alcohol (and their often inadequate knowledge of same) have little impact on their drinking. For some, however, alcohol becomes a medicine or drug rather than a social symptom. Of primary concern in this book are those drinkers who become dependent and compulsive users — alcoholics.

Problem and Alcoholic Drinkers

As one investigates what takes place in the developing alcoholic, one asks: Is it alcohol? Lack of willpower? The amount one drinks?

As most people do drink without ill effect, it cannot be the alcohol alone, except as it affects the alcoholic (his or her "allergic reaction"). The potential alcoholic must personally inject one or more ingredients, which, when combined with alcohol, can cause the onset of alcoholism. The alcohol may only serve as the fuse. Such drinkers are perhaps more sensitive and susceptible to the adverse effects of beverage alcohol. We cannot associate willpower with the development of any illness. By using willpower, can one control stomach flu, the common cold or tuberculosis? The amount the alcoholic drinks is not the essential characteristic of alcoholism either. Many excessive or heavy drinkers consume much more than some alcoholics. An individual, whether he or she is a light or heavy drinker, may develop a related problem because of alcohol, but not necessarily ever become an alcoholic. It is evident, therefore, that much more is involved in this illness.

The developing alcoholic progressively finds an importance in and acquires a dependency on beverage alcohol which is not the case with social drinkers. While problem drinkers may become aware of an increasing number of personal problems, at the outset they do not relate these problems to their use of alcohol. They may eventually see themselves unable to control "their kind of drinking" and as incapable of drinking according to initial intent regarding amount, time or place. Nevertheless, problem drinkers do not — and later, cannot — stop drinking. They begin to feel that, without alcohol, they cannot face the mounting pressures that surround them. This is unlike most social drinkers, who do retain the ability to stop regardless of other personal problems, even though they may overdrink or overshoot their mark at times.

Alcoholism: Treatable Illness

Alcoholics, in spite of personal intent, are notorious for starting to drink or for drinking too much at the most inappropriate time and place. The first drink triggers a chain reaction which they are powerless to control, no matter how it interferes with everything else that may be important to them. These factors can be put together as a working definition of alcoholism.

When one's drinking shows a progressive loss of the ability to drink according to personal intent, progressively interferes with one's normal relationships at home and work, financial affairs, and other interpersonal relationships, and in fact differs from or is unacceptable to the rest of the group with whom one functions, then some form of the illness alcoholism is indicated.

Alcoholism is characterized by several factors which distinguish alcoholic drinking from social drinking.

The illness is progressive. Alcoholics progressively lose control over the "how," "when," "where," "what" and "how much" of their drinking. The illness usually develops over a long period of time. The subtle changes that take place are not too easily measured or too obvious, either to alcoholics or to those around them, until the illness has reached a serious state. The alcoholic's kind of drinking becomes more and more dependent; each drinking bout is worse than the one before, and finally it takes less alcohol to reduce the alcoholic to a state of complete helplessness.

The illness is chronic. As an illness that in most cases progresses over an extended period of time and that becomes a permanent condition, alcoholism is a chronic illness. Most alcoholics regularly or periodically suffer prolonged states of alcohol intoxication which they sustain with the continued use of more alcohol. Excessive and prolonged misuse of beverage alcohol may result in physical and psychological changes, or both. *There is no known cure for this chronic state other than complete abstinence, which arrests the condition — unless or until more alcohol is consumed.*

The alcoholic is the last to recognize his or her illness. The most frustrating, exasperating and insidious characteristic of alcoholism is that the alcoholic is usually the last person to appreciate the onset and progression of the illness, and to recognize that he or she is indeed an alcoholic. You will recall the confusions, ambivalence of attitudes, the lack of knowledge and understanding that exists about alcoholism. Combine these with personal adverse attitudes and moral implications, and one can better appreciate the deterrents these factors represent to the alcoholic in accepting the illness.

For this reason, alcoholism — unless permanently arrested — may often progress beyond any point of possible recovery.

It is frequently difficult to pinpoint and separate alcoholism and social drinking. All drinkers, social and alcoholic alike, initially indicate similar behavioral symptoms in their use of beverage alcohol. Most alcoholics learn to hide defensively the outward manifestations of their developing alcoholism. In the early stages their illness is kept from becoming too obvious or different from the drinking of others.

Why some drinkers are more sensitive to beverage alcohol, and so develop alcoholism, is not yet fully understood. Nor is it possible to predict who, among social drinkers, will incur the illness. While several new and hopeful studies are underway, difficulty in making an early diagnosis remains a serious handicap. There have already been promising (albeit controversial) preliminary studies suggesting a potential link between alcoholism and one or more genetic defects.

We do know that at least one in ten drinkers will become an alcoholic and that complete abstinence is the only effective remedy. We also know that the physical, emotional, social and spiritual factors of alcoholism must be considered in unison, and that social pressures and apathy intertwined with attitudes to the use of alcohol are important areas of concern. The experience and techniques finally being learned are providing a growing basis of knowledge which may be applied to good purpose in dealing with the illness.

Types of Alcoholic Drinkers

Aside from the many individual "kinds" of alcohol-*isms*, alcoholics may be grouped into three general categories or types of dependency: dependent steady drinkers without benders; those with occasional benders; and periodics.

Firstly, there are those who drink regularly, and perhaps heavily, who never appear to go beyond a certain glow and saturation point. They have a real and definite dependence on alcohol, which they are never without, although they seem to have learned and will demonstrate better personal drinking controls than many heavy social drinkers. They are not to be confused with regular excessive drinkers. An excessive drinker may be told by a doctor, "Quit, or your liver will give out," or "Give it up if you want your heart to keep going," and so the excessive drinker quits. Quitting alcohol is not a major worry; the primary concern of excessive drinkers is still good health. As they basically drink according to intent and are not totally dependent upon alcohol, they still retain control.

I firmly believe that alcoholics in most cases are concerned, and would quit if they were not afraid to stop, or knew how to do so gracefully and with dignity. They cannot easily contemplate the agony of stopping or a life without alcohol. They would be noticeably uncomfortable if unable to maintain the level of saturation or concentration of alcohol — their life's medicine — to which they are accustomed. It is not merely a matter of taking or wanting a drink or two; it is the desperate urgency of *needing* whatever quantity it takes to maintain poise and physical and emotional comfort. The withdrawal of alcohol creates as much agony for the alcoholic as does the withdrawal of a drug for an addict. Like the addict, most alcoholics have to increase the amount they drink to get the same effect.

The second general type includes those who drink steadily and who manage to retain fair control most of the time; but, when pressures mount and opportunity permits, they explode into a spree or a binge, finally tapering back down to their "controlled" intake again. Progressively their benders come closer together, and the tapering down becomes ever more difficult, until one spree seems to follow right on the heels of the past one. Where a bender may start off as simply a heavy weekend of drinking, it will progress to a long weekend, and then perhaps to a lengthier period, involving the loss of another degree of control. Now it isn't only the amount consumed; it is the when and for how long. Attempts to regain sobriety, to live up to promises, to go on the wagon and even to quit, may now occur. The majority of alcoholics seem to fall into this group. They also incur a greater number of other losses and troubles: family, job, social status, driving arrests and other like problems. Members of this group predominate in the tragic treadmill with police, courts, jails and institutions.

The periodic alcoholic may remain totally abstinent from alcohol of any kind for weeks and months. Periodics have been known to have drinking episodes years apart. Some second type alcoholics, as the result of accepting partial help, are able to change their pattern from steady to periodic drinking. There are a number of these who seem to be able to achieve fairly long periods of sobriety, then relapse — and though they have improved, their slips are consistent. These pseudo-periodics are still fighting themselves. While they acknowledge an intellectual admission and achieve partial control over their drinking, emotionally they still maintain some reservations about their ability to drink normally. Though reluctant to seek help, they require further therapy. They must learn to make more sound personal adjustments and to kindle better drives to recovery. Otherwise, they remain a half success.

Periodic drinkers may include manic depressives who hit high and low peaks and so depend on alcohol to level them off; and people who suffer various glandular conditions.

The periodic drinker is perhaps the most difficult to approach. The periods of abstinence attained enable this alcoholic to build a defensive shell which challenges any need to resolve the matter completely. Most periodic alcoholics are usually well-hidden cases. Though some maintain the same period intervals indefinitely, most will sooner or later telescope drinking bouts, and will therefore of necessity eventually need to cope more decisively with their problem.

Developing alcoholics may attempt to change their own patterns of drinking, so as to be less noticeable and seemingly to better conform to accepted standards within their own drinking group. Once the alcoholic is aware that his drinking is different, he will make individual adjustments — perhaps a change to another group, one which condones more drinking. In this way, the finger cannot be pointed at "me" alone. A wife may say, "Why don't we play bridge with the John Does any more? Why must we only see your heavy drinking friends?" She feels they are a bad example to her alcoholic husband. And again, when reproached for his drinking after work, the husband might counter with, "Well, call Joe's and see if I didn't stop at two drinks." Of course, he doesn't add that he also stopped at Pete's and Frank's bar and other spots. No one saw him take too much at any one place.

Along about this time, the spouse may try to keep up with the alcoholic's drinking, or go to the other extreme and cease going out or having friends in, as all such gatherings become difficult and embarrassing occasions. The children too rearrange their lives and contacts.

All are affected in the many and continuing changes in drinking patterns. In the case of the periodic, the alcoholic may be allowed to be "sick" again. After all, it rarely happens! He — or she — is only hurting himself, not us. If the social pressures become too difficult, a change in job and a move to a new locale may provide a geographic cure. In the same manner, changes in the alcohol beverage are attempted, from the hard stuff to beer or wine. Among the skid row group, the changes are even more dramatic, as simple economics dictates the use of anything cheap. We see a transfer to fortified wines, canned heat and rubbing alcohol. There are known cases of economically secure alcoholics developing a preference for such toxic alcohol concoctions because of the "wallop" they derive. Unfortunately, the problem progressively gets worse for the alcoholic, the family and all others who are affected.

These three types do not cover the whole complex covered by the generic term "alcoholism." They merely provide a brief reference to general kinds of alcoholic drinking without attempting to cover the many forms of behaviour in each.

There are dependent problem drinkers whose drinking exhibits basic neurotic patterns. There are those people who require considerable individual attention. Drinking allows some to compensate for a lack of personal intellectual acceptance. There are perfectionists and moral philosophers who constantly strike a discordant note in society, but whose drinking balances them off with the rest of the group. Those who suffer from boredom with life and are unable to respond to the ordinary ways of life, gain an aesthetic lift from alcohol. These are the folks who have a mystic streak and who often find abstinence and recovery through religion. And there are those who suffer from depression and a feeling of deep unworthiness. Some of these may be suicidal. They will disintegrate under pressure or tension more quickly than others. They sometimes require deterrent measures such as the drugs Antabuse or Temposil to achieve abstinence. Alcohol has a very real meaning to them.

Alcoholism: Treatable Illness

Among other dependent drinkers would be found the inadequate personality types who use alcohol as a necessary and continuing crutch. Included might be such drinkers as those suffering from chronic physical and emotional or neurotic pains, who use alcohol to kill those pains. There are also those who cannot accept the emotional misery of a disease like cancer, who drink in order not to think about it. There are some who use alcohol dependently simply to pamper themselves. This group could include those who never seem to grow up: the woman who could not accept the responsibility of being a wife or a mother or a busy executive; the son still tied to his mother's apron strings; the playboy who can't become a responsible citizen. The prognosis for this group is good, providing they can be properly motivated to a realistic approach both to life and to their problem drinking. There are also those drinkers who abjectly submit to life. They are miserable all the time and are incapable of knowing any joy in living. To them, life is most painful. Alcohol relieves them of their pain.

Among the inadequate personality types could also be included those whose dependent drinking is representative of a dissolute character, including psychopathic personalities, social misfits, and those with pronounced emotional emptiness, who feel the world owes them a living. This is a difficult group with whom to cope. And, of course, there are the stupid excessive dependent drinkers who are the imitators and morons of society.

There is another pocket of dependent drinkers to whom the onset of alcoholism superimposes another illness over and above the serious emotional disorders they already suffer. In this group would be included those suffering from pathological disturbances such as psychosis, schizophrenia, manic-depression and the like. These are probably very much in the minority, though alcoholics are sometimes mislabelled with such disorders unwisely and improperly by psychotherapists.

Growing numbers of young adults — in their early teens and older — are now regularly using beverage alcohol (and often drugs too). They are naturally exposing themselves much earlier to an increasing number of both physical and emotional disorders.

Following a prolonged history of drinking, an alcoholic during withdrawal may evidence every possible emotional disorder. In most, these manifestations will disappear when sobriety is attained. Until the alcoholic is physically well, his emotional well-being cannot be fairly determined. Almost all alcoholics who do achieve sobriety — once both physically well and emotionally comfortable — are new people. Those about them find it difficult to believe they could have been the problems they were.

12. *Young Adults and Drinking*

Drinking experiences are the same for everyone, but the impact on each individual may be quite different. In mature and well-integrated persons such an impact is better distributed, as their emotional structure is sounder to begin with. Though alcoholism has not as yet been positively confirmed to be either hereditary or the result of a genetic defect, personality traits and parental metabolic and enzyme systems may carry on to the children. A susceptibility element may be present, but the other ingredients must still be added. As we mature we experience conflicting drives, such as pain against reward, which vie for recognition. We handle and adjust to these feelings through learned controls and self-discipline. The more stable person has fewer inner conflicts and demands less recognition. Alcohol retards the natural development and use of our controls. For some, it may appear to relieve pain, anxiety, depression, boredom, loneliness and frustration, thereby producing a false sense of comfort or well-being. For others it may produce extra rewards — more comfort, greater well-being, new kicks, added status.

These reactions to alcohol are particularly of adverse import to young adults, especially so to those in their teens. The adolescent boy or girl is ill prepared to cope with the potential dangers of "too early drinking experience." This adds unwarranted pressure on those who would otherwise become well-integrated individuals. The demands nature already makes, combined with the duress and competition of schooling, social activities, adjustments to sexuality and movement into independent adult status are impact enough without the adverse effects of alcohol.

Things have "progressed" to the point where most of us accept without too much argument that the majority of teenagers have tasted alcohol; perhaps half of these did so initially with their parents. A great many adolescents have done considerably more than taste it, as tragic statistics and accident reports (with which the media regularly bombard us) can testify.

It is one thing for young people to learn to use the odd light beverage at home, in familiar surroundings and under the supervision of careful parents whom they may never have seen drink to excess. It is quite another to join a group of associates

Alcoholism: Treatable Illness

for the teen equivalent of social drinking, under circumstances which are almost certainly illegal and probably adverse. Such experiences can only lead to painful inner conflicts, to confrontations with friends, school, parents, police and community authorities, and to disaster on highways and in the workplace. This is particularly true in view of the more general problems of substance abuse, illegal drug trafficking, violence, crime and economically disadvantaged subgroups in large urban centers and "inner cities." In this context, it has become increasingly easy for young people to obtain liquor (to say nothing of other controlled or proscribed substances), and to use and abuse it —either in conjunction with other substances, or as a prelude to the use of other drugs with a more immediate and apparently more dangerous impact.

One of the most disturbing aspects of the cultural morass in which many young people are growing up — apart from the spreading social problems of high divorce and unemployment rates, falling educational standards, sexually transmitted (and potentially fatal) diseases and corporate neglect for the public welfare (all of which we might regard as both symptoms and causal factors) —is a terrible sense of hopelessness and purposelessness in our young when it comes to fulfilling traditional expectations. We in North America seem to have taken the path of least resistance in key policy matters, with the perverse result that a substantial segment of our young, who after all learn by example, believe in many cases that no matter what they do, they are doomed to a cycle of failure if they follow the rules. Their actions often demonstrate a kind of tacit self-hatred or lack of belief in the worth of living, and they all too frequently pursue illegal avenues to get what they want from life. They come to see criminal behaviour among their associates achieving what appears to be great short-term success, and they conclude either that the price to be paid for this success is insignificant by comparison or that no price would be too high for it.

In the environments in which such attitudes, behaviours and problems are rampant, the demonstrable dangers of alcohol abuse and misuse might appear to be the least of one's worries. And, while this grim picture clearly does not apply to all young people, the scope of the problem has had the effect of "trivializing" the problems of alcohol for young people generally.

As a young man, I had every opportunity to drink at home. Anything was available, though my father and mother rarely drank, and then only sparingly. On the occasion of my first high school prom (more decades ago than I care to count), my gang decided to "do it up big," so we bought some bootleg whiskey. Before picking up our dates, we drove off to a country road and parked in front of a dog cemetery to sample our wares. I remembered little of anything else that night, spending the evening in a blackout; and though apparently not intoxicated, I ruined the evening for my date. This may not sound like much, but times and standards of behaviour were *very* different then, and it was a traumatic experience for me. In later years, as my alcoholism progressed, I always remembered that incident. At least three members of that class now are recovered alcoholics. One classmate, a capable doctor, died and another spent considerable time in a mental institution as a result of alcoholism.

Times may be different, but that hasn't made things better. Now, instead of knowing a classmate who disgraced himself by coming to a social function intoxicated and then throwing up on his date or into the punchbowl, most everyone can say that they have known someone whose drinking got them into some real trouble. The fact is that when young adults depend on alcohol to make them feel more acceptable to others or to lighten the tension of new activities, they are vulnerable to becoming marked drinkers. The crowd that demands, "Drink with us or you can't belong!" is simply a younger edition of the irresponsible group discussed earlier.

The very real concern of anyone using beverage alcohol is intoxication. Young people, with fewer learned, practised and experienced controls, are certainly more prone to an involuntary loss of control. Anyone, lacking an awareness of the potential adverse effects of alcohol, can more easily become intoxicated without volition. The likelihood of intoxication and the dangers arising from it can be intensified by the cultural factors we have noted, and by other factors. Cars are a necessity today. The structure of our cities often permits earlier and much freer association between young people. Despite rapidly shifting economic trends and severe unemployment problems in certain sectors, the buoyancy of our economy in recent years has allowed for greater independence than ever before. Greater ease of communication and transportation intensifies the freedom. An incredible range of group leisure pursuits, sports and recreational activities has become available and has provided further opportunity for social interaction in circumstances where the consumption of alcohol is viewed, not merely as acceptable, but as appropriate or even necessary if a good time is to be had by all.

The result is that the youth of this generation know a sophistication unparalleled in history. Although there is indication that youth matures earlier physically, it still takes all of the teenage years to learn the controls necessary to handle tension conflicts and to reach emotional maturity.

Remember, alcohol anaesthetizes the brain — it does *not* stimulate it. It relieves controls, negates learning and impairs judgment. It doesn't improve our abilities, though it may make us *less anxious* or *less scared* to drive, ski, surf, dance or date. Nor does it make that awkward or plain date more dashing or glamorous. Alcohol simply dulls perception and inhibitions. Wasn't it Ogden Nash who said, "Candy is dandy, but liquor is quicker"?

Young people generally tend to emulate the behaviour of those older than

Alcoholism: Treatable Illness

themselves. To learn to smoke, drive, dress older, have money and drink is to be adult. If the parents are problem drinkers, the children may go to extremes. They either hate alcohol and all who drink, or may go all out and say, "What's the use, look at them." Prejudice and ignorance of the realities and problems of alcohol are intensified by the unfortunate buildup given to the misdeeds of a few. Similar emphasis on attaining the right age to drink or to use some kinds of beverage alcohol is also misleading. This is not to minimize the tragic and tremendous costs in the rising problems of alcohol among young people; rather it is to stress the need for more factual and objective educational programming to cope better with those problems. Young people today more than ever before have the opportunity to learn about alcohol positively and without prejudice. They should do so. Young adults are in some ways better informed than we realize and must be approached as adults. They react violently to being patronized and to the "hell and damnation" tactics sometimes used.

Young people should be helped to distinguish fact from fallacy by replacing ignorance with knowledge. They should be taught the dangers and pitfalls everyone faces in using beverage alcohol and/or other drugs, *no matter who they are, what they do, or how old they are.* Remember that one in every ten who drinks incurs alcoholism. It is also well to learn to respect the prerogatives of others, whether they abstain or drink. And above all, one must learn that it is one's own opinion of self that counts. Your decision is your own. If made in good judgment it will be one of moderation in all things, and you will emphasize for yourself the proper time, the proper place and the proper way.

The young person who succeeds in learning some controls may think he or she is "out of the woods." In fact, this person may eventually be in a position of greater risk; if one enters the work force in some executive capacity, one may find that the pressure to drink in work-related contexts will stretch those controls to the breaking point.

I'm reminded of the head of a large organization who became concerned about the drinking of his junior executives. He was disturbed at the number of young men having drinks at the bar of his club before lunch. I pointed out that everything they see, hear and read suggests that successful people on the way up do drink, and that his own regular drinking with his employees confirmed this.

I advised him that he should play a different role. Rather than always ordering or saying "yes" just as often, simply refuse a drink when they are together. And when the opportunity arises, point out it isn't necessary to drink every day, at every place, to be successful. Many people drink simply because others do so, though they would prefer not to — and frankly, their budgets would fare better without it.

The executive tried this procedure and was pleasantly surprised to hear from several of his junior personnel that they did prefer not to drink, and that they worked better and spent less time at lunch when they didn't drink.

Parents and peer adults have a major responsibility for the manner in which they introduce the young people about them to beverage alcohol use. Any real hope for a positive influence will also be found in the attitudes and examples they personally demonstrate toward alcohol abuse and overuse and the quality of education brought to this generation of young adults. The alcohol education currently being developed and presented to young adults offers more hope to effectively improve attitudes, treatment and control than anything heretofore, though this does not mean we are as good as we can be. The insight, keenness, common sense and open-mindedness to change that young people possess are our most significant instruments. Let's use them!

13. Progression of the Illness

Is Alcoholism an Illness?

An early story is told about the late Dr. E.M. Jellinek's use of his "Phases of Alcoholism." A wife had brought her husband to the original Yale Clinic to have Dr. Jellinek see her spouse about his drinking. It was evident to Dr. Jellinek that the husband was both reluctant and disinterested. Nevertheless, after visiting briefly with them both, he took the husband into his office. Once alone, he put the man at ease and commented: "I can see you don't believe you have a problem. However, for appearances sake and to mollify your wife, visit with me for awhile." After going about some tasks, the doctor seated himself at his desk and began to doodle on a scrap of paper. "It will probably make things easier if you have something to talk about when you leave," he told the man, "so I'll show you what takes place in the development of alcoholism."

This Dr. Jellinek proceeded to do by outlining his now-famous "Bunky's doodle" (Bunky was the affectionate nickname by which the doctor was known). As the patient watched, the doctor doodled and described the progressive characteristics of the illness alcoholism. Near the conclusion of the doctor's remarks, the patient, involuntarily perhaps, but as if released by a spring, reached forward and placing his finger on one mark on the doodle, said, "Doctor, I am right there." Thus began his treatment.

The doctor's empathy was such that he could bring home to the alcoholic the knowledge that he or she was not alone, but rather one of many sufferers of the illness alcoholism who would be able to regain control of his or her life. Traditionally alcoholics are thought of as maverick drinkers who deliberately bring their disorder upon themselves; who stubbornly refuse to change; who rebel against all moral and religious ethics, and who repudiate every well-meaning offer of direction or help. Though this is largely the view most held of the alcoholic, a few scientists, truly interested in a study of problem drinking behaviour, sought to determine why most may use beverage alcohol with impunity; why some, though excessive users, remain controlled drinkers, and why some drinkers lose control and become alcoholics.

These were the interests explored in the early forties by Dr. Jellinek with his associates in the Center of Alcohol Studies, formerly at Yale and now at Rutgers University, and Harry M. Tiebout, M.D., a psychiatrist and physician in charge of a private sanatorium. They evolved the "Phases of Alcoholism."[1]

As scientists, interested in the well-being of their fellow men, these researchers realized that offhand assumptions were inadequate. They knew well the cliches surrounding those whose drinking evidenced a difference and a problem: "Oh, like most, after he sows his wild oats he'll get over it," or "After she's married she will settle down," or "When the children come and his job demands increase, this will all blow over," and like answers. Some don't settle down or get over it. Somewhere, during one of these stages, the alcoholic travels a different and solitary road.

A clinical illness, in order to be so described, must generally follow an established pattern and evidence a distinct and concurrent set of symptoms. While these properties are innate to alcoholism, they had never been set down in a comprehensive and conclusive manner. The studies behind the development of the "Phases of Alcoholism" had a most meaningful purpose and were to have a tremendous impact on the attitudes to and treatment of alcoholics. They heralded the advances we see about us today, for out of this work came conclusive proof that alcoholism is indeed an illness.

Alcoholics Anonymous and co-founder Bill Wilson played an important role in these developments. The membership, through their official house organ, *The Grapevine*, in May 1945 published a questionnaire to ascertain at what age and stage in the progression of their dependency the members experienced a number of phases and incidents. Dr. Jellinek, called upon to study the returns, amplified his investigations with a further study of more than 2000 drinking histories of male alcoholics. Drs. Jellinek and Tiebout saw considerable significance in the behaviour patterns of alcoholics. They found a syndrome or set pattern of concurrent symptoms in all problem drinkers who lost control — in other words, *they confirmed the existence of a distinct clinical illness in its own right.*

As all previous research had been conducted by psychotherapists, understandably the psychological aspects of those drinkers becoming alcoholics had been emphasized. Such therapy sought only to discover and rectify the patient's basic conflicts without giving attention to the alcoholic's drinking behaviour. This presupposed that alcoholism was not or could not become the number one problem. Such disregard of the history of the alcoholic's drinking behaviour and the resultant lack of any recognition of alcoholism as a distinct illness in itself are perhaps the basis for the antipathy demonstrated by most alcoholics to psychotherapists before, during and after their recovery.

Members of A.A., by emphasizing the significance of the drinking itself, see themselves (sick) again in another practising alcoholic. They understand and share

Alcoholism: Treatable Illness

his or her misery. This empathy or understanding for others assists greatly in achieving the recovery of fellow alcoholics. Drs. Jellinek and Tiebout learned to recognize this fact — thus their longstanding and close ties as non-alcoholic friends of A.A.

When I was working on the first edition of this book, I was involved with such a case. A female alcoholic whom many people had tried to help had relapsed again. We knew she had many serious problems; however, her alcoholism continued to prevent the treatment of these disorders. Though admitted to a hospital, she was peremptorily released as the bed "was needed by a *sick* patient." Since she was not considered to be an emergency patient, arrangements were made for her to go to a mental hospital and to come back for out-patient care. No one was notified of the new arrangements suggested until some time later when the patient called a friend to be picked up. The patient herself had no idea what it was all about; in fact, she didn't know what day it was. The friend sat up all night with her in a hotel room, feeding her soups and juices. Another brought her medication.

The following day, more rational, though still sick, she resented everyone and everything. On being told what the doctor had advised, she agreed to follow instructions but insisted on putting her house and affairs in order, paying her bills and getting leave from her employer. While those close to her knew that she was incapable of any decisions, there was no stopping her. Any hope she had at that time of working toward recovery would have begun in a hospital, but only under the guidance of someone who would understand and be willing to recognize her behavioral problems for what they were — a part of her sickness.

Though determined to show everybody she wanted to recover, disorganized and confused, she resorted to an open prescription for tranquillizers. Under their influence, she went to see her superior to request leave. Sympathetic and concerned, her work associates tried to put up with and ignore her behaviour. Ironically, her associates gave her a going away drinking party. Having leave of absence, her washing done, and her house in order (she was most fastidious in every way), she notified the doctor that she was ready to do as he had suggested.

This woman, without the constant supervision and care of friends and A.A. members, in those days could well have been a suicide as her depression and remorse were colossal. I have never seen anything more pathetic than this normally intelligent, well-groomed lady, completely incoherent, dishevelled, weakened by malnutrition (in fact, down to about ninety pounds), earnestly saying, "There must be some hope for me."

This case was not an exception. This was, and still is, the rule for all too many alcoholics. The addition of pills, a hopeless substitution for treatment, merely demonstrates our ignorance of the basic symptoms and needs of those suffering from this illness. Today, with the proliferation of exotic tranquillizers, relaxants and stimulants, the likelihood that a sufferer will compound the problem before he or she seeks treatment — perhaps with fatal results — is infinitely greater.

Phases of Alcoholism

The progressive stages of alcoholism may be divided into four phases: pre-alcoholic; premonitory or preliminary (also called the prodromal); crucial; and the chronic phases. The pre-alcoholic and premonitory phases make up the symptomatic period in the progression of the illness. The crucial and chronic phases compose the dependent or addictive phases.

Each phase has its own history of concurrent symptoms of behaviour denoting the progression of alcoholism. The basis for these materials and the chart on which the presentation of the phases is made are taken from the work of the late Dr. E.M. Jellinek.[2]

Most alcoholics are prone to think that they are not that "bad" yet and haven't reached this or that serious point in their drinking. It is wiser, therefore, to allow the portrayal to speak for itself. However, it should be pointed out that all developing alcoholics do not experience the symptoms in the same order or with the same frequency or duration. The symptoms of behaviour indicated are more pronounced in some alcoholics than in others. Nevertheless all alcoholics will generally conform to the path of the symptoms outlined.[3]

Pre-Alcoholic Phase (I)

Our portrayal begins with social drinking. Take any set of people — friends, relatives, acquaintances; for the majority, whether light, occasional and irregular drinkers or moderate, daily and regular users, their drinking is not an essential function. They will drink at home and participate in activities that involve drinking, including birthdays, weddings, dinners and cocktail parties. Some members of this group may gain an extra reward from their drinking. It may make them more relaxed or convivial and enable them to achieve social acceptance within their sets more easily. This would include the A, B and C drinkers on the chart (see figure 1).You will also note on the chart individuals D, DX and E. These are MARKED DRINKERS. For them alcohol provides a greater reward. They are affected somewhat differently by their drinking so they superimpose a new function for alcohol, over and above its use as a cultural custom. Individual D moves from OCCASIONAL DRINKING (1) to CONSTANT RELIEF DRINKING (2). It provides, for him, a relief from physical or psychological pain.[4] DX may feel more adequate to dance, to accompany others to parties and to meet other personal demands *after a drink or two*. Such dependency reflects even this early a form of pathological dependency on alcohol. Individual DX may thus bypass relief drinking and jump right to Point 5 and do some surreptitious drinking.

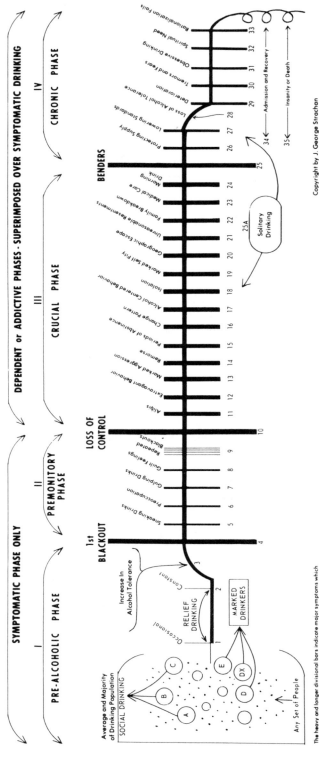

PHASES OF ALCOHOLISM

The History or Concurrent Symptoms of Behavior during the Progression of the Illness

I	II	III	IV
SYMPTOMATIC PHASE ONLY		DEPENDENT or ADDICTIVE PHASES - SUPERIMPOSED OVER SYMPTOMATIC DRINKING	
PRE-ALCOHOLIC PHASE	PREMONITORY PHASE	CRUCIAL PHASE	CHRONIC PHASE

1st BLACKOUT

LOSS OF CONTROL

BENDERS

Average and Majority of Drinking Population

SOCIAL DRINKING

Any Set of People

MARKED DRINKERS

Increase in Alcohol Tolerance

Occasional — RELIEF DRINKING — Constant

Symptoms labels:
- Sneaking Drinks
- Preoccupation
- Gulping Drinks
- Guilt Feelings
- Repeated Blackouts
- Alibis
- Extravagant Behavior
- Marked Aggression
- Remorse
- Periods of Abstinence
- Change Pattern
- Alcohol Centered Behavior
- Isolation
- Marked Self Pity
- Geographic Escape
- Unreasonable Resentments
- Family Breakdown
- Medical Care
- Morning Drink
- Protecting Supply
- Lowering Standards
- Loss of Alcohol Tolerance
- Deterioration
- Tremors and Fears
- Obsessive Drinking
- Spiritual Need
- Rationalization Fails

Solitary Drinking 25A

34 — Admission and Recovery

35 — Insanity or Death

The heavy and longer divisional bars indicate major symptoms which denote progression from one phase to another. Light and shorter bars indicate the progressive symptoms of behavior within each phase. Each symptom as numbered, is noted within the text.

It should be emphasized that these manifestations of behavior do not

Copyright by J. George Strachan

Taken from a presentation by the late Dr. E.M. Jellinek at the Yale Center of Alcohol Studies in 1950 (now The Rutgers Center of Alcohol Studies) and Q.J.S.A. Volume 13. No. 4. December 1952.

Drinker E may be one who will learn to take advantage of every social drinking opportunity to use beverage alcohol more often and in increasing amounts to achieve greater rewards in relieving pain, boredom and depression and in compensating for other inherent problems. Though several such drinkers get more satisfaction from drinking than do others, many will not necessarily overdrink for a long time. This varies with the individual. At this early stage these drinkers associate their satisfaction and relief with the group, time and place of the occasion. They do not immediately sense the relationship of alcohol to their feelings of well-being. A little later E, like DX, also begins to depend more and more on alcohol for both inner security and general well-being.

These marked drinkers may now begin to seek more frequent occasions on which to get the satisfaction they enjoy, involving more drinking. As the intake increases, abilities and controls will temporarily improve, so there is an INCREASE OF ALCOHOL TOLERANCE — THE DRINKING CURVE (3) moves upward. It is difficult to warn this drinker because he will argue, "I can handle my liquor." He is apparently more sober on several drinks than those about him who are on one or two. Unlike DX, who may become intoxicated on the first drinking experience, E (though he drinks more) is not conspicuous. Nevertheless, he soon learns it takes more drinks to do the job and begins to up his intake. The time element varies between drinkers.

Almost every potential alcoholic has lapses in memory, or "draws a blank" at this stage. While perhaps considered sober, he or she is unable to recall the events of a particular occasion on a given day or evening. This, the FIRST BLACKOUT (4), is a symptom of something new in the drinking history. It is the separation line between the pre-alcohol phase and the premonitory phase. These blackouts, in some persons, become more frequent and complicated. In others, they may not recur for awhile.

Premonitory Phase (II)

THE BLACKOUT, the demarcation between phases, is a form of alcohol amnesia. It has been suggested that some temporary physiological shifts occur — perhaps the withdrawal of vitamins or enzymes, impeding the oxidation of alcohol in the brain. The amount of alcohol consumed does not seem to influence this phenomenon. It does suggest a susceptibility to alcohol by some individuals. Whether this is caused by a physical or psychological factor of the illness is still being studied. It indicates a serious difference in what drinking does to the potential alcoholic as against other drinkers. Such blackouts rarely occur in non-dependent though excessive drinkers.

At this point, E may also feel a *need* to drink, and suddenly alcohol becomes a medicine to satisfy those inner needs. This greater demand now requires new ways

Alcoholism: Treatable Illness

to add the needed drinks. Not wishing to be misjudged or to have this need found out and so be known as a different kind of drinker, alcoholics will start to SNEAK (5) a few extra ones. While mixing a round of highballs for guests, or while alone in the kitchen, they sneak one or two straight ones. If asked about their over-drinking, they promptly reply, "Why, you saw me take just two." This also denotes the beginning PREOCCUPATION (6) with drinking. Alcoholics fortify themselves with a few before going to a party and change drinking groups to be with those who drink more; their occasions for drinking become much more important than formerly. Such occasions are planned and sought out.

Seeking to retain a happy glow, the developing alcoholic finds his or her system demands ever more alcohol, and now GULPS (7) drinks to feel more comfortable. Once caught up, one can coast again. The alcoholic begins to realize his or her drinking is different; behaviour toward alcohol is perhaps abnormal, causing the onset of early GUILT FEELINGS (8). Intoxicated at times, alcoholics may question their drinking pattern, or drink more to offset feelings of guilt. References to alcohol or to drinking experiences are avoided. Growing guilt will cause alcoholics to be irritated at their behaviour and to avoid being cornered about developing problems at home or on the job.

This creates a frustrating period for the spouse and family, who vainly hope that this will all blow over — so they too avoid discussions or confrontations about alcohol.

These initial warnings may be magnified by REPETITIVE BLACKOUTS (9). Though the drinking, and more regular intoxication, is not always conspicuous, the signs of developing alcoholism are there. The need for more alcohol, the covering up and the guilt, all begin to set this marked drinker apart. The alcoholic is edgy and impatient to drink to satisfy the need for alcohol. This period may vary in time from a few months to several years, depending upon the pampering and sheltering drinkers provide themselves or receive from others. The habits and patterns of one's drinking group likewise provide protection. Groups that cater to excessive drinking enable alcoholics to remain hidden longer than normal; or, if their drinking goes beyond group limits, they may change groups.

The infrequent or regular experience of blackouts is a major warning in the progression of the illness. Those drinkers, who learned to use beverage alcohol as a lubricant to adjust to society or to ease life's daily pressures, now find that their kind of drinking is separating them from the society they sought. As a different drinker, he or she now superimposes an entirely new set of behavioural problems over those for which the use of alcohol initially provided such comfort. *Even at this early stage, complete abstinence is the only positive remedy.*

Recent advances in educational and preventive programming on dependency are resulting in many such early stage alcoholics seeking guidance. Their fears and guilt, combined with growing awareness, motivate them to seek recovery. Not all follow through sufficiently to achieve complete abstinence. Some switch drinking patterns and become pseudo-periodics.

A number of so-called social drinkers, under certain circumstances, will experience the foregoing stages.

Crucial (III)

The critical symptom separating the symptomatic phases (pre-alcoholic and premonitory) from the next phase and denoting the onset of the crucial phases of alcoholism is an INVOLUNTARY LOSS OF CONTROL (10). The drinker finds himself or herself unable to control the amount consumed. With the best of intentions one takes a drink or two and is unable to stop — an innocent social drink ends up in a spree. The drinking triggers a chain reaction which is interpreted as a physical demand for alcohol, a compulsion over which the alcoholic is powerless whenever this need arises. The compulsion may continue until one is too intoxicated or "sick" to drink any more. This process doesn't always take place overnight, but varies with individuals over periods of days, weeks, and even months. As the ability and will to drink according to intent is lost, the episodes telescope and become progressively more serious.

While to all appearances everything in the drinker's life "couldn't be better," each drinking experience, without warning, becomes a serious episode. The alcoholic may not want to get drunk, and has perhaps even begun to hate the stuff — all he or she wanted was that happy glow. This drinker may now resent spouse, boss, friends and relatives, who accuse him or her of not drinking like a man or a lady — of failing to use willpower. Secretly he or she calls self a heel, is frustrated by his or her "kind of drinking" with its intermittent bouts of intoxication, and questions his or her own ability to quit. In between bouts, safe again, the alcoholic reasserts the ability to control the drinking, and so 'self-tests' time after time. Though retaining control over "when he (or she) drinks," once started, the drinker loses control of the amount.

Repetitive instances in the loss of control over the amount consumed increase the alcoholic's fear and guilt. Not wishing to be considered one of the other kind of drinkers and unable to answer questions on the "why" of the compulsive drinking, alcoholics now ALIBI (11). They rationalize excesses by blaming and projecting their problems on everyone but themselves. This is a desperate attempt to hang on to self-esteem and to protect the status of family and associates. Alibis become a constant part of everyday life — so much so, alcoholics themselves believe them.

With their alcoholism being conspicuous, and with others knowing more about their behaviour than they do themselves, there is a noticeable reaction to their problem drinking. Social pressures mount against it and them. In rebellion against

Alcoholism : Treatable Illness

these pressures and as a reaction to the veiled warnings of those near and dear, alcoholics respond with EXTRAVAGANT AND GRANDIOSE BEHAVIOUR (12). They attempt to regain stature by buying or spending extravagantly; treating everyone in high style, buying drinks for "the house" and developing "telephonitis." These actions are meant to salvage personal dignity and ego, but instead push alcoholics further away from society.

Since their behaviour is rejected by those about them, alcoholics now display MARKED AGGRESSION (13) to those who cross their paths by interfering with their drinking. Though they excuse their behaviour and drinking by blaming their many problems, they cannot understand that most of those problems are caused by and are symptoms of their own progressive illness. The alcoholic gets angry if dinner isn't ready and just as angry if no one bothers to wait. These are all reasons for aggression and for drinking more heavily and more frequently. The alibis and aggression are but a projection of one's inability to stop and face the pain or difficulties which the drinking is intended to solve.

At this stage of the crucial phase, in addition to the psychological changes, there is now evidence that some physiological changes take place. The loss of control is very apparent. Our drinker is beyond being just a social problem drinker; he or she is a very sick person — an alcoholic.

Alcoholics, completely entangled in compulsive drinking over which they have no control, find themselves living a pattern of behaviour which they despise intensely. They begin to suffer PERSISTENT AND INTENSE REMORSE (14). Each realizes what people are saying — that he is a good father and husband, a good wife and mother, or a good worker and provider — when sober. Each chastises himself more bitterly than any of those about him, though his defensive aggressiveness does not allow anyone to realize this. He makes innumerable promises and on breaking them is truly sorry — but still he continues. This only increases his remorse and creates new tensions, which call for increased drinking to blot out the added pain.

This intense personal shame, combined with growing family, job and social pressures, may cause the alcoholic to attempt varying PERIODS OF ABSTINENCE (15). These periods have a deeper meaning than previous attempts at "going on the wagon." They are sessions of repentance and reorganization of self. These periods of abstinence buy the time to retain a job, to hold a family together, and to think and work things through. During this enforced period of temporary compliance with outside pressures, the alcoholic reasons that he hasn't been going about his drinking in the right way. He may decide to drink other beverages, to change the time and place, and to establish a new set of personal rules, or CHANGE HIS PATTERN OF DRINKING (16). He will only drink after five o'clock, won't go to Joe's Tavern, will have his wife or friends accompany him.

Unfortunately he learns — as soon as he triggers another bout with a social drink or two — that the change of brand, time, associates or place makes little difference.

During this period, the alcoholic begins to withdraw more and more from his total environment. His need and dependency intensify his ALCOHOL-CENTERED BEHAVIOUR (17). Consciously and subconsciously, he centers every thought and activity around his "medicine." Under such circumstances, is it any wonder that family, job, and all other social associates suffer? With neither the time nor the interest for outside functions and with but one obsession in mind, the alcoholic regresses into a pattern that is completely self-centered. This behaviour causes him to ISOLATE (18) himself from every other interest. Finding his newly attempted change in pattern doesn't work, he will drop friends and change places and groups. He may try to drink alone and drop everything and everybody. If he senses a growing criticism from his business associates or employer, he may anticipate their reproof by resigning first.

Feeling very much alone, alibis rebuffed, with tensions mounting, the alcoholic is now led by the progression of the illness to bemoan fate and to wallow in SELF PITY (19). If offered help, he or she rejects it. Everyone is to blame but the alcoholic. This provides an excuse to go elsewhere and build up a new life — the GEOGRAPHIC ESCAPE (20): a fresh start, a new job some place where one won't be known, where all things that are against one won't hinder his or her way of life. The alcoholic still feels positive that if everything else is right, he or she can drink as others do.

The alcoholic's alibis, aggressions and self pity cause him to express UNREASONABLE RESENTMENTS (21) to everyone about him. Resentments are remorse turned inside out — the dimple becomes a pimple. He will accuse his employers of favouritism, his associates of disloyalty. When these avenues are closed, he will of necessity focus all of his resentments on those nearest and dearest to him. Naturally, the result is a COMPLETE BREAKDOWN IN FAMILY RELATIONSHIPS (22).

While many problems have developed within the family circle during each progressive stage, now matters are reaching an unbearable crisis. Spouse and children have become as isolated and ostracized as the alcoholic, or alternatively they have scattered in every direction, seeking for themselves an escape through numerous outside interests to compensate for the problems at home. Alcoholics may accuse their spouses of being unfaithful, or of deserting them in their trouble and of ignoring their needs. As they live more and more in an alcohol-centered world, they indicate less interest in a normal sexual life. This increases hostility and resentment. Jealousies are magnified as they see their last and dearest "possessions" slipping away from their grasp and showing less and less interest in them. They may chastise and berate the children for a lack of decent respect or

113

Alcoholism: Treatable Illness

affection. Everything seems to be closing in on them, so they are going to fight. Their behaviour is even more aggressive, and they may become physically abusive to those about them.

The alcoholic may now be influenced by the urgency of the crisis created to grudgingly seek help or MEDICAL CARE (23) and be coerced into visiting a doctor, psychiatrist, alcoholism clinic, Alcoholics Anonymous, or some counselling agency. If the timing and approach are right, the alcoholic may succumb and admit defeat at this stage, surrendering to the need for outside help to cope with the dependency. Unknown to others, he or she may be avidly reading everything in print to seek his or her own answers. The continuing emphasis on drinking has certainly had adverse effects on his or her health. Poor habits in personal care and nutrition will have taken their toll — so much so that he or she may need hospitalization. The alcoholic might even agree to go away to some private treatment center or, if less fortunate economically, may by now have been picked up and institutionalized. The alcoholic's physical condition, at this stage, is sometimes tragic and is intensely exaggerated by the emotional, social and spiritual disturbances he or she is going through.

The morning drink, or a drink at a set time, becomes an obsessive ailment in itself. At some point in the progression of dependency the alcoholic will learn, perhaps by accident, the benefit of morning drink. The first few occasions may seem to offer a wonderful new medicine. However, as alcoholics pass through these many stages, they reach a state of physical and psychological need that demands greater recognition. Physically upset and unsure of themselves, they seek and temporarily find reassurance with a REGULAR MORNING DRINK (24). This enables alcoholics to reorganize themselves for the day, or at least the next period, and to find the courage, strength and pseudo-stability to carry on. When the alcoholic evidences this regular symptom, he or she is proceeding into the final stage of alcoholism. Previously, they have confined themselves to regular, but not necessarily continuous, around-the-clock drinking, and to possible deliberate heavier use or intoxication during evenings or weekends or on special occasions. Regular morning drinking establishes a new and more serious phase in their dependency.

At the onset of the crucial phase the alcoholic, once started, loses control of the amount ingested. Now there is a loss of control as to when the drinking begins. Such drinking compels the drinker to neglect every duty and to violate all ideals and practices of character. The increasingly dominant role of alcohol, exaggerated by regular morning drinking (*or at such times as the individual establishes*), now truly denotes the drinker as a confirmed alcoholic. Finding himself unable to cope with the need to drink more often and in greater amounts, he explodes into BENDERS (25). These binges culminate in the alcoholic's rejection by all of society. Only a very sick person would take this risk.

Chronic Phase (IV)

The alcoholic's shift in pattern to drink compulsively and continuously, as in benders, moves him or her into the last and chronic phase of the illness. He loses all control, perhaps for days and even weeks, until his system gives out. He may remain holed up in a hotel, at home, or even in some dive, and could now be a SOLITARY DRINKER (25A). This symptom, denoted as a variable, could occur earlier or later. It could have started as an expression of extreme aggression — getting even with the world — or as a earlier expression of self pity and "What's the use?" Solitary drinking confirms that the alcoholic, withdrawn from his group or drinking set, family, even from his own sex, is using alcohol for an entirely different purpose. He is seeking oblivion from all he has become.

Dependent drinkers progressing into alcoholism learn to PROTECT THEIR SUPPLY (26). Preoccupied with a need for alcohol, alcoholics are careful of associates, of where they go and of what they do to better cater to their alcohol requirements. The alcoholic treasures his supply, perhaps hoarding for a bender. When stashing it away to be sure it is available, he sometimes even hides it from himself. Not to have a drink at hand, when he craves and needs it, is a dire situation that must be avoided at any cost.

These practices continue to ensnare the alcoholic deeper into an alcohol-centered existence. Rejected by related social groups, spurned by other drinkers, the alcoholic now undergoes a LOWERING OF STANDARDS (27), seeking out people and places who will accept his drinking behaviour. He is the well-dressed "lush" having a spree in the slums, or the hapless "visiting fireman" who is "tying one on" in another town where he isn't known and, more importantly, where he doesn't have to care. He may arrive home with some odd characters or be located in some strange places. Some lose everything, end up on skid row and try to fit in with a bottle gang. Here the alcoholic may learn to drink spiked wine or beer, bay rum, canned heat, rubbing alcohol and the like.

Just as the developing problem drinker achieved a greater tolerance for alcohol, now the curve goes down and there is a LOSS OF ALCOHOL TOLERANCE (28). Because of physical and psychological changes, it now takes less alcohol to bring about oblivion and complete intoxication. The alcoholic's ability to resist the effects of alcohol is much lower. If a regular excessive and continuous user, he or she is always well fortified. This phenomenon is noted in alcoholics who return to drinking after achieving lengthy periods of sobriety. On relapsing, they often express surprise at their inability "to drink very much any more."

Such drinking, amplified by benders, precipitates more marked disorders. In addition to lower personal standards of behaviour and of drinking habits, there is now a DETERIORATION (29) in the ethics and thinking of the alcoholic. He takes on an "I don't care," "I am hopeless," and a "What's the use?" attitude. Only

115

complete sobriety could regenerate more positive attitudes. The last problems and symptoms now quickly compound each other.

The alcoholic begins to develop continuing TREMORS AND INDEFINABLE FEARS (30). He may be afraid to sleep with the light off, to be in a small room or in a crowd. His imagination runs rampant with bizarre fantasies of all kinds, none of which he can diagnose or interpret. His tremors are persistent and recur violently when the concentration of alcohol is at a low ebb. To avoid these symptoms demands almost continuous intoxication. Without sufficient alcohol, he endures the shakes, gags, sweats, butterflies and the like. Without the proper balance of alcohol there is psychomotor inhibition, in which the alcoholic is unable to perform the simplest mechanical tasks, like tying a tie or shoelace. He must now drink to achieve coordination, as this ability lasts only as long as alcohol is present.

At this stage, the alcoholic's drinking is OBSESSIVE (31). Alcohol comes before everything else. The obsession is such that alcoholics exist to drink — while drinking to exist. Nothing else counts — family and self-esteem are meaningless, as are the normal concerns of all other persons. Nevertheless, most alcoholics, during some moment of temporary awareness have a feeling that this cannot go on much longer without some retribution. A drink or two and the feeling passes; but as the ineffectiveness of old excuses and alibis is demonstrated, the alcoholic has VAGUE FEELINGS OF SPIRITUAL NEED (32), a "*want to want* to quit." A vague desire for hope and help — perhaps as a reflection of past religious beliefs or moral convictions.

This indefinable yearning for spiritual help may be the last conscious or subconscious reasoning the alcoholic demonstrates. Tested too hard and too frequently, all RATIONALIZATION FAILS (33). Trapped on the treadmill of alcoholism the sufferer has no choice but to surrender and accept the terms of defeat: ADMISSION AND RECOVERY (34), or continuance on a torturous path toward INSANITY OR DEATH (35).

The treadmill (or "squirrel cage," as this stage is commonly called) of the illness is not irreversible. Complete abstinence and time can restore most alcoholics to health. Through sobriety, he or she can realistically achieve the life so mistakenly sought through the use of alcohol.

Though a voluntary approach to treatment is preferable by far, involuntary care is not to be ignored. As with any other illness, enforced assistance may be necessary initially, to regenerate faculties, judgment and motivation. This is particularly crucial today in situations where alcohol is taken regularly with other addictive substances which may deprive an individual of volition even more quickly than the alcohol itself. In circumstances where an alcoholic is incapable of seeking help or recognizing the aid offered, and no effort is made to create an opportunity to accept or reject recovery, the alcoholic must surely travel to the very end of the

alcoholic state. A percentage of alcoholics go beyond this point and develop ' ...
brain'' or alcoholic psychosis, which may be likened to being punch-drunk, and
from which recovery is usually impossible. Many alcoholics develop other
complications from which they die before reaching this sad state.

Some still maintain that the alcoholic *must lose everything* before he or she will
accept assistance. While this matter will be discussed under the heading of
motivation, I am prepared to state emphatically that this is not so. The surrender
process can be induced and a state of crisis and decision created. Sometimes the
recovery process can be achieved even in the final stages of alcoholism by calling
upon that last vestige of hope, the last spark evidenced in the alcoholic — namely,
that vague spiritual desire for help. This, however, must be interpreted only as an
evidenced desire for help. It must be nurtured and carefully guided with all the
techniques available, to bring the hopeless alcoholic back through his or her
spiritual, physical, emotional and social stages to total recovery.

Female Alcoholics Do Have Differences...

The preceding interpretation of the phases and symptoms of alcoholism did
not differentiate between men and women alcoholics. While their eventual patterns
are alike, female alcoholics do run a somewhat separate course. The physical,
physiological and emotional factors which differentiate women from men do cause
them to be more susceptible to an earlier and greater dependency on alcohol.
Additionally, despite the increasing and quite proper modern emphasis on the
equality of the sexes in our culture, we have a long history of viewing women as
taking a "proper place" in society. While we are outgrowing this, many of us still
have feelings which cause us to look at women differently and to attempt to shelter
them more. In women, the time and frequency between symptoms is often
shortened because women may telescope their drinking and reach a crucial stage
earlier than do men.

Women engage in solitary drinking more than men. More marked perhaps at
the outset, and as their lives' circumstances have traditionally permitted them to be
alone more, they may readily resort to a few nips to carry them through. A
housewife, caught in the web of mundane chores, once her husband is off to work
and the youngsters off to school, has the day to herself and can feel sorry for her lot.
Later in life, with her children gone, she has even fewer demands on her time and a
whole new set of reasons to seek an outside lift.

Some women, and men, may find this thumbnail analysis offensive, since it
appears to rest heavily on a view of women in society that is no longer in vogue. But
the fact of the matter is that there are probably two generations of women still living
who came to adulthood when traditionally applied stereotypes and cultural male
chauvinism were the norm rather than the exception. Some of those women became

117

Alcoholism: Treatable Illness

or are becoming alcoholics. This is a fact that has to be faced, regardless of one's views of propriety or impropriety. It is also a fact that, despite the achievements of recent years in the struggle for equality between the sexes, there are still millions of people in North America who do not see this struggle as applying to them and who do not measure their lives in terms of liberation or suppression. Many of these do not demonstrate cultural self-awareness, but rather live their lives as best they can. To the extent that they accept the status quo, for them many of the truths about female alcoholics that would have applied twenty-five or thirty years ago will still apply today. Finally, since the move toward equality is a process and since we clearly have not reached nirvana in this regard, there will be millions of young women who will subscribe strongly to the cultural values of their parents, the liberation movement notwithstanding. For those among them susceptible to alcohol, the analysis will continue to apply.

Career women do present different problems today in terms of how, when and why they drink. The obligations of business, marketing and public relations will provide both opportunity and pressure for many. The social side of modern business relationships acts as a lure, and the advertising industry has assisted the beverage alcohol industry in showing women as well as men that young, upwardly mobile people who work hard and achieve symbolic success should relax and blow off steam by having a drink or a few beers. The same business and career pressures which have driven men to drink are more regularly driving women to drink; and there is the added dimension of the career woman who, despite her success in the business world, may feel cheated or guilty about abandoning a traditional role as a wife or mother.

Circumstances between groups of women may vary, but the emotional and physiological aspects of their drinking are the same. Women who start to drink heavily at too young an age may be reflecting an emotional disorder. Those starting about middle age, with no background or neurosis, may incur problems because physical differences. In many instances, a woman's alcoholism can more easily be traced to a specific time or event. Female alcoholics therefore may compress the progression of the illness into a shorter period. Where a male alcoholic might take fifteen years to travel through the phases, a woman, whether she enters early or late, can experience the whole gamut of symptoms in one-third the time.

In seeking relief from their drinking or other problems, many women inadvertently became addicted to the use of tranquillizers and sedation. This has become a cultural phenomenon to the point that police in major urban centers must face a burgeoning criminal traffic in substances like valium and quaalude, to name only two. The abuse of such drugs has become so familiar that we have even started to see a kind of sick humour in it, as most movie-goers will attest. The over-prescription of such substances for women may well be related to the training of a whole generation of medical practitioners who viewed women paternalistically, and who, in some cases, may have been attempting to treat with drugs a problem which was tied to the use or abuse of alcohol.

As society loses the straitlaced sensibilities which prevented women from entering so many areas where they are making vital contributions, it paves the way for more of the women who are susceptible to alcohol to become members of one of those groups of drinkers who will pursue a course through all the phases of alcoholism.

Sometimes, membership has no privileges.

The Alcoholic Couple

When both husband and wife are alcoholic, the problems created are compounded many times over. Until recent years, the male spouse usually developed full-blown alcoholism first. Often the spouse's alcoholism results from "desperation" drinking while trying to keep up with the alcoholic partner. With the pattern set, the spouse's alcoholism may only manifest itself after the partner achieves recovery and sobriety.

It is tragic indeed when either partner, after a lengthy and sound period of continued and happy sobriety, is insidiously drawn back into a daily life of torture through the other's alcoholism and then seduced to relapse by the practising alcoholic's need to cover up his or her drinking. It is heartbreaking to see the illness recur and destroy everything that was regained.

Some years ago, a man with everything to live for called me over to his home for help. On arrival, I found him and his wife both sadly the worse for wear. His remorse and disgust with himself was beyond words. A proud man at the top of his profession, with family grown and gone, after a decade of sobriety he had tried controlled drinking to please his spouse. At an age when life should hold everything for both, the shambles of their home life told the whole story. It is possible to recount several identical experiences of couples whose lives were devastated by alcoholism.

Whether a new or recurring case, it is rarely possible to achieve sobriety for both mates at once. Unless both are well-motivated and determined to achieve recovery, it may be better to attempt to separate the two practising alcoholics and achieve beginning positive recovery for one member on which to anchor the recovery of the other. This is not an easy task. In such cases, when there is no strength to draw upon from either partner, it is helpful to seek outside support from other members of the family, particularly stable and aware adult children.

Stable recovery and happiness, with mutual respect by each partner for the other, are not compatible with fear. Thus, if one spouse is in constant fear of the other partner's recovery and sobriety, something must be done to achieve common

Alcoholism: Treatable Illness

goals of sobriety for and with both alcoholics. Circumstances will dictate whether programs are initially instigated separately or together. Eventually, however, every effort must be directed to achieving joint participation and involvement in a common approach to the illness alcoholism. Then it will be found that mutual understanding, love and happiness are indeed compatible.

Young adults and even younger children should be involved in the recovery program evolved. While most children are usually anxious and willing to cooperate, some have also learned the game of manipulating parents one against the other for personal protection and gain. There are, therefore, two essential objectives to be sought. One is a common denominator of understanding about the illness to be learned and applied; the other consists of common and unselfish but rewarding goals of achievement for all.

In the case of a relapse by one parent, it is not uncommon to be met with, "Not again, what's the use?" Associates and friends repeat the attitude. Despite this, an attempt must be made to find an approach that will work with one partner and to motivate that alcoholic with a desire, through personal recovery, to assist the other.

Each partner must also respect the prerogatives of recovery and sobriety of the other. In other words, "No kibitzing, and play your own hand!"

The Alcoholic Personality

A knowledge and understanding of the phases of alcoholism, together with the confirmation of alcoholism as an illness, does not permit any conclusion that there is an identifiable alcoholic personality, though recent research suggests that there may be a genetic identifier in some individuals. This precludes a possibility of determining that a particular kind of drinking will in itself result in alcoholism.

Alcoholics superimpose secondary behavioral problems over a wide variety of personality types and, as drinkers, may have several traits in common (perhaps including low levels of coping energy in dealing with tension).

While excessive drinkers may demonstrate many of the symptoms described, as non-dependent drinkers they still retain control. At no time does alcohol become a drug on which they are completely dependent as are alcoholics. They rarely have blackouts, have no need for rationalizations (though they may use them), and do not necessarily ever change patterns. If desired, or if the acknowledgment of family, medical, social or other pressures important to them demand it, abstinence is still within their control. The alcoholic's dependence forfeits any ability to acknowledge similar demands. While the non-dependent excessive drinker may lose face because of his excesses, the alcoholic cannot help losing everything once beyond a given point in his or her kind of drinking. It must be apparent, therefore, that there are other factors involved. Under the circumstances, how can a special personality be identified from such a morass of drinkers — social, problem, moderate, excessive and alcoholic?

It might be said that a drinker, after incurring alcoholism, does develop a distinct personality pattern as he evolves his own social position and world, and so prevents his own return. He doesn't feel guilt over the kinds of problems he makes and leaves, because his drinking dulls any feelings about them. By sanctioning himself, developing his own extravagant ideas and making his own laws, he becomes isolated. No one can stop or stimulate him to change, correct or modify his actions. This is the oblivion the state of alcoholism creates.

The bender state is a complete breakdown from social reality, wherein the alcoholic renounces every custom or use of social interaction, every traditional or cultural value, every shred of self-respect, and every law of God and society through the domination of his own needs. Having lost all options, opinions, ideas and ideals, he gets angered because his system, differing entirely from the systems of others, isn't acknowledged. His fears, being his own, cannot be shared. He may fear for his own sanity or be deemed insane. Nevertheless, his only hope for recovery rests with the society he rejects and which rejects him.

Notes

1. *Quarterly Journal of Studies on Alcohol* (Volume 7, Issue No. 1, June 1946, and Volume 13, Issue No. 4, December 1952) — with permission. "Disease Concept of Alcoholism" — Jellinek, Dr. E.M. — Hillhouse Press. "The Syndrome of Alcohol Addiction" — Tiebout, Harry M., M.D. (Q.J.S.A. Volume 5, No. 4, March 1945) — with permission.

2. Jellinek, E.M. — Phases of Alcoholism as presented at the Yale Summer School on Alcohol Studies, 1950, (now the Rutgers Center on Alcohol Studies) and from the *Quarterly Journal on Alcohol Studies*, Volume 13, No. 4, December 1952 — with permission.

3. The reader notice that there are times when, in speaking of 'the alcoholic', I refer to 'he,' and times when I refer to 'she'; there are times when I say 'he or she.' In all cases save those where I am referring to specific case histories or examples, I mean my use of one pronoun to include the other, and vice versa. Alcoholism does not respect gender, and I have tried to strike a medium between grammatical convenience and overtly non-sexist language.

4. NOTE: Please note that in the use of an example case moving through the phases of alcoholism, the individual or person is at all times meant to represent women *or* men. For ease in reading and in interpretation, the masculine pronouns may be used for individual and/or personal emphasis. Thus the reader may more readily identify with the examples portrayed. Remember that today there are probably at least as many female as male alcoholics.

Part III

Treating the Illness

14. *Understanding the Alcoholic*

An eminent university professor, a recovered alcoholic, in making public addresses on alcoholism began by saying, "I am an alcoholic — do you know what is the matter with you?" He went on to add that he had done something for himself and always asked, "What have you done about yourself?"

We tend to forget that most people have problems, which though less evident are just as serious as alcoholism. The shadow of past prejudices and ignorance have downgraded the alcoholic to the extent that he or she is not always thought of as normal. There are patterns of compulsive behaviour that are socially acceptable; alcoholism is not. Let me illustrate this point with a story.

Following its annual golf tournament, a country club held an awards party. The chairman presiding made much of the winner's dedication to his game. He jokingly noted the doctor had earned his award by stealing every spare moment from family and duties to become more skilled — a typical golf addict! The doctor had even delayed a patient's labour to finish a round!

Standing nearby, an unpleasantly plump lady helped herself generously from each tray of food that came her way, while a man helped himself as regularly from each tray of drinks offered. The lady finally turned to him and said, "You know, sir, you are getting drunk." A little later she added, "Sir, you are drunk!" Finally she lashed out, "You are disgustingly drunk."

The man took each remark with a whimsical smirk, but the biting contempt of her last thrust got to him. He replied in kind, saying, "You know, ma'am, you're fat!" A pause, then: "You are disgustingly fat!" After a few seconds hesitation, looking her in the eye he added his last barb: "In the morning I will be sober, but you will still be fat!"

In the compulsive behaviour indicated, the excessive golf and eating are socially acceptable; excessive drinking is criticized. Though heavy drinking is acceptable in some settings, the alcoholic's rejection goes further; he is ostracized even by other drinkers.

As it is essential in treating alcoholics to understand better the forces which drive them, let us now relate the illness to the individual.

Alcoholism: Treatable Illness

The World Health Organization extends its interpretation of alcoholism by defining alcoholics as: "Those excessive drinkers whose dependence upon alcohol has attained such a degree that it shows noticeable mental disturbance or an interference with their bodily and mental health, their interpersonal relations, and their smooth social and economic functioning; or who show the prodromal signs of such developments. They therefore require treatment."

I would re-emphasize: when a drinker no longer uses beverage alcohol according to intent and no longer feels comfortable about, but must defend or conceal his or her drinking, then he or she gives every indication of having a serous problem with alcohol.

Alcoholism is analogous to a three-legged stool. The legs represent the physical, emotional and social components of the illness. The physical aspects are self-evident: the inability to eat, the shakes, sweats, gags, butterflies, the hangover state, and all of the other physical symptoms reviewed. The veneer of alcoholism may hide both the complications brought about by malnutrition and poor physical care, and other existing ailments.

The alcoholic progressively indicates the many serious emotional or behavioural symptoms outlined in the phases. Whether these psychological components are primary or secondary to the alcoholism cannot be determined until the physical dependency on alcohol is eliminated. *Alcoholic behavioural symptoms do not invariably reflect serious but underlying emotional disorders.*

The social or third leg, a paramount factor in itself, affects and is affected by the other two components. Many alcoholics and those about them find the social implications inherent to alcoholism more difficult to surmount than the physical or emotional factors, notwithstanding the increasing rate of change which is resulting from new educational and prevention programs.

When alcoholics recognize that their kind of drinking is different, primarily because of social implications, they feel intense shame and defensively "go underground." Though willing to acknowledge having a drinking problem, they cannot envisage themselves as alcoholics. The image of the stereotyped derelict hangs over their heads like the sword of Damocles. It forces them onto the defensive, to protect innate dignity and remaining status with family and associates. They use other acceptable ills to cover up their hangovers. I have known fathers to disown sons and daughters, doctors to refuse to care for their wives and employers to terminate key associates, rather than allow alcoholism to infringe on their lives. Similarly, social attitudes and their implications prevent spouses and families from seeking guidance for their alcoholic member.

It follows that such adverse forces have a combined social and psychological effect on the alcoholic, causing more drinking and greater physical suffering. Each "leg" compounds the suffering arising from the others, culminating in a vicious circle of cause and effect.

A major but intangible element in the alcoholic's torment is the impact of this cycle of events on the spiritual substance of every inner person. *This is quite distinct from acquired religious influences.* While this spiritual aspect may arise from religious teaching, it may also arise as a matter of cultural influence, upbringing and tradition, and does not necessarily involve even a belief in a supreme deity. It is that inner moral quality in each of us that causes us to aspire idealistically for the best in our own lives and for those about us, and that permits us to have faith in self and belief in others. Seeing life's aims ebb away, the alcoholic starts down the path of intense remorse, guilt and hopelessness. When this component collapses, the alcoholic is truly in conflict.

In a state of despair, fearful of the progressiveness of the illness, anxious and depressed, questioning his or her own sanity, the alcoholic's problems are compounded by the confusion of existing social attitudes, misconceptions and prejudices. Though urgently requiring treatment, fearful of new labels, he or she rebels against and defers help. Is it any wonder that the alcoholic, unable to forgive self, feels trapped and that his world would collapse if he were to quit or reveal his dependency on alcohol? Nor is it remarkable under these circumstances that he or she is unwilling to show hurt on being injured by the barbs of others; and so the individual is contrary, possessive and jealous, lashing out insanely at those who are closest. Don't those who criticize the drinker know how desperately he or she feels or has tried?

The alcoholic's only recourse is to attempt to drink just enough to get over the shakes, feel physically comfortable, think things through, and determine how to get even with those "enemies." However, after a few drinks restore a comfortable edge, he or she cannot remain there and all the plans and dreams go awry again.

The alcoholic's problems are further intensified by the very attributes with which he is endowed. Rarely phlegmatic, he is an extremist and perfectionist, a driver who makes intense demands upon himself and others and wants everything now, not tomorrow. My own experience suggests that most, if not all, alcoholics are idealists. They display a deep sensitivity and, because of this idealism and sensitivity, they are at war with themselves and at odds with the world. Because they sense keenly a disparity between the way events turn out for them and the way they wish events to turn out, they are supersensitive to the antipathy, rejection and jibes of those about them. They readily distinguish between sincerity and hypocrisy, but for them the real is exaggerated by the imagined. Seeing two heads together, they become paranoid — "those people are talking about me." If conversation stops when they join a group, again they become paranoid. They bolster their alibi system

Alcoholism: Treatable Illness

with fancied slights and grudges. Living in the fantasy of their alcohol-centered world, they become completely out of touch with reality.

To defend his drinking the alcoholic may successfully manipulate and fool those about him. He will seek a doctor agreeable to blaming his problems on an ulcer or on his wife's nagging, lack of understanding and companionship. He is in seventh heaven when he finds one who agrees that his drinking is not the problem. He will appear at work earlier than others and leave later. He will rush around, papers in hand, and look very busy, though he accomplishes nothing. He straightens up to meet an emergency — and then falls to pieces later. These and many more machinations become second nature to the alcoholic as the illness progresses.

To suggest that alcoholics lack courage or willpower is absurd. They have been known to perform heroic deeds, alertly measure up to tremendous demands, and then not remember anything about what happened. They can walk straight lines and perform other tests of sobriety after accidents. In emergencies, they often function more capably than others about them, but later fall apart. There comes to mind an alcoholic who returned home on the death of his father. He managed the funeral arrangements, settled all necessary family affairs and was commended by everyone for his composure and stability, though he drank incessantly throughout the two weeks at home. On returning to his own city he let go, and was admitted to hospital because of the severity of his condition.

In another instance, a man left a party, apparently intoxicated, and drove his car. When an accident ahead forced him to stop, he immediately gave first aid to two children. He got traffic moving, drove one youngster to a hospital forty miles away and assisted the doctor in clamping her scalp! Then he took a few more drinks and went on home. When reporters looked him up the next day, he didn't remember what he had done.

Such actions make the alcoholic even more difficult to understand. The cry is raised, "Why can't you be this controlled all the time?" Even these protective devices deteriorate as the alcoholic reaches the later stages of his or her illness.

It would be simple indeed if the spouse of an alcoholic could beg, "George (that's my name, so no inference intended!), you are an alcoholic, therefore you must stop drinking!" But George does not, much as he would like to please her. Nor is it possible for any parent or other relative to plead, "George, if you love and respect your family and your children, surely you can stop for them?" Again George does not, though he writhes in anguish over their hurt. George cannot stop, even if a friend or business associate — after ignoring the issue as long as possible — warns and demands, "George, you are throwing away everything you wanted to accomplish! Why won't you stop?"

If controls were attained that easily, a sea of tears would not have been shed in vain. If alcoholism could be cured, arrested or even curbed that easily, this illness would not remain the enigma and problem that it is today. Nor would this book and others, or the many efforts now under way, still be searching for desperately needed answers.

"George, why don't you stop?" George might well answer, "Stop and die? If I stop, what do I do to live?" Or if George could voice what he really feels, he might say, "God knows I am not happy with my kind of drinking. I hate both the stuff and myself. If I knew how to stop with dignity, without fear of embarrassment, without dying a thousand deaths when the shakes and the fears start again, then maybe. Stop? I want to stop! But not because I am considered a moral leper, a spineless sot, or a hopeless drunken bum, whom you pity. My God, don't you see — I am the George you married and loved; who fathered your children, made you the belle of the gang, the George you proudly cherished and showed off. That's how I want to stop. As a man, a meaningful somebody. Now tell me, with what you, everybody else, and even I feel — can I stop as that kind of man?"

False pride, you reply. I disagree. This is human dignity. It remains with us to the last, regardless of how we fare. To approach and help the alcoholic, we must respect and understand that dignity; we must "feel" empathy — a genuine liking with true sincerity of purpose. To help the alcoholic to help himself, we must truly understand that he or she is another human being, but just now a very sick one.

Alcoholism might be considered a cancer of the soul. The initial trauma of recognizing and accepting the illness as *something that is happening to me* is completely shattering to one's ego and dignity. The emotional hopelessness, despair and remorse are demoralizing beyond belief; the physical deterioration and pain are demeaning; the social regression and rejection by associates and family is akin to being labelled a leper, and the spiritual recrimination, guilt and self-condemnation drives many an alcoholic to consider or take suicide as the only way out.

The alcoholic does want to stop. But driven by dependency, pursued by nameless fears, haunted by guilt and remorse, hurt by adverse attitudes, he or she is cornered by the complexities of a chaotic existence in society. Voluntarily or involuntarily, alcoholics must be helped to seek a way out. If too ill to ask for help of their own volition, then you and I — the well ones of society — must provide the recognition and response required. That is our responsibility to sufferers of any illness.

15. Motivation

Alcoholics who voluntarily seek help demonstrate their motivation to achieve recovery. After all, the majority still retain meaningful personal "assets": spouse, family, economic and social position. Though it may be unwise to deny some patients the experience of a personal sense of desperation to propel them to ask for help, in most instances it is wiser to use honey rather than vinegar. All too often the alcoholic has known little else than gall. A spark of hope and desire can usually be fanned into the warmth of life by one who understands.

When confronted by an alcoholic who, of his or her own accord, seeks help and asks what he or she can do, I promptly reply, "You have just done seventy-five percent of the job yourself. You are speaking about it, requesting aid and demonstrating your desire and need for help. The rest is now a matter of learning about your problem and yourself. You need never suffer it alone again!"

Those outside the alcoholic's world should learn to appreciate the immense relief it is to the alcoholic to be able finally to talk to someone in a positive manner, someone who is not blind to his need and who does understand. This enables the alcoholic to hang on. That initial spark of hope, when properly fanned, may be ignited into sincere motivation. Shared and nurtured, it enables the alcoholic to begin to be relieved of self-blame and to learn forgiveness of self, a major factor in the recovery process.

A female alcoholic, defeated and alone, travelled home to the scene of happier days. She walked countless miles over the once familiar farmlands of her childhood. Lost and alone, she could only wonder why. She had spent months in a private sanatorium seeking answers. Her doctor had pleaded with her to want something, a new hat, anything. Because her future offered only a repetition of a drinking past, it was too bleak to permit her to want that something. Her simplest plans would go awry the moment the compulsion to drink overcame her again. After her sojourn there, which left her drained emotionally, she walked into an A.A. meeting and by good fortune met a person who said the right things at the right time in the right way.

She remembered little of what he said, but his empathy and understanding rekindled her vital spark of hope. Little by little that spark grew to faith and action.

For the first time, she learned she was neither alone nor hopeless. Above all else, she recognized she had been an ill person, and though she might need to travel a long and difficult road, she could be completely well again. Recovery with dignity, without self-abasement, could be hers.

That was almost half a century ago. One would never associate the woman she subsequently became with the forlorn and desperate person walking that farm. There are those who, seeing her poise, dignity and composure, cannot believe she was ever an alcoholic! Conversely, when she approached A.A., in those early days some said, "Look at her — look at her clothes and her walk! She'll never make it; she has no humility. She hasn't been hurt enough yet." How incongruous and contradictory are the ideas some people have about "being ready," and how little all too many non-alcoholics and recovered alcoholics alike really know about motivation. It is not always apparent when or how an alcoholic is truly motivated and ready for recovery.

As a result of growing awareness, more and more drinkers, suspecting a problem, are taking a look at themselves and changing, limiting and even quitting their drinking entirely. What is more, they may even take this self-inventory quite openly. Most of us recognize that it is becoming far less fashionable to disparage the alcoholic, recovered or not — he or she could be the boss, the doctor, the attorney, the clergyman, or the host!

When recovered, alcoholics like to feel that they made the first decision of their own accord. However, in almost every case, some outside influence by coercion or prodding helped to bring the patient to a point of decision. Well-planned approaches will help bring reticent people to a recovery program. Families, industry and the professions are learning to take suggestive, but positive and firm measures with excellent success. Often it is the first logical, impersonal and objective approach the potential patient has had and usually the patient is relieved to have it over with.

It should be re-emphasized that as alcoholism progresses, many patients are too ill to make a decision to seek or ask for help of their own volition. Many alcoholics are alive and sober today, simply because someone had the fortitude and intelligence to step in and force the necessary care on these patients by compelling them to recognize their problem and by helping them find a permanent way out. Enforced care does not always demand arrest and incarceration, as was thought in earlier times. Would it not be ridiculous to see someone have a heart attack and to await their recovery to ask if the person wanted help? No, we get all the emergency help we can for that person, and for sufferers of all other illnesses, without asking questions. In alcoholism, too, good judgment and action must prevail, without prejudice and ignorance.

Alcoholism: Treatable Illness

The desire or motivation to accept guidance can be self-imbued, or it can be influenced, coerced and instilled by those close to the alcoholic. Improving attitudes and resources, together with an increasing knowledge about alcoholism resulting from the educational and treatment activities of alcoholism resources and the splendid work of Alcoholics Anonymous, are attracting earlier, less damaged referrals for treatment. The publications of these services, reflecting such improved attitudes and knowledge, are now being pointed toward the needs of the majority of the alcoholic population — the hidden alcoholics. No longer geared only to the stereotyped image of the past, publications play an important part in creating motivation. Experience proves that many patients are better read on the illness alcoholism than some of their counsellors. A growing number of alcoholic patients are also being motivated to seek help for themselves through the effective example of recovered alcoholics from treatment centers and Alcoholics Anonymous.

Nevertheless, early and voluntary referrals remain very much in the minority. Far too many alcoholics are still literally condemned to a continuation of their illness. Because of misconceptions that linger on, both the alcoholics and those about them defer any positive action, waiting for something to happen in the hope that the illness will rectify itself. Most of us have incorrectly learned to believe that alcoholics must personally want and personally ask for help. Tragically, this will remain so until public recognition and response and the image of the alcoholic are completely changed. Despite modern inclinations to "come out of the closet" on a variety of issues, this causes ninety percent or more of the alcoholic population who are of average and higher status, professionally, vocationally, economically, socially and educationally, to remain hidden. They find it difficult to overcome embarrassment and use every protective and sheltering device possible to delay seeking treatment. Remember, however, that all alcoholics, men and women alike, regardless of who or what they are, do "get sick and tired of being sick and tired over alcohol." With help, their status can be used as a motivating factor for recovery.

To accuse people who are ill of lacking motivation, of "not being ready yet," of needing to "hit bottom," or having to "want or personally ask for help" is more often than not a projection of our own lack of understanding, prejudice, inadequacy and failure in dealing with the situation — not the sick alcoholic's. The same element of responsibility applies to the manner in which we assist or contact those close to the alcoholic (spouse, family, doctor, clergyman, employer and others) to reach the patient who is of real concern to them.

Crisis

Many alcoholics are brought to treatment as the result of some turning point or crisis in their lives. This crisis may be a single event or shock, or a combination of several adverse experiences; or it may be that the alcoholic is finally fed up with what he or she has become.

The first meaningful approach on a broad scale to those suffering from alcoholism was achieved by the Fellowship of Alcoholics Anonymous. The early members pulled themselves out of a bottomless pit of despair, tragedy and loss. Hitting bottom became the first criterion to motivate recovery. From that grew such expressions as "being ready," "wanting help," "being hurt enough," and the like. Because, too, most early members were literally bankrupt in every department of life, the impression grew that an alcoholic must lose everything before seeking help. There are those who still insist that this is the one most important experience that will change the alcoholic's thinking — all alcoholics must "rise from the gutter." This is absolute hogwash, and elimination of this notion is a critical part of the unlearning we must go through if we are to do away with the absurd myths surrounding the illness alcoholism and its treatment.

Today we know that it is not necessary for every alcoholic to lose everything. There are high and low bottoms. There are several points in the progression of the alcoholic's illness, each of which is a major crisis in itself — blackout, loss of control, threatened loss of family or job. With guidance and direction, those close to the alcoholic can use these traumatic situations and through a precipitated crisis achieve a positive response in the patient. Through cooperation, awareness, knowledge and understanding, when such a crisis arrives the alcoholic can be brought to discuss treatment and can learn that just as the diabetic shows good judgment to seek and accept the help needed, the alcoholic may be assisted toward the same insight.

We must appreciate, therefore, that attitudes, misconceptions and confusions hamper a positive approach to instituting motivation in both the alcoholics and those close to them. The alcoholic is a sounding board for all our confusions and ignorance.

Often one must spend many hours interpreting the position of spouses to overcome the false impressions they have learned. Through ignorance, the collaterals of alcoholics make endless mistakes and hence continue to deal inadequately with their problem drinking situations.

I remember the case of a wife who required two years of counselling from several workers to help her appreciate the role she must learn and play in bringing her alcoholic husband to treatment. This was finally achieved. He accompanied her to the clinic. At the end of his initial interview, he stood up and said to her, "Why the devil didn't you tell me what you had learned and bring me in here two years ago?" Following counselling, both were referred to Alcoholics Anonymous and Al-Anon and have remained active in those programs ever since. This was thirty-six years ago! It is interesting to note the wife has done much public speaking since and,

Alcoholism: Treatable Illness

to my knowledge, never refers to the two years required for her own education. While much more should and could be said about motivating the alcoholic to seek help and about the education of spouse and other collaterals of the patient, this may better be done indirectly by allowing the sense of motivation to be implied in the ensuing chapters, as we deal directly with the treatment of the patient and the role of the spouse and those others concerned.

The following experience interprets some of the elements of motivation. After an address on alcoholism to high school students, I was introduced to the president of the graduating class. He was a fine looking, strapping young fellow, an honour student and a three-letter athlete. He asked if he might come to see me one day, so we arranged an appointment.

In telling the story of his family life, he revealed that his father and mother were alcoholics. He hardly remembered seeing them in any but adverse conditions. A younger brother and sister were being seriously affected by the home conditions. He remembered hearing someone say he should rise above his environment and set his own goals regardless of those about him, so he did.

He determined to be the most successful student and athlete in his school. He was. He already had an athletic scholarship to a major university. He had also set two goals for himself: the first was to do everything possible to get out of that home as quickly as he could. He had supported himself for years by doing odd jobs. His second pledge was that on graduating and leaving home, he would beat up his father and spit in his mother's face and get the rest of the kids out of there. This was his motivation.

My talk had been the first he had ever heard concerning alcoholism as a treatable illness. A bright and sound young man of good basic principles, the talk had disturbed him; hence his desire to see me. Learning his parents' actions and condition were perhaps due to illness, he questioned his feelings and wondered if it were too late to do something. We had several sessions together planning what might be done. Through the cooperation, help and understanding of a very able family service worker and a wonderful chaplain from a veterans' home who had himself been through the mill, we resolved the case. The mother's sobriety was initially achieved through hospitalization and commitment; the father's a few months later was achieved with the added support of his employer. In each instance, orientation was required for all involved.

Their sobriety and recovery were continuous and gratifying. The children became excellent young adults. In the course of time the oldest son, who became an All-American football name, graduated from medical school. On graduation day, the chancellor who presented the degrees (pre-arranged and at the son's request) gave the young man's degree to the father, who in turn presented it to his son. That boy today is an eminent physician and friend of many alcoholics. This is motivation.

16. *Progressive Stages of Recovery*

Once alcoholics are motivated to seek recovery, their spouses and families — and, most importantly, those responsible for their counselling — must be aware of the changes to anticipate during the recovery process. The patient relinquishing a dependency on alcohol manifests a definite set of symptoms, physical, emotional, social and spiritual, as significant as those that took place during the development of the illness. The interpretation of these changes follows the order presented on the chart "Progressive Stages of Recovery."

Not all patients will necessarily follow the order in which these changes are described. Some patients attempt to by-pass elements vital to total recovery. A.A. members call this "two stepping" — admitting one is an alcoholic and then jumping right in to save everybody else, without resolving other disorders which *must* be addressed if one is to achieve total and meaningful sobriety.

Some alcoholics will immediately accept and, through positive therapy, cope with all their personal problems. Those less damaged by alcohol require less time and effort to achieve total recovery. Hence the advantage of seeking help early.

The chart denotes four stages in the recovery process: *Admission, Inventory, Recovery* and *A New Way of Life*. Significant changes are denoted by heavier and longer bars. The lighter and shorter bars indicate the gains made during each phase of the recovery process. The individual manifestations described are numbered to follow the outline of the chart.

The Admission Phase (I)

We pick up the path of the alcoholic where it leaves off at the end of the progression of the illness through the phases of alcoholism. As before, *it is essential for the reader to remember that when we use the masculine pronoun we do not imply exclusion of the feminine, and vice-versa. The illness alcoholism ignores gender.*

You will recall that the alcoholic reaches a crisis in his or her drinking by which he or she is motivated to seek recovery. In the Crucial Phase (III) of alcoholism, this crisis is usually the complete collapse of the drinker's rationalizations, or the failure

PROGRESSIVE STAGES OF RECOVERY

The History or Concurrent Changes In the Alcoholic During the Attainment of Sobriety

NOTE During the Progress of Recovery all Alcoholics will not necessarily experience those changes in the order outlined. Some may · by possi' resolving problem factors vital to complete and contented Sobriety. Others 'willingly accept' and resolve all areas of concern without reservation. Those less damaged by alcohol may require less time or effort to achieve recovery.

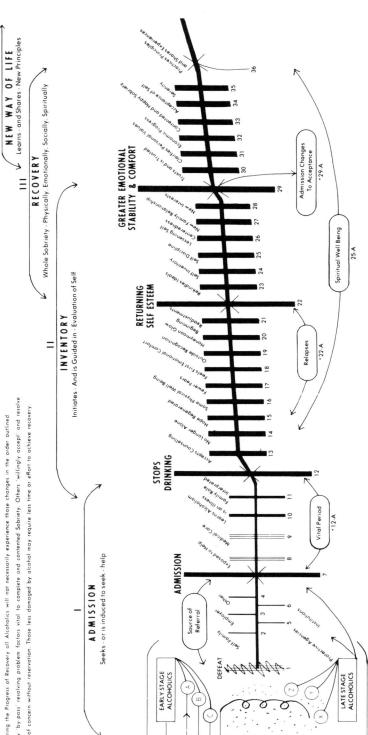

Copyright by J. George Strachan

of his or her drinking system to provide the benefits which brought about the onset of alcoholism in the first place.[1] When this crisis brings about acknowledgment of DEFEAT (1), also referred to as being ready, hitting bottom, and having had enough, the recovery process can be instituted.

Recognize, however, that the alcoholic may be too sick, reticent or scared to seek help on his or her own. Some alcoholics are SELF-REFERRED (2). Others are induced to seek help through their SPOUSE or other members of the FAMILY (who may need guidance to achieve the referral, which will be discussed later). The patient may be referred by his EMPLOYER (3) or by OTHERS (4) — clergy, friends, physicians, other recovered alcoholics, treatment centers and agencies. Referrals from these sources (1,2,3,4) include mainly early- and middle-stage alcoholics (A,B,C):

A. those in the early phase, who, because of greater insight, or concern with a first blackout, loss of control or remorse, determine to seek help; or

B. those in the late stages of the crucial phase, who have been hospitalized, who have repeatedly tried to quit alone and have already known serious setbacks, threatened loss of family, job and the like; or

C. those who, at some early point in their problem drinking, experience a spiritual or religious concern and so are imbued with a desire to live better.

As noted during the phases, this may occur soon after the loss of control is indicated. Early stage alcoholics may, of their own accord, make a personal admission, stop drinking, by-pass early symptoms and move directly into counselling or go to A.A. A higher percentage of early referrals attain recovery as they still retain more personal assets, are less damaged and are better motivated.

Those alcoholics who progress into the chronic phase may reach their crisis and be referred for help through a PROTECTIVE AGENCY (5) (police, probation officer, judge or magistrate, family court); others may be referred during custodial care in INSTITUTIONS (6) (mental hospitals, sanatoria, jails). Most late stage alcoholics (X,Y,Z) will institute recovery through these sources of referral, as they very often require enforced care.

X may have reached the bender stage, finding herself on the fringe of everything. Y is bankrupt in all departments of his life, separated or divorced, jobless, close to the end. Z is an outcast, perhaps on skid row.

Earlier we spoke of acknowledgment of defeat. This is not necessarily ADMISSION (7). Though the alcoholic may admit to himself the failure of his controls, he may be unable or unwilling to do anything about it. The crisis, whatever it may be, will help in initiating action with the admission of his alcoholism, to self-propel or to be guided to EXPOSURE TO HELP (8). This exposure to Alcoholics Anonymous, or to any of the sources previously mentioned, should bring him to MEDICAL CARE (9), which can be from a private physician, alcoholism clinic, a

Alcoholism: Treatable Illness

hospital, a private treatment center, or simply first-aid remedies by others like himself. This is a critical point in the alcoholic's possible recovery. If approached with knowledge and empathy, he learns to appreciate that ALCOHOLISM IS AN ILLNESS (10). It is vital to include the spouse or close family members, and sometimes other associates — for example, an employer — in understanding the concept of alcoholism as an illness. Greater progress and eventual success is achieved when the alcoholic and spouse are approached together. It is essential to thoroughly INTERPRET THE ROLE OF THE SPOUSE AND FAMILY (11).

During these stages of initial approach and care, hopefully the alcoholic has been induced to STOP DRINKING (12). Many early stage referrals will have stopped. There are those who, retaining greater pride and self-esteem, won't make the first contact until they are sober. Later stage alcoholics have perhaps, through enforced custody, been abstinent. Some alcoholics, unable to stop drinking alone, may require enforced care; a few may continue to nibble and naturally there will be those who will have regular drinking bouts while making a show at quitting. It is not unusual for a patient to bolster himself with one or two, simply to have the courage to talk about it. All should be directed to attempt at least an experimental period of abstinence.

These initial contacts represent a VITAL PERIOD (12A) in moving the alcoholic to seek and accept recovery treatment. I cannot stress this point enough. In my opinion, the opportunity of talking to the patient face-to-face is ninety percent of the recovery process.

Inventory (II)

Once the alcoholic stops drinking, it is possible for him to initiate (or be guided in) an evaluation of what drinking means to him as an alcoholic. If induced to understand that as person suffering from the illness alcoholism he should not drink, he can then be helped to appreciate the need to ACCEPT COUNSELLING (13). Critical to this approach is the need to make it very clear to the alcoholic that one cannot recover alone, and that help may be needed from many others along the way. It is always a relief to the practising alcoholic to learn that he is NO LONGER ALONE (14).

There is no therapy that can replace the day by day growth and stimulation that a continuing relationship with other sound, stable, recovered alcoholics may provide. This is not to minimize the value of meaningful professional care, not at all; it is a supplemental form of care that complements any other service provided. Aware and knowledgeable alcoholism clinics recognize and use this tool. These alcoholics are encouraged to meet others like themselves from the same walks of life and vocations, with the same demands and problems. More than any other influence, during the early stages, this helps to relieve remorse and guilt, and *enables the alcoholic to begin to forgive self.*

When the alcoholic, spouse and other family members meet those who have successfully faced the same conflicts, they receive stimulation and support, and HOPE IS REGENERATED (15). With new-found hope, a combined physical and emotional change occurs. There is greater PHYSICAL WELL-BEING (16) which must be protected through unlearning former adverse traits and relearning better personal habits, such as proper rest and diet, regular medical checkups and all the measures taken during convalescence from any illness. This results in FEWER FEARS (17). While one may still dream of drinking, the alcoholic will not shake from imagined problems, will begin to avoid the need to escape, and thus, will begin to achieve FIRST FEELINGS OF EMOTIONAL COMFORT (18). He will know less frustration, see or feel a potential hope for recovery and begin to do some realistic thinking about himself and where he is going. Emotionally, too, he is happier if his spouse and family are incorporated in his program, as this also ensures greater comfort. Much of the new physical and emotional comfort has its basis in a beginning sense of spiritual ease with self.

Recognizing alcoholism as an illness has alleviated feelings of "sin" and failure. This progress shines through, and the alcoholic will begin to enjoy OUTSIDE RECOGNITION (19) from family, work associates, friends and others. If in close contact with doctor, clergyman and superior, the alcoholic will confirm the evidence of progress.

Regardless of the source of help (Alcoholics Anonymous, an alcoholism clinic or other), it is nearly impossible to prevent the alcoholic from experiencing a HONEYMOON GLOW (20) as the result of improved feelings and the increased recognition received. He or she is back in society. This can be useful if properly channelled as it will enable the patient to make BEGINNING READJUSTMENTS (21), make amends to those harmed, renew relationships with relatives and friends, and continue the process of "growing up" which the drinking interrupted.

These many changes are most apparent and recognized by the alcoholic in RETURNING SELF-ESTEEM (22), which through sobriety he or she once again enjoys. However, this is also a dangerous period: with everything righting itself again, the newly-sober alcoholic can become over-confident, and may decide to stretch the honeymoon glow into false security, and may then decide that, as he or she once believed, "If everything else in my life is alright, I should be able to drink like others."

He may harbour this reservation for some time; then, inadvertently or deliberately as the result of some petty incident, he may try his luck again to test himself and suffer a RELAPSE (22A). A return to drinking can create serious disturbances in the recovery process. A relapse often occurs because the alcoholic, and those near and dear, are ill prepared for the euphoria resulting from sobriety. Though this may sound like heresy, for some a relapse serves as the convincer, the final payment on the initiation fee to achieve acceptance of total recovery and sobriety. Every alcoholic has one last "drunk" to get it out of his or her system. However, this is an awful risk for one to take. Once again sober, he or she must be reassured and strengthened and made to recognize that nothing can take away the progress achieved through the initial period of sobriety. The experience, therefore, can serve to good purpose with proper guidance and support. Relapses may be prevented by helping the alcoholic to keep uppermost in mind the knowledge that one cannot achieve recovery alone, and that one should use every available source of help.

The recovering alcoholic, following a rebirth of self-respect, begins to REKINDLE IDEALS (23). As this occurs, one places more importance on an honest SELF-INVENTORY(24) and tries to master the ropes of SELF-DISCIPLINE (25). These qualities, together, enable the alcoholic to change from an uncontrolled person of undisciplined behaviour to one who does control himself. Through self-discipline one achieves tolerance, avoids anger, self-pity and resentments, and learns that these are luxuries an alcoholic can ill afford.

The alcoholic who regenerates these qualities feels at peace with self. There is quality to one's sobriety. The quantity or period of time involved is not as important as the depth of that sobriety. No longer fighting with self, the recovering alcoholic definitely knows a sense of SPIRITUAL WELL-BEING (25A). This must not be confused with formal religious observance. This is a very personal feeling which even self-acknowledged agnostics and atheists sense, but in another medium.

The rebirth of such qualities and the changes they denote are evidenced to others in an apparent LESSENING OF SELF-CENTEREDNESS (26) the alcoholic has always indicated before. The sober alcoholic establishes NEW FAMILY RELATIONSHIPS (27), and is recognized and again enjoyed as a person by the family — who sometimes cannot believe what is happening! He or she evidences many NEW INTERESTS (28); broadens his friendships; indicates much more interest in work; may start a few hobbies; works around the house; returns to formal religious observance. These changes evidence a GREATER EMOTIONAL STABILITY AND COMFORT (29).

Recovery (III)

This new stability marks another significant change: it reflects the recovery of the whole person — physically, emotionally, socially and spiritually. This is SOBRIETY, not mere abstinence from alcohol. Unobserved, ADMISSION CHANGES TO ACCEPTANCE (29A); the alcoholic, relieved of reservations, takes the chip off his or her shoulder and quits fighting with self. Alcoholics

Anonymous interprets this vital change in another way. They suggest that for a time the alcoholic chases after A.A.; then suddenly, without the individual's knowing when or how, A.A. reaches out and overtakes the alcoholic. After this, even if one could drink normally again, one wouldn't — *as drinking is no longer important.*[2]

With this improved outlook, the recovering alcoholic learns to TRUST AND IS IN TURN TRUSTED (30); CLARIFIES PERSONAL VALUES (31); determines what he or she wants out of life, and begins to enjoy ECONOMIC PROGRESS (32). As personal drives become more realistic and are satisfied, and as interpersonal relationships improve, the alcoholic demonstrates an enthusiasm for sobriety. Thus he begins to enjoy CONTENTED AND HAPPY SOBRIETY (33), something once considered to be impossible. To be sober and happy — or happily sober — was unimaginable. Now the sober alcoholic is both!

New Way of Life (IV)

During these stages of progressive recovery, a major phenomenon takes place. The alcoholic gradually experiences and evidences a complete change in personality. This change for the better is the key to an entirely *new way of life*. It is without a number, as it represents the spectrum of all the recovery symptoms and the goal of sobriety.

As this phenomenon of recovery probably began with the return to self-esteem, the chart denotes the several stages as overlapping one another. Just as the developing alcoholism was not apparent to the sufferer, so are the subtle recovery changes that take place. The continuing improvement is apparent to everyone else, but least of all to the alcoholic who feels, "I am what I always wanted to be, and I am doing what I always wanted to do!"

Though only sensing improvement, the alcoholic feels good, is happier, is enjoying an abiding well-being the like of which he or she never knew before. Much of this contentment is due to AN ACCEPTANCE OF SELF (34). Learning to accept oneself as "I am, I must also realize that I will be an alcoholic as long as I live." However, through recovery, one regains judgment and reason and the power of choice: the option is to die a practising wet alcoholic, or to retain the precious gift of sobriety, to live a meaningful and happy life as a whole person and so to achieve finally and know SOBRIETY (35).

Serenity reflects true faith in self, a sense of peace with one's God and world, and the feeling of achievement which comes with mastery of self and whole recovery. Those alcoholics who by-pass personal disorders seemingly never enjoy more than "frantic serenity." This gift is not wrought overnight. As the alcoholic perhaps took years to reach the pit of her or his own alcoholism, so too is time required to recover.

An enlightened acceptance of self enables the patient to unlearn false ways, to

Alcoholism: Treatable Illness

relearn lost qualities and values, and to acquire new and improved principles. Consciously or not, the recovered alcoholic PRACTICES THESE PRINCIPLES and SHARES THE EXPERIENCES LEARNED (36) with others to retain the sobriety gained.

Such new attitudes are an example to others who watch this miracle of recovery and sobriety, first with skepticism and then with curiosity and wonder. Recovered and sober alcoholics learn to protect their sobriety and in gratitude to share it with others like themselves.

Though the stages overlap and the recovery process varies with individual alcoholics, one factor is common to all: the return of hope, faith in self and spiritual well-being. The recovered alcoholic is returning to life and now has newly borrowed time to live that life to the full. One belongs again to oneself and no longer to a bottle.

This is not to say that one will not be faced with life's normal tribulations. However, as the alcoholic's recovery progresses, he or she learns to live a more normal pattern. High and low points are not as pronounced, reducing from jagged peaks and bottomless crevasses to gentle swells. Initially, one's ability to cope with life's demands requires a conscious exercise in faith. Later it is an accepted prerequisite for self-discipline — so much so that most wonder how one could really have had such a problem or been such a person.

These individuals are to be trusted; after all, they have accomplished what few men or women are called upon to do. Each has been tried and tested, and then has achieved the insight, courage and intelligence to master self. Most of us are never called upon to get out of the rut of our own existence. As my late friend, the professor, put it, "I'm a recovered alcoholic. Do you know what's the matter with you, and what are you doing about it?"

Notes

1. Please note that in the use of an example case going through all the phases of alcoholism, the individual or person is at all times meant to represent women *or* men. For ease in reading and in interpretation, the masculine pronouns may be used for individual and/or personal emphasis. Thus the reader may more readily identify with the examples portrayed.

2. The development and acceptance of a growing number of qualified private and public facilities and resources is resulting in an ever-increasing percentage of patient and family member referrals to A.A. and the Al-Anon family groups for aftercare.

17. *Attitudes and Prerequisites to Counselling*

Preparatory to approaching the alcoholic and discussing the roles of the spouse, family and other collaterals, we need to repeat and re-emphasize a few pertinent factors.

From the onset of obsessive drinking, alcoholic men and women alike, acutely aware of the attitudes of those about them, consciously sense reproof, distrust and rejection. The alcoholic's intolerance of a seeming lack of appreciation of his or her problem is defensively projected as resentment to any relative, friend or collateral seeking to assist. This is magnified many times over in the case of the spouse and those dearest to the afflicted individual. Therefore, it is vitally necessary that those approaching or counselling the alcoholic understand both the progressive phases of alcoholism, and the progressive stages of recovery, if their help is to be accepted and beneficial.

As with any other illness, an initial prerequisite to achieving treatment for alcoholism demands sincere empathy. Even trained workers disqualify themselves if they have innate prejudice toward alcoholism or the alcoholic. A study was done to learn why an institutional program was not working. The program apparently included all the ingredients necessary to a successful operation. It was learned that it was the antipathy of the personnel to the patients that was at fault.

Other studies have indicated that more important than the medication, the place, the kind or the source of treatment, is the attitude, empathy and technique of those concerned with the alcoholic that make the difference. Even some recovered or abstaining alcoholics remain most unsympathetic to alcoholism and intolerant of drinking. They,too, are useless as counsellors.

It must also be taken into account that many forms of emotional disturbance will be evidenced during early stages of alcohol withdrawal. Initially, a patient may be as irritable and unreasonable as before when preparing to go on a bender. In the majority of cases, these disorders are behavioural symptoms and do not necessarily reflect serious mental impairment. As the period of abstinence progresses, such manifestations usually disappear.

Those approaching the patient should refrain from dropping ''labels'' that may be heard by the alcoholic or repeated to the spouse, members of the family or

Alcoholism: Treatable Illness

other collaterals and passed back to the patient. The most unintentional remark by a staff member of a clinic can be blown up out of all proportion and cause the patient to break contact, accusing these helpers of belittling him or her further. Care must also be taken in discussing the patient with other agencies. During early treatment, ashamed and fearful, the patient imagines everyone to be watching or talking "about me." An alcoholic who learns inadvertently that someone has deemed him psychotic, psychopathic or neurotic feels his fears were justified and that he really can't trust anyone after all. To be told by a beloved member of the family that he isn't, never was and never will be any good is not the sort of admonition which is likely to bring the alcoholic to treatment.

A psychiatrist working in the development of new inpatient and outpatient facilities for alcoholics visited Dr. Jellinek to seek his guidance in counselling the alcoholic. Dr. Jellinek summed up what the psychiatrist should know and do in these words: "Forget everything you think you know about alcoholism and alcoholics, set aside the usual tools of your profession, and when dealing with alcoholic patients try to express and convey to them the same warmth, appreciation and understanding of their ills and overall needs, as did the old-fashioned general practitioner. In his day he was counsellor, doctor and confessor, expressing in word, manner and action a fatherly concern for each of his patients."

Most alcoholics of middle age and up will not always easily relate to very young counsellors. Regardless of innate ability, academic training or presumed experience, if counsellors (clinical personnel, clergymen, doctors, agency workers) do not evidence maturity and experience, an initial block is raised that defers an acceptance of treatment. This is especially so with the alcoholic who is a success in the business or professional world, and who wonders why he can't lick this thing alone. Those related to the alcoholic, who know status in their own lives, cannot help but feel the same. Similarly, the growing numbers of younger people with alcohol problems may have difficulty relating to counsellors who are much older than they are, especially where those counsellors' spiritual strength and position prevents them from addressing young alcoholics in language and in a context to which they can relate.

This obviously does not mean that counsellors cannot be quite young or quite old. It does mean that the counsellor must be mature in attitude, flexible in approach, knowledgeable and sensitive to the patient's feelings. Without these characteristics, the counsellor will be unable to establish that credibility which needs to be created quickly in order for the counsellor to be of real assistance. With discretion and careful supervision, such counsellors may contribute in meaningful ways in education, research and group activities for alcoholics of all ages, and in counselling with collaterals.

One can appreciate how critical this is in a family counselling situation. A reputable surgeon and his wife had almost reached a parting of the ways because of his drinking. It was suggested by their lawyer that they have a discussion with the pastor of their church, who was known to be an understanding, knowledgeable and capable person, wise in dealing with the problems of his parishioners. An appointment was made with him. However, when the couple appeared in the pastor's study they were greeted by a young assistant minister to whom the matter had been entrusted. The couple had a son with a Ph.D. in psychology who was about the same age. The wife was president of the women's auxiliary in the same church. Though outwardly calm, the couple were rankled, and thus an opportunity for counselling was lost. They separated.

A prominent criminal attorney in a like situation agreed to counselling. His estranged wife had received excellent guidance from a knowledgeable and mature lay therapist. The attorney was confronted with a chic young thing in a very efficient and businesslike way. He broke off the interview and left.

A hardened loner with some fifty arrests, on leaving an institution, hopefully arranged to visit a clinic. Known as one of the best men in his trade, he had once owned and managed a good business. Contractors would pull him out of institutions to finish key jobs. When his family gave up, he hit the skids. His initial reception and intake were admirably handled and well received, but the counselor to whom he was assigned was a young psychologist, a part-time trainee, working toward a master's degree. The patient's reaction is unprintable. He broke contact.

In another clinic several students were working on a study project involving both active and closed cases. A former woman patient, sober a number of years, agreed to assist with the project. On visiting the clinic, she was greeted by a female social work student who in a thoughtless and tactless manner said, "You may sit down now," and then officiously sat down behind her desk. The student counsellor proceeded to question the patient with the intent of drawing our her presumable "lurid alcoholic past," taking it for granted that as an alcoholic, the woman must be uneducated, promiscuous and from "across the tracks." The patient, reserved, well-bred and educated, and the wife of a college dean, broke off the interview and left. While wishing to cooperate she plainly found that the student lacked manners and training. Fortunately, this patient had a solid period of meaningful sobriety.

Such experiences create many problems. In the first three instances patients were doomed to continuing their alcoholism. Only with great care and considerable work by others were they returned to effective counselling. All were reunited with their families. The "loner" is a well established, successful man again today. Each could have begun positive programming on the initial contact had more emphasis been given to the attitudes and prerequisites essential to effective counselling.

Several other principles are involved. One of paramount importance indicates that the supervision of the personnel involved in these cases had failed to acquaint the trainees with the responsibilities of their role. Certainly, too, their basic training was sadly lacking in the "how" of establishing patient rapport.

Alcoholism: Treatable Illness

The damage created by such negligence and training is not merely to the patient alone, though this is serious enough. Indirectly, the harm done is compounded by the patients and collaterals who voice their opinions to others involved in the services being offered and received. Thus the adverse effects are amplified to a disturbing degree.

Patients with any illness should never be subjected to disdain. Counsellors must always be prepared to learn that their patients may be better educated, experienced and trained than they are. A common reaction of alcoholics to alcoholism clinics is, "What the devil do they know about life? They're not even dry behind the ears yet. What do they know about waking up in a strange place, alone, broke, friendless, with the shakes and gags and with my kind of remorse and fear? What do they know about waking up in a jail when I am supposed to be performing an operation this morning? I have thrown away more on one drunk than they will earn in the next year." And so on.

In the case of the female former patient who gladly offered to help with the study, the counsellor properly oriented might have said, "I am a student worker interested in working in this field. It is fascinating. We are trying to learn as much as we can about this illness and would like your help with the study we are doing. I know only a little of your history and background [which the counsellor should actually have carefully studied before the patient came in], so please forgive me if I tread thoughtlessly or unkindly."

This honest and more humble approach, combined with a warm greeting and expression of gratitude for the assistance offered, would have made a friend and a helper. In the case of our advanced "loner" friend, the selection of a recovered alcoholic as a counsellor would have held a patient.

A number of years ago a friend of mine was loudly sounding off about how he had sought and found sobriety entirely of his own volition. In his self-satisfaction he forgot many things. This chap is a fine person, a successful professional man. His alcoholism had brought him to a serious state in life, to the point where he was close to losing everything. His family sent him to a famous sanatorium. While there, he received the finest of care and counselling, and he has never looked back. But much care was involved. Before his discharge the doctor had contacted a recovered alcoholic of the same profession and city to whom the patient was personally referred. His background was well interpreted beforehand. That A.A. sponsor met his plane and introduced to him a selected group of people for his first few contacts. They nursed him through a series of initial A.A. meetings; arranged daily contacts his first few weeks; helped him organize his affairs at home and in his practice, and were ever available to guide and counsel him, in close cooperation with the doctor. This is kid glove treatment, of course, but it pays off. That was years ago, and the recovered alcoholic has since sponsored, in identical fashion, countless numbers of other recoveries. This sample case evidences many related factors. The wife and family received counselling, both on the progression of the illness and on what to anticipate as recovery begins. Several other people were tuned in on the case, non-alcoholic business associates and others.

The managing director of one of North America's largest organizations was advised by the executive committee of his company board to take a leave of absence and seek treatment. The wife was brought into the picture and honestly advised of their decision and asked to cooperate. She sought my advice. On a number of visits, she was accompanied by her six year old son. She learned to understand and accept alcoholism as a treatable illness. Her husband agreed to go to a private treatment center and did so for four weeks. He returned physically and emotionally healthier than he had been in years, though it was evident that some reservations still persisted.

When on the job a month, he attended an important business meeting, followed by a cocktail party, at which he felt he would test himself again. After a couple of weeks of willed and controlled testing of "one or two a day," following another meeting and cocktail party, he returned home later than usual — just over the edge. Though dinner was waiting, he immediately went upstairs, saying he would skip dinner. The wife joined the family and said, "Dad isn't feeling well so we will have dinner without him." Though hurt and scared, as counselled and forewarned, she remained calm and collected before the children. The young lad of six as matter-of-factly answered his mother, "I guess Dad is sick again, alcoholic sick, isn't it? We will have to start over and help all we can."

The father, dejected and remorseful, standing on the landing upstairs, overheard the conversation. It was his second shock of the day. The first had occurred at the party. A board member, seeing him with his third or fourth drink, had said, "Not again, George, you really shouldn't, you know." With that the man had turned on his heel and left. George, with chagrin and resentment, had dashed home to be confronted with his family's awareness. Both confrontations had been without anger or the usual threats or scenes. Both got through to him. He rejoined the family and announced, "I guess if being 'alcoholic sick' is acceptable to you it had better be to me." He called me that night and asked if we might start over. He has never had another drink.

Understanding, achieved only through conjunctive personal effort, paid off. A top executive was salvaged, a husband and father retained, and a social being regenerated to make a meaningful contribution, through recovery, to himself, his family, his vocation and his community. The attitudes of each are closely intertwined. How does one express in words a meaning that will get through in every situation? Position, level or kind of patient doesn't really matter. To me, the essence of reaching any kind of patient is wrapped up in the attitude, awareness, knowledge

Alcoholism: Treatable Illness

and understanding we learn, first of the illness alcoholism itself, and secondly of what we are prepared to give and feel toward the alcoholic as a person. The attitudes, learned as a prerequisite to dealing with their problem drinking situation, enabled George's board members and family to deal with his relapse constructively and positively, without fear or panic.

Problems and Tensions Brought to Counselling

It must be recognized that, regardless of the alcoholic's status in life, during the progression of the illness many new problems develop. Over and above life's normal pressures, the patient intensifies personal difficulties with new and added tensions, the degrees of which are dependent on the stage of the alcoholism. It is essential that the patient and all who work with the alcoholic appreciate the depth and weight of these problems.

Initially, alcoholics seemingly agreeable to counselling may only be seeking relief from another pressure: how to retain spouse and job, get a bed and a meal, get tools out of hock, find a ticket home or receive medical attention to get over the shakes or a killing hangover. These immediate concerns must be dealt with in their proper order and manner to provide sufficient relief to patients and to encourage their continuance as patients. Other cases may only be seeking to learn how to drink moderately, to hopefully continue social drinking with their group. Others may just be curious as to how far along they really are.

Naturally the alcoholic, preoccupied with the need to drink and the importance of alcohol in his or her life, minimizes the seriousness of his or her emotional and physical condition, and *conceals the extent of his or her drinking*. Though clouded by all of these issues, in my opinion a greater number of potential patients seek some kind of outside or professional help than we realize. They may skirt about issues with spouse, family or boss; they may avoid with their doctors any honest discussion on drinking by discussing their nerves instead, and perhaps they may reject religious counselling because of spiritual despair. Some even call upon or attend A.A. meetings — but deny doing so. These feelings and the demands of other practical needs must be recognized and constructively met.

Proper and controlled tension is a major influence in our lives — ambition, work, goals, material security, personal responsibility, and other daily responses and drives — producing personal gratification and success. A daily response to the alarm clock can be a normal tension or a hatred for it as a symbol of slavery to life. In a well disciplined life, rounded out by the usual demands of family, church, club, sport and hobbies, these are normal social tensions, which with others complete life as we know it in our society. Alcohol has a mild role for most people in this setting. It is a social lubricant, a tension relaxer, a convivial means of enjoyment.

In the developing alcoholic, these kinds of tensions or demands take on negative implications. While people with too little or too much tension may develop other kinds of problems, alcohol for the alcoholic magnifies any other problem. As a result there is greater frustration, anxiety, failure, resentment, isolation and negative reaction to daily demands, creating new symptomatic pressures. As pointed out, it is difficult during the early stages of problem drinking, for the alcoholic to realize or acknowledge the relationship of his drinking to these increasing tensions. He or she believes alcohol to be a necessary medicine to relieve these tensions. Therefore, it is important for anyone preparing to assist the alcoholic to understand how such drives, which make up hope, ambition and success for some, create frustration, resentment and failure for alcoholics.

As alcohol dependency mounts, it is soon difficult to determine the chicken or the egg — particularly as the "medicine" becomes a new and paramount tension in itself. Increasing family, job, social and other tensions, resulting from the dependent use of alcohol, explode into a vicious circle. Because of "his kind of drinking," family problems outweigh family satisfaction; alcohol dependency demanding more alcohol makes budgeting an increasing problem; job demands necessitate the easement of a few drinks, creating more inner fear, remorse and resentment. Sooner or later, as the phases progress, the dependency on alcohol becomes the number one tension; all others are secondary.

Spouse, family, friends or counsellors who want to help the alcoholic must learn to recognize and understand these pressures. Crying jags or grandiose behaviour are but outlets for the internal pressure the alcoholic is undergoing. In the advanced stages of this kind of drinking, the only relief from these tensions for the alcoholic is more drinking.

Recognizing the critical role that alcohol plays in the alcoholic's life and the vast spectrum of problems related to the abuse of alcohol, anyone who helps that patient achieve sobriety must discard normal procedures of approach. The counsellor must indicate an awareness and understanding of what the alcoholic feels and suffers, and must gain cooperation by making no impossible demands. To initially say, "Now you must stop drinking for good," or "Stop because I say so and want you to," will have little effect. If sobriety is to be achieved, a new outlet or relief for the alcoholic's tensions must be found. This will be found in the firm but understanding support of the spouse, in A.A., through a clinical counsellor and additionally in part from doctor, employer and/or clergyman — providing each has acquired a knowledge of the prerequisites and attitudes of a sound approach in dealing with the alcoholic so as to provide a safe and sober means to relieve these internal tensions.

Importance of Initial Approach

I submit that almost everything that is to be achieved in bringing an alcoholic to treatment is generated, with pointers to success or failure, in the initial discussion with the patient as a sober person. However, even that which is said and done with a

Alcoholism: Treatable Illness

hung-over patient somehow gets through, at least in part. The patient especially, but also the spouse or other related collaterals, should realize that it may be necessary for each of them to discuss the alcoholism and other problems with several specialists. This is not to shunt them around, but rather to explore every possible means of assistance and to use the special skills of the various workers to cope with their total needs.

As acceptance and empathy represent the key to reaching the alcoholic, an unwarranted number of patients may be lost to treatment if the initial approach is an unacceptable one. The alcoholic is thus committed to a continuance of drinking for another indefinite period.

Since more and more alcoholic patients, their spouses and families are making an initial contact through alcoholism agencies, reference to the important role of clinics is included in this discussion.

Bear in mind that many patients may seek help on their own during the early stages of their illness while still retaining physical, emotional, economic, social and spiritual assets conducive to their recovery. These assets, if the drinking continues and the illness progresses, may unfortunately deteriorate. It is not unusual for alcoholics seeking help to give no indication of ever having sought assistance before. The experience of most alcoholism agencies indicates that over fifty percent of those seeking help — seemingly for the first time — have already been to A.A., a clinic or a doctor, perhaps several times. This isn't disclosed for fear of ridicule, rejection or chastisement over personal inability to follow through.

It is also important that, on the initial or reopening contact, the alcoholic is received with warmth and understanding, as a person who is very ill and urgently in need of reaffirming his own dignity. The manner in which he is received will help re-instill his hopes. This procedure, as stressed repeatedly, is vital to an initial approach to the alcoholic regardless of the means or sources of contact. In an alcoholism center this attitude must begin and be evidenced continuously with the receptionist, the nurse, the doctor, and the individual or group counsellor to whom the patient or spouse is assigned.

A sure way to start things off on the wrong foot is to ask, "Why do you drink?" or "Why did you start to drink again?" If the patient had that answer he would not need to seek help. His self-abasement and discouragement are already intense enough without such questions adding to them. Despite claims to the contrary, the alcoholic does desire recovery, though he may not manifest that wish. His desire is sometimes strong enough even to surmount the obstacles and adverse attitudes of those from whom he urgently and earnestly seeks help.

A patient seeking assistance was refused care by several doctors and hospitals; he was told he "wasn't ready yet" by members of his A.A. group and given an appointment at an alcoholism clinic ten days away. Finally, he was taken to a police station to be locked up under their protection. The sergeant on duty called, and we arranged for the alcoholic to be hospitalized as an emergency case. An organist in his church and a successful businessman, it was his first relapse after over five years of sobriety. Though sober again, he died several months later from the after-effects of his relapse.

As upsetting as it may seem to the established routine of agencies or clinics, when an alcoholic finally seeks treatment he is unable to sit patiently and wait — nor can he be given an appointment days or weeks away. For the alcoholic to wait can have tragic results. A receptionist, oriented to the needs of new and active alcoholic patients and their spouses, can help immeasurably in bringing patients to treatment and in retaining them. Similarly, a receptionist can relieve the urgency and panic when problems which seem unsurmountable arise for a member of the family. Having an extra member of the staff free to greet, meet, and put at ease ill and distressed patients is most helpful. Patients awaiting appointments will understand if the nurse or counsellor provides immediate attention to new and disturbed patients, since they have been in that position themselves. It is inexcusable for patients in the waiting room to sit and shake while jocular staff members laugh and converse over coffee.

I recall an experience in which a group of counsellors assembled to wish happiness to an associate who was getting married and to present a gift over coffee. Their banter and laughter filtered through to the reception area. Waiting with other regular appointments were two new cases, both very sick and upset. Two patients had taken time off to keep their appointments.

Unfortunately, staff well-wishers took longer than planned at the little celebration. No one apologized to the patients in the waiting room. The regular receptionist, who normally would have handled such a situation by sharing coffee and visiting with the patients, was away ill, so an "unorientated" worker was at her desk.

Suddenly there was an explosion, as one patient, with language appropriate to his opinion of the occasion, let go with a real head of steam and led all but one patient out of the clinic. Two made official complaints. An ordinary incident became a serious episode; though blown out of all proportion, it was embarrassing from a public relations standpoint, with unhappy results for the patients. No treatment facility can afford such adverse publicity, however innocuous the causal event may seem.

To greet a patient with a long questionnaire is ill-advised. Counsellors who cannot get all necessary information on the first contact without these usual tools of the trade are not worth their salt. Vital information should be procured in an understanding and sympathetic conversation and noted to memory for later recording. A request for name and address (to get it properly), with the result

Alcoholism: Treatable Illness

written on a scratch pad will do. The details may be added later during routine sessions.

Anyone dealing with an alcoholic situation must learn never to be shocked by the appearance, mannerisms, language or resentments of a new or relapsed patient. This principle, while important to the spouse and family, is critical to the orientation of the counsellor, doctor, clergyman or others seeing the alcoholic, as their previous training ill prepares them to cope with the illness alcoholism.

As the initial contact with an alcoholic may be made by a doctor, a member of a hospital staff, a counsellor at a clinic or institution, or an employer, the proper orientation of these sources of referral to the illness alcoholism may initiate a positive treatment approach, with later follow-up for the patient.

While in the hospital being "dried out," I found my whole life changed by a few constructive words from a supervisory nurse, who managed in a few short sentences to initiate my recovery process. She simply said, "You know, you don't need to be like this; whether you recognize it or not, you are sicker than you realize. Alcoholism is an illness, and if you will let me, I will try to help you learn something about it. Call me when you feel a little better and we will talk about it." She then inquired about my care and needs. Was my family okay? Did my office know where I was? I did send for her later and learned that she had a brother who had found help in the same hospital. That was the beginning — her understanding, kindness and willingness to help gave me hope for a different life.

There is nothing more damning than to have a patient or the spouse go to a clinic and admit having tried A.A., only to have the counsellor say, "Why did you go there? Why didn't you come here first?" — or conversely, to be referred to an A.A. contact and admit having visited a clinic previously, and then be greeted with, "Why did you waste your time going there first? Don't you know only an alcoholic can help an alcoholic? If an alcoholic doesn't want or ask for help, he or she isn't ready yet, and doesn't really want to quit."

It doesn't take too much imagination to appreciate the damage such a reaction creates for either the alcoholic or the family. Nevertheless, such deplorable attitudes continue to exist, deterring objective treatment.

Thoughtless and glib answers are just as damaging. On initial contacts, everything possible should be done to permit the patient or spouse to feel comfortable and to talk. The alcoholic and the spouse desperately need to "ventilate" their problems — whether the alcoholic blames the spouse, family, boss or whatever, let them talk. In particular, allow patients to wear out their own excuses. Be prepared to offer understanding, never maudlin sympathy. Self-pity should not be condoned. Again, a reminder, do not use "highfalutin" labels. Sometimes a light but appropriate comment can be especially effective in establishing a bond of understanding with the patient.

There comes to mind an alcoholic who was literally carried into my office by his aggressive wife. One could readily see that he was the "milquetoast" type. She started right in doing all the talking and pulling that poor fellow to pieces. Finally I asked her to listen so that we could hear his side of the story. After a few hesitant comments, he said, "You know, I have seven women running my life, a wife and six daughters." With momentary inspiration I promptly stood up, reached over, shook his hand and said something to the effect that, "Any man who has seven women running his life needs to drink!" It was as if a whole new world had opened up to him. With a broad smile on his face he sat bolt upright as much as to say, "Here's somebody that understands." He told about the doilies under his ashtrays, the frills around all of his personal things and of the horrors of life in that house. Being a small man, he resented his inability to participate in physical sports, but loved them all. Can't you just see him drinking — a typical Napoleon standing on a chair and telling his family off!

By seeing the family as a group, continuing counselling for both patient and family, and arranging a new relationship for him in a suitable closed men's group, we were able to help this alcoholic achieve complete sobriety and learn to be the man he wished he could be. The wife and daughters perhaps gained equally as much.

In the majority of problem-drinking situations, the family is still intact. Even when separated, the spouse can be the most important and helpful contact in establishing an initial approach to the alcoholic, especially when the patient does not personally seek treatment. Though the family role is covered in a later chapter because of its importance to treatment and whole recovery, a few "family" comments are pertinent here.

Initial orientation of the spouse, family and other collaterals is vital to the recovery of the patient. As emphasized in the early phases of recovery, what they learn and how they apply themselves may mean the difference between success and failure in bringing the alcoholic patient to treatment. The initial approach sets the basis whereby the patient, the spouse and other family members or collaterals learn how to relate to and be a part of the treatment process.

These few thoughts cannot begin to cover the many essential attitudes and prerequisites involved in counselling. Every person involved in any relationship with recovering alcoholic patients must be exposed to adequate and proper orientation. As the spouse and family are deeply related to every facet of the illness, and as counsellors will be exposed to every type of question and enquiry, they should have considerable knowledge about A.A., local alcoholism agencies, and every resource available that the patient or those close to him may use in the community. Only in this way can each understand the language of alcoholism and the symptoms of the illness; only in this way can each assist in better interpreting the alcoholic's experiences, his needs, and obstacles to accepting treatment. This is essential if the

Alcoholism: Treatable Illness

alcoholic is to be motivated and then adequately supported to eventual recovery.

With information and education on the increase, many (if not the majority of) initial inquiries regarding treatment are being made by the spouse and families or other collaterals of the patient. Each must be dealt with as positively and thoroughly as possible, and treated with the respect and importance such inquiries deserve.

Not all inquiries are made by individual personal contact. Many are by telephone, by letter or in informal conversation with a recovered alcoholic or someone purportedly informed about such things. While making every effort to encourage a personal visit, these types of contacts should be handled as seriously and thoroughly as a personal interview. Where possible, a procedure of following up these inquiries will produce rewarding results.

It is not unusual for a completely sober person to enter a clinic or an A.A. office seeking information for a distant relative, friend or employee, when in effect the request really concerns the individual personally. Hence, the continuing reminder regarding labels, discouragement and attitudes.

Every contact made with patients and those close to them must relate to the total treatment effort, in as much as treatment is an educational process. Alcoholics and their collaterals, as a result of their newly found awareness, knowledge and understanding, must learn a totally new approach to their problems. They must also unlearn former attitudes and dependencies, and must recognize the ineffectiveness of measures taken in the past. Patients and their families, together with those responsible for providing treatment services of any kind, through repetition and practice must continue this learning and unlearning process until all have a feeling and a sense of the illness and an appreciation of the concept of alcoholism as a treatable illness, the most vital factor in the treatment process. This is the essential attitude for effective and successful counselling.

18. Face to Face

A face-to-face interview with the alcoholic is a major breakthrough to the patient's potential recovery. As the first contact may be a request for help from someone other than the alcoholic, equal importance must be attached to the person making the initial inquiry. Regardless of the source or type of inquiry received, every encouragement should be given to the patient or the referral source to arrange to talk about it face-to-face.

Pertinent information concerning the patient prior to a first face-to-face interview is helpful in determining the individual best suited to the needs of the alcoholic. A few simple questions will provide a glimpse of marital and family status, age, level of work and responsibilities, the home situation — without requiring more intimate disclosures. This procedure applies to inquiries directed to any resource for help, including an alcoholism clinic, a doctor, a member of A.A., an A.A. office, a hospital and an E.A.P.

Occasionally, the alcoholic may be the one to phone. Again, tact will elicit the information needed. At times a patient, a member of the family or a collateral may show up at a clinic, an A.A.'s home or a doctor's office and simply ask for help. Sometimes the person seeking information for another is really looking for self-guidance.

The alcoholic may hesitate to make an appointment unless the interview is arranged on an anonymous basis, in the evening, over the weekend, at lunch, in the home or office, in any way which will permit the patient to be at ease. Though preferably the alcoholic should be seen in a counsellor's setting, exceptions are not out of order. Patient interviews may be arranged in a doctor's office, a hospital, a clergyman's study, or under other circumstances. The level of inquiry, the source of referral and the type of contact will determine the arrangements made.

By way of example, an alcoholic might call a doctor, teacher, boss or even a clergyman. The "contact," following a beginning interview could, with permission, invite an A.A. friend to take over. A doctor, with an alcoholic in a hospital, might call a counsellor from a local alcoholism agency; or there might be an alcoholism worker on staff, and again there may be an available list of A.A.

155

sponsors on call to serve such inquiries. These and many other arrangements may be used to establish the first face-to-face interview with the alcoholic. These inquiries and the role of other collaterals are dealt with more specifically in later chapters. Those "beaten down" by their alcoholism, though embarrassed, feel less reticent about going directly to an alcoholism agency, an A.A. office or any other resource suggested. Professionals or those in "high places" may want to see someone in confidence, or they may want to see the person in charge, especially if they know him or her. Such demands are not unusual from patients, their families and collaterals alike.

I was often asked why I saw so many people myself to initiate treatment. My answer is simple: "If an interview with me will start an alcoholic on the road to recovery — that's what I'm here for." This is sometimes upsetting to counselling members of a clinical staff, but most patients can be moved into routine treatment channels once the ice is broken.

In the early days of program development, there weren't too many guidelines to follow. Deeming it important to my role and education, I sought the advice of professional counsellors, alcoholism agency directors, and particularly A.A. members. After all, at that time the Fellowship of Alcoholics Anonymous was essentially the only working medium available.

It was my privilege to learn a great deal from a successful physician and health director. This friend, a recovered alcoholic whom I shall call John, was a dedicated worker both at the public level and in Alcoholics Anonymous. He answered many of my questions about programming needs, particularly in the area of treatment, by relating a number of his experiences with patients. He had developed a free and easy manner of resolving direct requests for information and assistance. When I asked him how he handled requests for personal interviews, he related the following case experience.

"Dick, a social acquaintance, telephoned to discuss a personal problem so I suggested he drop into my office at his convenience." On arrival Dick looked hale and hearty, seemingly without a care in the world. He opened the conversation expressing concern about his drinking — not that he got stupid drunk ever, but because he found himself drinking much more than ever before. He found that he was getting high more often and looking for excuses to attend more parties. This was causing discord at home since his wife did not drink. He had seen doctor friend who had advised him he wasn't an alcoholic. Nevertheless, matters weren't getting any better. After further discussion I learned that although Dick felt guilt about his drinking, and it was upsetting him no end, he still persisted in trying to drink socially and be 'one of the boys.'

"I pointed out that no one could tell him he was alcoholic but himself — that only he could determine the extent of concern or the number of problems his drinking created. If it interfered with his home life and the relations he enjoyed with his wife and children, he was doing the intelligent thing to think about it and look into it. A person married to someone of temperate beliefs, of necessity is faced with determining what is most important to him: drinking, or a happy relationship with the family. Sometimes a spouse's fears are a carryover from an unfortunate alcoholic experience with a parent or the result of rigid early training.

"I suggested that in such situations one's drinking must be carefully assessed, or one must suffer the adverse results. A decision concerning the use of alcohol is often confused and prejudiced by the social pressures existing concerning the importance of alcohol to our society.

"Further conversation revealed that Dick was really drinking more than he indicated; that he was sneaking a few drinks on the side and keeping a bottle handy in case he needed it or woke up and couldn't sleep. He told me he liked the stuff, especially the taste of it. I countered his rationalization with the comment that whether he knew it or not, it was really the effect he was after. A lot of people like ice cream; in fact, some are quite addicted to it. However, I didn't know of anyone taking ice cream to bed with them and keeping it handy in case they woke up! I interpreted the insidious factor of alcoholism — that it crept in and created a dependency, the seriousness of which he would be the last one to recognize. It was evident that it concerned him, why else was he in my office?

"The hopeful and really fortunate aspect of our discussion was his ability to discern a developing problem and his concern with it. This gave rise to the need for a vital decision. What was important to him? And did he want to resolve his drinking problems?

"To cope with his problem, I proposed that he and his wife attend a series of group counselling lectures then available at our alcoholism agency. This would help her to understand what alcoholism really is, and, by teaching her the differences between drinking, drunkenness and alcoholism, help to resolve some of her convictions and prejudices. In Dick's case a discussion of the phases of alcoholism would help him to determine whether or not dependency existed. Guided by that knowledge, he could take it from there. It was further agreed that he visit a few A.A. meetings, following his counselling sessions, which I agreed to arrange through an A.A. friend.

"As it later transpired, Dick was an early stage alcoholic. Certainly, he did not tell me the extent of his drinking. I didn't expect him to. His wife, on the other hand, magnified the problem because of her own deep-seated aversion to his drinking. Through joint counselling, he saved face as far as knuckling down to her 'you can't drink' edict and was able to establish a continuing program of contact and sobriety with a closed A.A. group that met in home. Both have every reason to be satisfied. His recovery and their joint education will be most useful when they are faced with

Alcoholism: Treatable Illness

guiding their children to make similar decisions.''

John went on to point out that his approach to patients reflected the experience he had gained in A.A. He emphasized that the personal touch that had worked with him, and which he practised sponsoring others, is effective for anyone wishing to apply it —A.A. members or professional counsellors alike.

Inquiries arise from the most unlikely people and in the most unexpected fashion, time and place. Alcoholics, preoccupied with their problems and having no sense of time, are subject to "spur of the moment" decisions. They ignore established channels of service or routine — a fact anyone working with alcoholics must anticipate and accept at least on initial contact and under emergency circumstances. Anyone unwilling to do so may as well stay out of this field.

Another of John's experiences emphasizes this point quite clearly. He put it this way:

"When the phone rang at about 11 o'clock on a Saturday evening I wasn't surprised at the call, but was by the calling party — my friend Ann. Because we are mutually interested in a business matter I presumed this to be the purpose of her call. Her voice, though urgent, gave no hint of disturbance. I started right in on the last news of our enterprise. She broke in with, 'No, John, this is a personal matter concerning your kind of business.'

'What member of the family is involved?'

'It's me. Will you help me?'

'Of course I will.' I hoped she hadn't noticed the long pause that indicated I was caught up short. 'When do you want to see me?'

'I'd like to come right away, but I just got home. I'm scared! Can we talk about it?'

'Of course — tell me about it.'

'Well, John, I was away and I guess blacked out for two days. We had a family squabble over our son, who is at that age. When he didn't get home I went looking for him, found some liquor missing, panicked and drank too much myself, I guess. This blackout scares me. Last week, after a small cocktail party I drove some girls home, returned home myself, evidently drank more and fell. The folks found me all bruised. I don't remember any of it. John, I'm scared silly.'

"Calm reassurance is needed at a time like this. 'Let's take it easy. From your voice I believe you have hold of yourself, so take a warm bath, drink some clear soup and hot chocolate, and get to bed. First thing in the morning if you need a drink, drink fruit juice, and then come on over, or I'll go see you and we'll see what to do.'

"Ann went on, 'I never believed it could happen to me! It's only the last couple of years. John, I never get drunk when I go out. I've never embarrassed myself or anyone else, but I do sometimes drink alone. I should be ashamed I suppose, but knowing you and many of the people who work with you, I'm more scared than embarrassed, so after putting the car away I dashed to the phone and here I am. What is happening to me, and what should I do?'

'Ann, don't worry; feel real good about what you are doing. You did ninety percent of the job by calling me and talking about it. Now go and follow instructions: remember, a hot bath, some bouillon and chocolate and get to bed. Leave the worrying to me for tonight. We'll look for you in the morning. My wife will have the coffee pot on.'

"After a few pleasantries and assurances Ann said goodnight. She seemed relieved. Promptly at ten the next morning she drove up. My wife, knowing in these situations, stayed out of sight. Apart from a tense and questioning concern on Ann's face, she was bright and seemingly cheerful.

'John, this is terrible of me. I didn't realize how late it was, or even the day for that matter, when I phoned. I'm all mixed up, but not as scared since talking to you.'

"I welcomed her warmly: 'Ann, you couldn't have done a nicer thing. It's a privilege to have your trust. Maybe it will ease your mind to know that you are one of many women and men like ourselves caught in this illness. The simplicity of it all evades every alcoholic. As suggested last night, the worst is behind you because you are here and had the insight and courage to call at once when you felt you needed help. Alcoholism is an illness, Ann, not a matter of morals or willpower. You can get well, have no fear! You may bump your nose along the way, but really you don't need to if we can get you started right, and if you remain as honest and sincere as your start indicates.

I would say you have more insight than some. The most serious aspect of alcoholism is that all too often the alcoholic is the last one to recognize the symptoms and progression of the illness. As an alcoholic's problem drinking progresses it is as if he or she were caught in a glass cage with everybody else able to analyze his or her actions. The first misconception to get out of your mind is that all alcoholics are from skid row. Secondly, contrary to what you may think, you do not need to be drunk all the time to be an alcoholic, or thus embarrass yourself and those about you. This can happen, but it doesn't need to. Another thing to remember, Ann, is that the only opinion that counts is your own true opinion of yourself.

'Well, Ann, I can see you feel a little easier. If what I've said has opened the door a little, suppose you take it from here.'

'My husband has been worrying over my drinking for some time. When I questioned my son about his drinking he told me I had better check my own! I didn't even know he knew about it. I thought other people wouldn't know because I never take more than a drink or two in public at any function, and you know I am active and busy all week long with something. But I have been rushing home and

Alcoholism: Treatable Illness

taking a few drinks alone every day before facing up to all the family demands and problems.'

'Always remember, Ann, that, right or wrong, if you are drinking you are deemed wrong. Problems at home and relationships between yourself and your family cannot be satisfactory until you resolve your drinking problem. With that in hand, one by one, you can face any issue that arises. If you achieve self-respect and stability in your own life, it will then be easier to establish a better sense of values in the lives of those about you. Your example of sobriety will do more for your children than a thousand sermons.'

"I went on to point out to Ann that abstinence from alcohol is only the beginning, sobriety means recovery in every department of one's life. 'You will find that you can't afford the luxury of resentment, anger and intolerance and all those traits of character we develop as our drinking becomes serious. What people don't realize is that you criticize yourself more severely than anyone else ever could. That's the reason you are here now. Your own remorse and guilt are causing you to question your actions as a wife, a mother and a woman of education and position.

'You may find it is harder, Ann, to surmount some of the social pressures of this illness than it is to get over the physical and emotional turmoil it is causing you. Getting over the word alcoholic was your first fear. In fact when we spoke about it last night, you immediately said, 'But John, I'm not that bad yet.' The word *bad* and the word *sick* don't mean the same thing. Every alcoholic is sick, very sick. Alcoholism is a progressive illness. Sooner or later you would be drinking to overcome the effects of your drinking, and then it all becomes a vicious circle. Ann, it isn't that you can't drink, either. You can drink anytime you want to — as long as you hold out physically. However, you can save yourself an awful lot of suffering, by learning that as an alcoholic you *shouldn't* drink. That's the simplicity of it all. If you'll appreciate that one fact, you will eliminate the heartbreak of fighting it to the bitter end. There is only one end if you, as an alcoholic, continue to drink — the loss of everything you hold dear, and the shattering of every ideal and value you have built up during your life.'

"To this Ann replied, 'Well, at my age I have the usual problem. My doctor warned me not to drink and referred me to a specialist. I lied to him and told him I drink very little. He probably feels my problems are mental, whereas I guess a lot of them are the silly fears I have and the problems brought about by my drinking. I feel better now just talking it all out. How do I start?'

'Ann, begin by going back to your family doctor and telling him what you've told me. Ask him for a complete physical checkup in view of this new angle. With your permission, I will also phone him. By the way, no dieting yet. Weight in many cases is alcohol bloat, and right now you need all the food value you can get.'

'What about my family, John?'

'Well, there are several things I want you to do. I am going to introduce you to another friend, a girl I am sure you know. She will invite you to an Alcoholics Anonymous group. I rather fancy both of you have been friends since you were youngsters, but I must get her permission to use her name. Another thing I would suggest, to answer your first question, is that we bring your husband into this as quickly as possible and tell him exactly what plans we are making, as I think you should have his immediate cooperation and support. You should both participate in a joint counselling program at the local alcoholism clinic, so we'll arrange an appointment there also.'

'Let me tell you in advance you aren't going to like everything or everyone you meet in these several efforts. That, too, is normal. I defy you to like every dress on every woman in the pews ahead of you in church. I know you don't. Still you go to church, not to see dresses but to satisfy a special need. Now you will be going to do these things — clinical counselling, the A.A. person — and will be receiving the joint support of people like yourself for a special need, your illness alcoholism. That comes first.'

'With the rest of the family, for the moment say nothing. With everything red hot after the blow-up last week, we had better choose an opportune moment to begin to set the record straight. First, let's have you O.K. Decisions can wait until you are physically and emotionally sober and comfortable. They'll be better decisions when you're at ease with yourself.'

"Ann talked on for some time about her problems: the emotional disturbances; the growing friction between herself, her husband and her family, her rift with her folks, and the many other things she needed to express. A little later my wife joined us for coffee, and we decided to call Claire. She was happy to be called on to help and soon came over. After a visit, we left them alone. They had been friends since childhood, so Claire was a sound choice as an A.A. sponsor. Ann left carrying some selected literature and books.

"Ann followed through with all her contacts. There were visits with her husband. Claire introduced her to an A.A. group. She 'levelled' with her doctors and was relieved to find they approved. Suppose that when she first called I had said, 'Phone me next week,' or 'Go see the clinic or tell your doctor.' It might have worked — but if it hadn't, where might she be and where, in conscience, would I be?"

When face to face with an alcoholic, the first requisite is to achieve a meaningful relationship. The setting, the person and a recognition of his or her needs influence much of the early conversation. It is important to keep the discussion pointed to alcoholism and to impress upon the alcoholic the relationship of his or her problems to the dependent use of alcohol. The alcoholic can be led with understanding and firmness. He or she cannot be pushed with moralism and sermons.

The emergency needs of the alcoholic must be recognized and dealt with. They

Alcoholism: Treatable Illness

may range from talking to the spouse to get permission to allow the patient to go home, to providing a room or a meal elsewhere. It may mean talking to an employer, a family physician or other collaterals, and a dozen and one other things. It is not unusual for a new patient contact to require endless phone calls and conversation to put all the pieces back together and to start things off on the right track. I have heard many say, "Shouldn't they do these things ourselves?" Perhaps. If patients are led and helped to do them, they are making commitments which they will try to honour. Remember, most alcoholics are desirous of recovery, are grateful for help, and — given the right direction and chance — will try to measure up. This is my philosophy, and it is one which helps to breed understanding and patience in would-be counsellors.

When a patient is working through an alcoholism agency, if other community resources are unavailable, necessary services should be provided within the clinic itself, though it may be emphasized that the center is a treatment facility rather than a welfare agency. Particular attention must be given to providing any emergency medical care indicated. Though few alcoholics really require hospitalization, when needed it is a vital part of treatment. Each personal interview presents a challenge during the early period of recovery. Alcoholics will alternately feel sorry for themselves or be ready to set sail alone without outside help . . . the moment the pain or fear of the last drunk is gone. However, if all conjunctive resources available are utilized, each will contribute in a meaningful way to help resolve the continuing problems and questions that arise. Regular and stable contact with other recovered alcoholics plays an important role in these face-to-face sessions. In this way the alcoholic will learn, link by link, to weld the chain of a personal recovery program which will work for him or her.

The same answers do not necessarily fit all alcoholics. Each case, being different, must be handled individually. Some alcoholics must be shocked out of their smugness; others out of their despair. A kid glove approach will reach one alcoholic; with another, a sledge hammer "put it on the table" discussion may be required. It may be necessary to use one's whole bag of tricks. Alcoholics learn to be first-class manipulators and to use those who are their benefactors.

The immediate families of alcoholics are constantly faced with the dilemma of dealing with the alcoholic skeleton in the closet that pops up out of nowhere when the sufferer needs some form of emergency care. Normally there is one family member left whom the alcoholic feels safe in approaching time after time, when all other doors have been closed to him. A handout of money is not the answer. Relatives faced with such demands — and they always come at inopportune times — should consider something like this.

"I don't resent your coming back to me; at least you know that I would do anything I can to help you. However, since seeing you last I have learned that you suffer from a very serious illness. I also know that I have said and done all the wrong things — giving you money, putting you up in a room, sending you away, burying your clothes. It's all a waste. Oh, I know that you mean your promises, or at least once you did, but now I realize that you have no control over breaking them.

"This time my help has a condition. I will do everything possible to help you — to recovery and to sobriety — but nothing to promote your continued drinking. You have broken the hearts of everyone else in the family, including your wife and children, and have been the despair of us all. I won't permit you to hurt them any more, nor to impose on me or my family. I will help you try a positive program of recovery — nothing else. If this is agreeable, I will see if we can find help together, but remember it is your decision and your right to drink if you want to — but not here."

Let us consider an example involving an alcoholic who reached this stage. Bill, a man I met through services he rendered my office, dropped by the house late one evening. When I answered the door he told me he hated to presume on me at home, but, finding the clinic closed over the weekend, he had to do something. He was seeking advice for his brother, Tom, who was "just out" again. Tom had taken a few drinks and had come out to Bill's house to seek a place to stay until he could find a job and get started again. I agreed to see Tom and then to help him get whatever help was needed. My friend added, "He's outside in the car with me now."

Bill fetched Tom and the two of them came in, with Bill looking relieved and Tom somewhat sheepish and defensively belligerent. We visited briefly and then I asked Tom, "When did you get out?"

He replied, "This time I was in a mental institution. I got drunk right after being in jail sixty days, so the family asked the judge to send me there for treatment. My wife won't let me come home, so I went over to Bill's house. I haven't been able to find work. I hope to sign up on the DEW line again. They need good electricians. I did a good job up there before."

"Do you think that is the final answer, Tom? It seems to me that you are only running away again. Did you ever go to the Alcoholism Clinic?"

"Yes, I went down there and stayed sober awhile, but that's when I went north. I had to eat and take care of the family so I took the first job that came along. However, I blew most of the bundle I saved as soon as I got back in town."

"Well, I think, Tom, that we should take these problems in the proper order. It would seem to me that the first thing you should do is face up to the drinking problem. You can't mend your life a piece at a time. You will have to deal with the whole thing sooner or later, and it starts with the drinking. Nothing will fall into place until that is resolved."

"I do want to quit," replied Tom. "I've tried a dozen times but everything is against me. What chance does a guy have without a family or job, and with

Alcoholism: Treatable Illness

everybody breathing down his neck? In my condition, it's easier to bum a drink than a loaf of bread!''

"That may well be, Tom, but you know there is a big difference between *wanting* to 'want to quit', and really wanting to stop, once and for all and above everything else, to control the kinds of problems you have because of your drinking. You must decide just what you want out of life. Whether you realize it or not, your drinking is at the root of all your present problems — not your family, or being out of a job, or anything else that you blame. Right now you are probably planning what you're going to say to your brother for bringing you here! Perhaps it's time that your brother Bill, like your wife, understands that no one can stop your drinking for you. If you continue, more and more doors will be closed. Several are closed now: your family is gone, you can't get a job, and now when you're drunk they are starting to put you away, for your own protection as well as theirs. Have you ever tried A.A.?''

"Yes, I have been to a lot of meetings in several places, but I can't stomach some of the stories I hear, some of the preaching I get, and the God stuff. Besides, I'm not that bad yet, and I can do it alone."

"Well, I don't know what you call bad. You haven't much left to show for your efforts of trying to prove to yourself and the world that you can drink. If you can do it alone, why haven't you? I don't know any alcoholics that have. You have said that to yourself and others many times before — and all you've proved is your inability to control your drinking.

"As far as what you heard at the meetings, there is one thing those people do have that you don't: they're sober; they know where they're going to sleep tonight; they have their families and they're working. You can't tell me that you're happy with yourself and your kind of drinking, and what it has brought you.

"And as for the preaching and 'God stuff,' perhaps it's time you decided to listen and learn, instead of telling everybody you can do it alone. You've made a mess of it alone and that God you scoff at is a pretty good ally, when you're friends again. You don't have to like everybody and everything you hear in A.A. or the clinic, but you can take the best of what you hear and apply it yourself. All Bill and I can do is give you some of the tools to work with. You have to use them and be willing to stay sober long enough to give them a good try.

"Every alcoholic pictures himself as something different. It's being an alcoholic that bugs you. But it won't take too long before you are as 'bad' an alcoholic as the kind you don't want to be. Alcoholics are sick people, not bad ones, and your recovery could start here and now, if you'll let it. Try to stop drinking for the next twenty-four hours; learn to eat and live properly, get cleaned up inside and out, and as you learned in A.A., start another twenty-four hours every day.

"Don't make pledges to Bill or anybody else. If you agree, you can go through the clinic properly and be introduced to some people in A.A. I'm sure if you will give it an honest effort you can stay with Bill until you're on your feet. We can find you a job here and take things step by step, one day at a time.

"How about working as hard to stay sober as you work at getting a drink when you need it? If you put as much into trying to stay sober you will make it, never fear. Tom, try to be willing to make an honest experiment of staying sober just for yourself, and then let's make a decision about how long you want to stay sober later. If what you find isn't as good as what you have, you can always catch up with your drinking by bending your elbow again.

"Let me ask you something. The gang that helped you drink up your bundle, have any of them a place for you to go tonight? Do any of them worry about you, your wife or your kids? Are any of them going to see if you eat tomorrow? That's what I mean when I say you decide what you want. If you want to keep on drinking your way, nobody can stop you.

"I say these things because, in my opinion, most alcoholics would quit if they weren't afraid to quit and didn't have to face themselves. You're lucky. You have a brother who cares and no doubt a family that's wondering what happened to the man you were. They left you because they couldn't stand by and see you destroy yourself and them, too. You aren't stupid, Tom — you have a lot on the ball; that's why I'm putting it right on the line for you. Bill wants to help; that's why he brought you here. So think about it. It takes guts to throw everything away as you are doing, but that's the wrong kind of courage. Properly applying the brains and the courage you have will get you back where you belong.

"Tom, it isn't that you can't drink; as an alcoholic you shouldn't. You well know that after a few good meals you are over the hump again and will make a thousand promises to yourself that it won't happen again. Of course you mean them, but when you take a drink it starts something in you that you can't control until you are drunk again. The only way to answer that is to learn never to take the first drink, always one day at a time. You can believe that guy inside of you who makes you feel guilty and remorseful, who makes you call yourself all those rotten names and forces you to hate yourself after every drunk. That guy inside of you wants the best for you. Why not try it?"

In our continuing discussion, we suggested Tom should have a thorough medical checkup, go through the clinic and avail himself of all their services. We expressed our strong belief that when he was sober, doors would begin to open and he could go back to work.

Tom was reminded that those who would tease him to take just one drink or to try again didn't give a damn about him as a person. He was told that a lot of people and resources were at his disposal if this time he would also put everything into it himself.

Tom remained with Bill for almost two months. In that time, he was a patient at the local alcoholism clinic, where he received personal and group therapy. He was referred to an A.A. group, and through the efforts of an understanding employment counsellor got a job in his own trade, a good job. His reputation as a worker and qualified craftsman was well known. His new character as a sober alcoholic is now also known. He learned to be completely honest about his problem and found that when he was sober, more people were on his side than he realized. His family was brought into the picture and though reluctant at first, his wife joined him in the group counselling and later attended some A.A. meetings with him. It was like a courtship all over again. That was years ago. They had a new baby, and Tom became the foreman of his crew. Nothing much else needs to be said.

I must repeat that the manner of approaching an alcoholic is essentially the same for everyone, whether a non-alcoholic professional counsellor or an A.A. sponsor. Regrettably, all too many workers seem unwilling to learn from the effective experience of Alcoholics Anonymous, in spite of the fact that their way is achieving results.

19. *Treating the Family*

Once when interviewing the wife of a particularly difficult alcoholic, I was trying to make her understand that her husband was really a very sick man, suffering from a serious medical and social illness — alcoholism. She interrupted with: "Yes, and I'm sick, too — sick and tired of him! Sick to the eyeballs of all he's done to me and my kids! Sick of looking for him, sick of picking up the pieces after one of his drinking spells, and sick of supporting his family! Don't talk to me about being sick!"

Very often those closest to the alcoholic require as much therapy as the patient — sometimes more. When a spouse or member of the family seeks guidance it usually comes as a shock to learn that they have an integral role to play in the recovery process, both for themselves and for the patient. Many have said and tried so many things for so long to no avail, that they feel helpless, desperate, frustrated and incapable of doing anything more to change matters. Many hope for a pill to effect a cure, or for some magic wand to create a change for the better. Various family members may require guidance and therapy over an extended period of time to understand the illness and to be oriented to their role.

The Spouse

A wife or husband who has been exposed to alcoholism for a lengthy period is bound to have suffered extensively. Though stable and mentally healthy individuals, they cannot help but be confused and even seriously affected. For that reason, even while requesting aid, they may feel that help is useless and the situation hopeless, since they've tried everything already. Made to feel inadequate, often rejected by the alcoholic, and usually blamed vociferously at home and on the outside for the alcoholic's kind of drinking, the spouse may not realize that most personal problems are the result, rather than the cause, of the alcoholic's illness.

Remember, too, the spouse is confronted with the same confusion and complexity of outside attitudes and pressures and learns to assume many fronts to combat the situation. Once he or she begins to feel responsible for the drinking, then he or she too suffers from guilt, remorse and self-incrimination, while developing even greater hostility. Accused of driving the alcoholic to drink, the spouse may be

Alcoholism: Treatable Illness

blamed and repulsed by relatives and friends alike, thus increasing guilt and hostility. On confronting the alcoholic, the spouse may be told that he or she — and not the alcoholic — is the one who needs help!

Defeated, the spouse withdraws and becomes isolated, as does the drinking partner. Becoming even more dependent upon the alcoholic for crumbs of acceptance and approval, the spouse becomes embroiled in a confusing conflict with the alcoholic. The non-alcoholic spouse thus begins to evidence as many physical, emotional and behavioral symptoms as does the alcoholic. Though threatening to leave, he or she can't, and so loses all individuality and objectivity.

These are the problems the spouse brings to counselling. None may be ignored or neglected. Each adjustment required may take painstaking effort, tolerance and understanding. Counselling will enable discussion, examination and resolution of problems. As recovery progresses, it is then possible for the spouse to assume a positive role in aiding the recovery of the alcoholic. This explains why such extensive and extended care is sometimes required for the spouse before the alcoholic may be treated.

The spouse must learn that threats, tears, anger, pleading and preaching are of no avail. Maudlin sympathy, babying, support of self-pity or assumption of the role of breadwinner only exacerbate the situation. One must appreciate the fact that though criticism and name-calling seem to fall on deaf ears, the alcoholic chastises himself about the drinking and is a seriously sick person, as unhappy in that state as the spouse is in the corresponding state. He or she must learn to be objective and positive, understanding though firm, and helpful without being bitter. When a spouse seeks guidance in coping with an alcoholic partner he or she needs to be given reassurance and hope, and to have his or her confidence and worth as a person in his or her own right reaffirmed. Able and astute men and women often look upon themselves as failures because of the alcoholism of their mates. Some, in addition to being blamed by the alcoholics, blame themselves for everything that happens in their deteriorating relationship. Like the alcoholic, they do not see the relationship between their problems and the illness alcoholism.

There are those wives or husbands of alcoholics who revel in the martyrdom, sympathy and attention they receive from other members of the family. These types may do considerable damage to their children by warping and prejudicing their entire outlook toward the alcoholic. Even when refused a role by the alcoholic, the spouse should be encouraged to make one. It is not unusual for the alcoholic, when encouraged to include his wife in a recovery program, to say, "Why should she be a part of this? It's my problem, not hers." My immediate rejoinder is to say, "That may be true, but your problem has created as many and perhaps more problems for your wife. Selfishly, therapy will get her off your back; unselfishly, since you gave her all the hell of your drinking, why not let her share some of the fun of your recovery?''

Mrs. Baker and I had been visiting for some time about her husband Bob. Finally I summed things up by suggesting she take a firm but understanding approach at some opportune moment when Bob was remorseful and hung over to talk with him — something like this:

"Bob, I want to talk to you. This time, please have the courtesy to hear me out! We must discuss something that is of vital importance to our well-being. Please don't get mad and stamp out. I'm not threatening, nagging and preaching any more; nor am I leaving or going home.

"Bob, I think you are ill and much sicker than you realize or will admit. I'm worried about you — about us both. After all, as your wife and the mother of your children, I have a responsibility in any illness you have. If you had a heart attack, I would take every means possible to get you all the emergency care available — this illness is even more tragic. I don't know whether or not you are an alcoholic. I do know that your kind of drinking is affecting our relationship, the children, your job, our budget, and everything we have together. You're no longer the man I know you want to be, and I think it's time we do something about it.

"I want you to know I am learning all I can about alcoholism and I want to help. No, I'm not asking for a separation or divorce, I simply want to protect all that we mean to each other. I've decided this can't continue. I'll do everything I can to help you if you will let me. If you are determined to continue your drinking your own way, then know that I will not be a part of it any longer. If you don't care what it does to you, then I must take care of the health and well-being of myself and the children. Therefore, something must be done before we're all destroyed. I know now that I have also been at fault — and that your disturbing behaviour is the result of your abnormal drinking.

"You've promised to stop drinking in the past and think you can do it alone. This is as impossible as treating a heart problem or any other illness alone. We both need help. All I am asking is for you to be *willing to try with me* to find an answer and to save our lives together."

"I've said all these things a thousand and one times and only received criticism and abuse in reply," Mrs. Baker said to me hopelessly.

"No doubt you have, but probably in anger and with tears or threats. This time, Mrs. Baker, approach Bob when he is comparatively sober, preferably when his remorse is at its peak, following an especially rough time. Remind him of his previous promises, and of the fact that he hasn't been able to do it alone. This time speak your piece with firmness and decision. If you are not prepared to speak decisively, don't approach him. You must be prepared to follow through, if for no

Alcoholism: Treatable Illness

other reason than to resolve your own life and that of the children. Your manner must provide the necessary shock to get through to him. It will, if you can be decisive and clearcut in your statements. No tears, no screams, and by all means no anger. *Your decisiveness and finality must be apparent!* Bob must sense it, just as he always knows that a few kind words, a silly present and a lot of new promises can twist you around his finger again. He will know when you truly mean it. Only then will he react positively."

"What if he tells me off again, or threatens to send me packing or to leave himself?" Mrs. Baker countered.

I advised her to be prepared for that reaction. Her reply must be calm, decisive and to the point — something like, "Very well, there's not much more I can say. I have offered my help. If that is the way you want it, remember, you made the decision, not me. If you continue your drinking, you leave me no choice but to do whatever is necessary and best for all of us. We can't go on as we are."

"This approach, Mrs. Baker, may be the means of making Bob really think and decide to reach for help. He may get drunk to see if you really mean it. This will test your determination to follow through. Don't make a secret of the fact that you have sought outside guidance."

"Supposing Bob asks me, 'Why did you go there — and what did you learn?'"

"Your reply should immediately indicate that you have learned that the illness alcoholism no longer holds any embarrassment or fear for you, and that you have some hope again. You now know his alcoholism can be treated. Tell him that when you saw your doctor, he wondered why you were so upset and nervous; that he sensed Bob's drinking was the source of much of your trouble, and so referred you to us for further help. Also tell Bob that more people know about his problem than he realizes. Ask him to make the decision unanimous and to join you in doing something about it — or at least to look into it."

There are instances where a wife can include the employer. The alcoholic's superior may have sought her assistance, being concerned by the adverse effects of the alcoholic's drinking on his work and stability. If this is the case, it should be brought out with the admonition that, "Everybody is concerned about you. Can't you see they want to help? Won't you please let us?" The wider and more solid the sphere of approach the more effective it will be, providing all parties agree and follow through with the same approach. Other family members can also join you in this intervention — as long as they are aware and in agreement.

"If Bob agrees to see someone what shall I do?" Mrs. Baker asked.

"Don't look like the cat that swallowed the canary! Tell Bob, with whatever affectionate terms and manner you know will please him, what it means to you to have him well and himself again. Let him know how deeply his well-being concerns all of you. Tell him you know your own ignorance has caused you to make mistakes and probably hurt him without realizing what you were doing. Share some of the blame and then tell him that you will make a joint appointment to talk it over — and leave the rest up to me. You just get him here at any time convenient to you both. We will work it out together.''

It is sometimes necessary for the counsellor to work with the spouse for an extended period to have him or her learn about alcoholism and thus to understand and play the proper role. Many times the spouse will be bitter and belligerent, or may be beaten to a pulp emotionally.

My experience suggests that it is always possible to effectively regenerate deep affection or to transmute explosive animosity into understanding action. Both extremes evidence sincere feeling and interest in helping the alcoholic. It is extremely difficult to regenerate hope or interest on the part of alcoholics' wives or husbands who have reached a point of complete apathy, not caring what happens. When a husband or wife feels nothing but disgust and ''all dead inside,'' wanting only to escape the trap they find themselves in, they may be better off separated until some spark of feeling is regenerated. This could require a lengthy period of sobriety on the part of the alcoholic. The gap may never be bridged. In some such situations, separation and divorce have occurred even after sobriety is achieved by the alcoholic.

The husband or wife should be encouraged to maintain an extended therapy program of his or her own. Similar to the alcoholic, the spouse will need to face many problems and to get well physically, emotionally, socially and spiritually; to regain individuality; to fit back into the society from which he or she felt ostracized by the behaviour of the alcoholic. The spouse can learn the fun of having sober friends in the house, of sharing in the recovery of others, and of growing spiritually together. He or she may be referred for additional support to group counselling, either at a clinic or through Al-Anon, an auxiliary of Alcoholics Anonymous — preferably both.

Should separation be considered, this must be a personal decision, and rarely the direct recommendation of the alcoholism counsellor involved with the alcoholic. If such a decision is necessary, every cooperative resource should be brought into play through legal counselling to protect their joint interests and — hopefully — to leave the door open should the alcoholic achieve sobriety. The same cooperation and coordination of services should be invited from other agencies, when and if they are involved. Several resources and a great deal of care and therapy may be necessary to have the spouse play a meaningful role in finally bringing the alcoholic to treatment.

Less attention has traditionally been paid to husbands of female alcoholics than is given to wives. As with preparing the husband and father for the birth of a child, he should not be ignored in this instance, particularly in view of some of the

Alcoholism: Treatable Illness

cultural trends discussed earlier. He should be included in every aspect of therapy and treatment, and may have to be finessed into overcoming some particularly male traditional attitudes he may not even acknowledge that he demonstrates. He is a most important factor in the total and happy recovery of the alcoholic wife as a whole person in a whole family. Much more planning and effort usually go into the treatment of the spouse as a wife than the non-alcoholic husband receives. This can be averted through meaningful direction and cooperative guidance and counselling. Personal and group therapy in professional or A.A./Al-Anon family settings for husbands, fathers, and single male parents have come a long way. For the husband to re-establish pride and respect in his wife is to rekindle and increase the depth and sincerity of his affection and love. All persons — especially husbands and wives — like to know or rediscover that their original decision and feelings were indeed sound. It's good for their egos.

The spouse may have been drastically affected by the alcoholic's behaviour. Ill, distraught, and having carried the whole load, he or she may be as taut as a fiddle string. When the alcoholic begins to recover and things look safe again, the spouse may suddenly collapse. While the alcoholic should be cautioned during recovery to be prepared to be strong enough to carry on for both and warned of this possible reaction, he or she may not realize the seriousness of the spouse's condition. Here any counsellor must be prepared to sense the symptoms and to move in ahead of time if possible, to forestall a serious physical or nervous breakdown. This is another reason why close cooperation with the family physician and other collaterals is essential to the "whole" recovery of the alcoholic, the spouse and all others concerned. Though much excellent progress has been made in this area, continuing emphasis should be placed on this point. No one recovers or lives in a vacuum.

Conversely there is the spouse who, on the recovery of the alcoholic, suddenly sees his or her role pushed into the background. Having laboured long and hard to keep the home and family intact — and perhaps revelling in the martyr's role — the spouse may consciously or subconsciously deeply resent the alcoholic's new-found poise, status and independence. The wife, perhaps the breadwinner or the one who held fast to the purse strings or picked up her husband's check at the office, is suddenly faced with sharing the planning of the budget. Once sober, the alcoholic no longer relishes having an allowance doled out. He or she doesn't like to ask for money to join friends for an outing.

The spouse may sometimes determine to make the alcoholic pay for every past hurt and transgression and will demand everything at once, refusing to sacrifice any longer, materially or socially. Perhaps without realizing it, the spouse may even wish the alcoholic drunk again to regain the control he or she feels is being lost. Others may want to be waited on hand and foot, demanding continuing penance from the alcoholic. Some complain their former alcoholic partner is not much fun any more: "We don't go out and kick up our heels like we used to." These are sick people, too, who have not been able to resolve the hurt and disappointments inflicted by the alcoholism. They require a great deal of aftercare and help, which they can get from proper Al-Anon and professional counselling.

During initial stages of recovery at least, the spouse should guard against drinking and especially over-drinking beverage alcohol. Though the alcoholic's recovery should permit those close to the alcoholic to drink, it is not conducive to recovery or even to a compatible relationship and to marital harmony for the spouse to get "high." In the close relationship of marriage, a drinking spouse can be a negative influence. Often the non-alcoholic spouse, through trying to drink with the alcoholic and control personal drinking, may have or be on the verge of developing an alcohol dependency as well. In such cases, the matter should be discussed honestly and thoroughly, and the recovering alcoholic should be counselled to generate the strength and perseverance necessary to cope with this problem.

Roles with the children change. The long-suffering spouse may see the children he or she has sheltered from the adversities of the illness alcoholism looking up to and running after this "big, new, sober hero" in the home, while the spouse no longer receives the sympathy or attention that once were taken for granted. This calls for considerable readjustment and the sharing of credit. He or she may require guidance to learn to accept the new role and to become able to appreciate the quiet gratification that is truly his or hers. It is not easy for a spouse under such stress to recognize that youngsters really need a father and mother both. There is a period in the lives of children when the stability of their relationship with their parents as individuals and as a couple makes or breaks their lives. This is particularly so with daughters and their fathers. In similar fashion, sons, once re-established as sound male offspring, gravitate back to the mother and thereby determine their continuing relationship with the women in their lives. Alcoholism more seriously affects all of these relationships than is sometimes generally acknowledged.

As the alcoholic achieves sobriety in its fullest sense with recovery in every avenue of life, and as that recovery is reflected in every relationship of the family, there comes a point in time when a male alcoholic's old self-centeredness is reflected in another way. As the result of the miracle of recovery, he becomes the center of everything, and his wife is left to bake the cakes for the gang and to keep things running as hard as ever before. She may deeply resent his working with other alcoholics or spending time at A.A. meetings and clubs, or the time he spends in his new outlets and hobbies. She might even say she used to see more of him when he was drinking!

Similarly, as an alcoholic wife recovers and renews social and economic activities in a life of her own again, the non-alcoholic spouse can feel left out and

Alcoholism: Treatable Illness

jealous of his wife's time with and attention from others; he may be resentful of what he views as his secondary role in the family. A recovered alcoholic, a doctor's wife, is an excellent example in point.

Charming and personable, Mickie radiates good health, poise and vivaciousness. Gregarious by nature, with her sobriety came renewed demands and invitations, both within her own circles and in A.A as a speaker. With four young adult children — two boys and two girls — in high school and college, and with recognition as a popular hostess and guest, her schedule of activities was something indeed.

Leslie, her husband, who after the chaos of the past, wanted nothing more than a period of peace and quiet and a measure of personal attention, was beside himself.

Of course the situation required open assessment and adjustment, and it was achieved with proper compromise on both sides. Mickie remains active, but with some restraint, and Leslie and the young people are all more than content with the attention and love they receive — and they respect and are proud of and grateful to their Mickie.

The spouse's recovery is not complete until he or she also has that independence necessary in everyone's life — the need to belong a little to one's self. I recall such a case in a large family. The alcoholic made a tremendous recovery in every way. There were seven children in the home. They did not want for anything as the father was a very successful professional person. But the wife was a servant to the whole family.

With some guidance, one day after a holiday dinner, she called them all to attention and announced, "I want my innings! I love every one of you, and I don't resent being taken for granted [actually, she did, but had learned how to handle it]. From now on, one day a week belongs to me, and I want each of you to treat me as a person, an important person on that day. We will vote on which day you want to give me." She handled it very adroitly, made them all think, and their affection and respect came to the fore. The household gradually became an entirely different home, so much so that one of their tiny tikes was heard to say to an older brother, "You've had the floor long enough! It's my turn for you to listen to me!"

The spouse must learn to turn hope into trust and faith. Every time the alcoholic comes in the door, he must not be greeted affectionately — as a ruse to sniff his breath. The non-alcoholic partner must understand why the spouse may come home with flowers or candy when one of the youngsters desperately needs shoes. The non-alcoholic should take the flowers and be happy and grateful. The alcoholic is trying to make amends. He or she is a little child relearning to grow up. With care, the alcoholic will learn to share his or her problems, fears and depth of gratitude. Do not disparage a gesture that may seem foolish or absurd. Accept it with the knowledge that you have done your job well.

It is important to learn that the elimination of the alcohol problem does not answer every problem of life. Couples will still disagree, and maybe even fight; they will take different sides on many things — all the things we call normal behaviour. Not drinking simply brings everybody back into focus — presumably to be normal again. There is an advantage, though, that recovered alcoholics and their spouses have over others. They have had an opportunity to learn, together, how to live better and how to practise sound principles of recovery in a serene, happier and more meaningful way of life.

The Children

It is no secret that in North America today, the divorce rate is alarmingly high, and a generation of research suggests that over fifty percent of divorces are caused by alcohol-related problems. Studies indicate a higher incidence of alcoholism among children of alcoholics and a tendency to increased rates of delinquency, crime, emotional disorders and dependency on other drugs.

While these investigations indicate that children of alcoholics more easily fall prey to social, physical and emotional disorders than do the children of non-alcoholic parents, not enough is known about the behavioural pattern of the bulk of children from the homes of "hidden alcoholics." Remember that this group, though being reduced, represents ninety percent or more of the problem-drinking population. There must be a vast number of children managing to make the best of it. They either learn how to live with the problem in the home, or are immune and hardened to it as the result of parental apathy and the frightening public acceptance of the deviant misbehaviour associated with drinking in society today. These problems, hidden like the parents' alcoholism, are perhaps reflected in the overall incidence of mental illness, promiscuity and suicides.

Nevertheless, the families of many alcoholics· are effectively combating the situation — some with the support of the Al-Anon Family Groups, and others with professional guidance. The non-alcoholic spouse who diligently maintains a home with proper status and stability for the children under the trying condition of alcoholism is to be commended indeed. It is remarkable that so many wives and mothers, husbands and fathers do as fine a job as they do under these difficult circumstances. Unfortunately, there are many who don't or can't guide the children because of factors beyond their control.

Many children seem to develop an insight and stability at a very early age to cope with the alcoholic parent. It is a continuing marvel to meet as many well-adjusted children as there are under the adverse conditions of alcoholism in the home. Not all children are so fortunate. With some, the tragedy of this illness carries through to young adulthood and to adult status, affecting personal

Alcoholism: Treatable Illness

relationships throughout their whole lives, for themselves, their mates and their children. Certainly, when both parents are alcoholic the children are most seriously affected.

A youngster of about fourteen was released from a "home" to visit an ailing aunt. His parents, both alcoholics, were separated. The mother was on skid row. The elderly aunt had raised him. When he did not return to the home, the police were sent to pick him up. They found him on the floor of the aunt's home, near death from an overdose of sleeping pills. The lives of many children entrapped by this illness are of necessity vagrant, disturbed and unhappy. Such experiences are more numerous among "street kids" at every level society than we realize.

The emotional stability of children in an alcoholic environment is to a great extent controlled by the non-alcoholic spouse and other relatives or older children, who may promote the acceptance of alcoholism as an illness. While it is essential for every non-alcoholic spouse to seek the understanding necessary to cope with alcoholism in the home, it is vital that the awareness and knowledge gained be passed on to the children. Good intentions alone are not sufficient to help any illness, much less alcoholism. Often children are so disturbed that they are considered slow learners or retarded, when in reality they are only emotionally upset by the alcoholism. It is particularly unfortunate when the children are made pawns of the conflict between the parents and entreated or forced to take sides one against the other. Children can become excellent manipulators under such circumstances. In most instances, children love both parents and are hard pressed to keep from being utterly confused and frustrated.

A dramatic example comes to mind. In this case, the alcoholic was the husband. A physician, he had lost practically everything. In fact, arrangements had been made for him to live in a rented furnished home. Suspended from his profession, he was referred to me by the medical director of a mental institution where Art (not his real name) had spent three months. His wife, in a general hospital recovering from a 'nervous breakdown,' suffered several other ills. A daughter, who was failing in school, was said to be somewhat retarded; and a younger daughter was 'different.'

On arrival at the clinic, Art was quite belligerent and wanted it known immediately that he wished no part of A.A., God stuff or further professional counselling; that he could manage things alone, etc. I learned that earlier on, he had suffered an unfortunate experience in A.A.

After his opening defensive comments, I countered by saying this: "Regardless of your concerns, your referral to me is for but one reason, to assess and help you to face your alcoholism. Perhaps if you will be honest with yourself and me, and willing and open-minded enough to seek answers, it may be possible for us to find a solution and recovery. Your way failed. Now let's try mine."

We had several good sessions together. I arranged for Art — on an experimental basis — to meet a few close A.A. friends (including another physician) with whom we formed a cocoon around him. After a period of internship in a hospital, we were able to have Art reinstated and practising his profession. He and the new A.A. group grew together. A new and much more open and empathetic person, Art went on to be a tremendous success — he even became the medical director of that same hospital. However, perhaps the most dramatic change was in the wife and children.

She became one of the most popular hostesses in the city and very active in Al-Anon. There was nothing wrong with her or with either child. Both girls soon led their classes, developed sound careers and married well. The only thing that needed to be resolved for each of them was the husband and father's dependency on alcohol. With everyone learning and working together, they developed an aware, close and loving relationship. With Art's full recovery and sobriety, everything else fell into its proper place.

It is not unusual in a family counselling situation to find that the children need reassurance about the integrity of purpose of their parents during a beginning recovery. Lacking attention, and sometimes affection, the children, old and advanced beyond their years in some ways, remain very immature in others. The pressures existing in the home of an alcoholic often prevent the children from studying or doing well at school, and cause them to refrain from normal activities with others. One never knows what might be going on at home. Thus, they isolate themselves, or seek all their enjoyment away from home. In the past, sons planned to get away as soon as possible; daughters married to escape. Given the changes in our culture over the past few decades, the differences in the respective reactions and behaviours of male and female children may be much less marked once the children are beyond a certain age.

When the child of an alcoholic evidences continuing disturbance, physically or emotionally, such problems should be dealt with positively and given every possible attention — before it is too late. The children of alcoholics, unless treated, may evidence the after-effects of alcoholism as a continuing personal problem long after the alcoholic recovers.

It is my experience that most children earnestly wish help both for themselves and their parents. Having more insight into the problem than we may appreciate, they can be guided to an understanding of the illness with mutual benefit to themselves and to the alcoholic. It is essential in counselling the offspring of alcoholics to treat them as adults. They sometimes know more about the hard facts of life than the counsellors. I have known children to scrounge for themselves and to support both parents in one manner or another. I have seen children cajole and plead with a parent and effect a positive attitude, when neither the spouse nor the counsellor could get anywhere with the alcoholic. Many recovered alcoholics owe their recovery to their children.

One of the most progressive changes in attitude finally taking place is the provision of adequate and informed prevention education in schools, beginning in kindergarten through high school and college. Young adults from twelve to twenty often seek the advice of counsellors after being exposed to such education. Youngsters cannot easily be swayed by "hell and damnation" material. They are attracted and informed by non-controversial, non-moralistic and factual teaching. In a like manner, children cannot be given advice on "intelligent drinking." They can be advised about alcohol; they can learn to understand the illness alcoholism correctly, and thereby make better decisions both for themselves and those about them.

These factors, though general, are relevant to the philosophy to be assumed in treating the offspring of alcoholics. Young adults ideally fit into group counselling, with professional or Alateen (as an auxiliary of Alcoholics Anonymous). They are usually more forthright and positive than their parents. Their cooperation should always be sought, and they should be completely informed on the program established for the alcoholic parent. They are an integral part of the treatment team. Their questions, problems, suggestions and treatment must never be ignored.

The Immediate Family

With both children and other immediate members of the family — parents, brothers, sisters and other close relatives — the same philosophy and regime of therapy is indicated as those previously covered for the spouse. The wider and more solid the sphere of approach, the more effective the treatment will be to the alcoholic's total recovery, as a whole person in a whole family.

The alcoholic and the spouse can be seriously affected by an unwarranted and overly dependent relationship with another immediate member of the family, from either side. Parents who continue to cling to their children, who spoil them or baby them, and who find fault with the spouse rather than the alcoholic's drinking, pose a real threat to the recovery process. In-laws who will not assist the spouse in a positive approach, but urge a breakup of the marriage instead, induce tragic results. Parents may seek counselling for an adult "child" whom they have "taken home" to nurse back to health. In effect, they are requesting help to undo the damage their "baby" suffered "away from home." Like the alcoholic, they cannot or will not associate the problems incurred with the alcoholism. This seriously compounds the treatment of the alcoholic's illness, and where this problem exists, all immediate family members must be brought to counselling to achieve a common approach to the alcoholic.

There is no worse situation than for a spouse to be between an alcoholic mate and well-meaning but possessive, spoiling parents. When faced with such a situation, the spouse is occasionally well advised to let the parents have their fill of it and deal with it on their own.

Sisters, brothers, aunts, uncles, and other immediate family members all may fit this category. A maiden sister or aunt who has raised the alcoholic since childhood can sometimes be more domineering and possessive than parents. It is not unusual for such relatives to refuse to accept the individual as an alcoholic, as the alcoholic dependency is their tool to keep the alcoholic jointly dependent on them. Relatives have been known to sneak drinks or a bottle to "a beloved patient" even while the latter is hospitalized for the alcoholism. Such conditions make it very difficult for the alcoholic to admit to or accept the illness.

There comes to mind a case of an alcoholic whose sister mothered him from infancy. With no life of her own, his life was all she had. She shadowed him through two marriages and families, and as his alcoholism progressed, his hostility toward her was colossal. Only through complete separation was it finally possible to reach him and, later with his help, to have her understand her proper role.

Because of innate prejudice and their misconceptions about alcoholism, many families will not accept the illness as being something that could happen to them. They won't let it happen! A top executive and community leader had a son who developed a serious drinking problem in his late teens. After shipping him off to several schools, as much to get him far enough away not to embarrass the family as to educate him, the father contacted several sources of help including an alcoholism agency — but always the same block reappeared. Never had there been an alcoholic in his family, and he wasn't going to have the first one! A heavy but controlled drinker himself, he could not condone his son's kind of drinking or dependency.

The boy wanted help. On referral, and later of his own volition, he came in for treatment. Again the father took this as a personal affront and, wanting him elsewhere, disowned him. The boy went away but, as suggested, made contact with the treatment center in another city. His own concern and insight enabled him to continue his treatment with the clinic, to join A.A. and to follow through to recovery. An astute and energetic lad, he found employment, met a lovely girl and was married. Through a chance meeting with a family friend, the father learned the boy was doing well and had a son. He was not going to let an alcoholic son raise his only grandchild and male family heir! Then he learned his son had been completely sober for almost two years. Returning to counselling with a more open mind, the father later wrote his son, admitting his own failure in the situation. Now a proud grandfather, he brags about his son's recovery. It might be said the boy reached "bottom" this way — but isn't it tragic that one should pay such a price when

Alcoholism: Treatable Illness

positive fatherly affection and insight might have found an earlier and better way? An alcoholic may be without family, or his or her alcoholism may have prevented contact with any relatives. When family remains, even though in an area distant from the patient, they may still be brought into the recovery picture. Those assisting the alcoholic to recovery should encourage the patient to contact his or her family and help to seek out and refer family members to an alcoholism center or an Al-Anon Family Group in their own community. The family may not be willing to believe the patient any more, but they might listen to a counsellor, and thus be helped to appreciate their role and later accept referral to local resources.

The patience and emotional support of immediate family members, aided by positive counselling, have resulted in the recovery of many an alcoholic. Through their efforts, many families have been united and otherwise broken homes repaired. Possibly the greatest benefit Al-Anon Family Groups render is the hope provided initially to all those near and dear to the alcoholic, and the understanding and direction family members are thereby enabled to receive. This attitude must precede efforts to "force the alcoholic to recovery." Al-Anon and alcoholism agencies provide a means of educating family members to their role.

Mobilizing the Family

Let us recap some factors essential to recovery. The alcoholic must recover as a whole person, in a whole family and whole community. The guilt, remorse and fear that intensify the illness can seriously deter complete recovery. These feelings are strongest within the family setting. The patient will more easily learn to forgive self, if he or she senses forgiveness in those who mean the most to him or her.

Meaningful and continued sobriety also hinges upon the family's ability to accept the illness concept of alcoholism, both intellectually and emotionally. To that end, the family should work with whatever sources of counselling assistance are available — Al-Anon, an alcoholism agency, a knowledgeable and understanding doctor or clergyman. The family must learn to repudiate feelings of embarrassment, moralism or punishment. This acquired awareness and understanding will enable them to interpret the adverse actions of their alcoholic member as symptoms of the illness without intolerance or rejection.

The spouse and family must not blame themselves for the alcoholic's abnormal drinking, though they may be blamed for it by others. Realizing this, they will not resent the alcoholic's wild conversation, false accusations and deviant behaviour. Such symptoms in an otherwise fine, loving and kindly person, though hard to tolerate, are evidence of the seriousness and the progression of the illness. Often they are the patient's only defence for his or her own self-abasement and bitterness. Pleading, threats, scolding, throwing away the supply, or expecting the alcoholic to stop for love or respect of spouse, children or family are all to no avail.

180

Drinking with the alcoholic only condones and expresses family sanction of the drinking. Recognize, too, that as with any other illness, the family cannot be the doctor. They must seek all the special care required.

Once the onset of the illness is recognized an attempt at treatment is agreed upon; the member(s) approaching the alcoholic should choose the most appropriate and effective time. The person(s) should remain calm, positive and prepared to follow through. When approaching the patient, it is necessary to evidence personal understanding and acceptance, without embarrassment, of alcoholism as an illness, and to recognize that you as a concerned family member have also been at fault in dealing with the problem. Share all the knowledge learned, and, if the alcoholic indicates interest in seeking help, make every effort to initiate treatment promptly and participate with the patient.

Once the patient has begun the recovery process, each member of the family must be a cooperative member of the team; they must indicate faith, trust and affection, and also agree with whatever measures of recovery the alcoholic takes. It is very damaging to disparage the alcoholic for going to A.A. or to a clinic because in your heart you feel he or she "is not that bad yet." Be cautioned also not to be jealous of those who help bring recovery, or to resent the interest and time the alcoholic may give to a recovery program. Never throw up the harsh or unfortunate experiences of the past. Don't allow envy or false pride to create resentment of the alcoholic's new relationships and independence. Do learn to encourage and help the alcoholic to assume his or her rightful family role.

Be forewarned: the alcoholic, suffering from an illness, may relapse. Learn in advance how to cope with this possibility, though without undue fear that it will happen. The relationship with the alcoholic should be one of understanding and firmness, never one of maudlin sympathy, or conversely one of eulogizing his sobriety. After all, the alcoholic is striving for everyday normalcy. Don't hide drinks because you have an alcoholic in the family. Let the patient make his or her own decisions, thus eliminating fear and distrust. In like manner, allow the alcoholic to tell whomever he will about his problem himself. The family should never "post signs" with everyone about "not drinking."

While leaving the alcoholic on his own and allowing him or her to assume responsibility, be willing to share the relearning process. Recognize, approve of and express gratification and pleasure with the improving recovery, and do indicate affection, without babying or being overly protective. This will help to restore the alcoholic's confidence and regenerate faith in self. Initially, the abstinent alcoholic will be irritable and tense as he or she gives up the crutch of alcohol, so try to establish a warm and tension-free atmosphere in the home. Encourage and join in new outlets and interests. By all means jointly participate in continuing recovery activities. Comparisons with others or unwarranted demands, materially or socially, are out. Be happy and satisfied with the progress made.

The alcoholic who enjoys the complete understanding and cooperation of an aware family has a much better chance of making a complete recovery. By sharing the happiness of recovery together, the family learns to laugh again, to appreciate life, and usually to enjoy a relationship they never knew before. This inevitably happens when all the family resources are mobilized as a team to work in unison with a loved one suffering from any illness. After the despair of alcoholism, these feelings are magnified many times over.

20. Role of Other Collaterals

First inquiries regarding alcoholics are often initiated by people other than the alcoholic or the family and may be made by one or more of several sources. Increasing knowledge and interest among those who regularly deal with problem drinking situations are enabling them to take an aware or knowledgeable approach to the alcoholic with gratifying results. Though in the past an employer, doctor or clergyman might give up in despair, now each is learning that as a member of a team working in harmony with the family and other resources, recoveries of once seemingly hopeless cases can be achieved.

Foremost among these contacts are: medical resources, employers, lawyers, clergymen and related alcoholism agencies. An employer may seek the advice of the company physician or nurse in handling an alcoholic employee; a clergyman might seek guidance from an alcoholism agency about a family in his congregation; a visiting nurse might seek the advice and assistance of an A.A. friend about a home where she is calling. All inquiries may be made to outside resources by interested people other than the patient or family and without their knowledge. While there are many avenues of initial approach, we will emphasize the medical and employee resources related to the recovery of alcoholics; less will be said about other contacts of equal importance who should follow a similar approach.

The Medical Profession

Traditionally, the medical profession was frustrated by alcoholics. Setting them apart as "untreatable," it formerly did little to improve individual attitudes, in spite of official admonitions to Medical Association members to take a more objective look at the care and treatment of alcoholic patients. The neglect — even rejection — of alcoholics by medicine is not justified, given our current understanding of the concept of alcoholism "as a treatable illness."

As reported in the early '80s by Joseph Skom, Chairman of the ad hoc Committee on Dangerous Drugs of the American Medical Association (AMA):

Public action must be taken to force medical schools to include courses on alcoholism and drug abuse because all professional efforts for change have failed.

Alcoholism: Treatable Illness

Dr. Skom said his organization "for the past 15 years has petitioned (U.S.) medical schools to provide the time for alcoholism and drug abuse (training) and we have been unsuccessful. The only success has come about through the career teachers in the sense it has been an infiltration into the schools of people who are interested in doing this."

Dr. Skom told the National Conference on Prescription Drug Misuse, Abuse and Diversion that the only way now "is for public pressure and public demands to make medical schools respond. They certainly have not been responsive to attempts by organized medicine or by specialty groups."[1]

Though there is still reticence at the grassroots levels to becoming involved, more and more of the medical association hierarchies are acknowledging and responding affirmatively to the need for action on their part. One major improvement is a beginning in teaching and orientation about alcoholism within the academic mainstreams of medical faculties. Even more important is the growing movement to initiate IMPAIRED PHYSICIAN PROGRAMS to reach and bring to recovery alcoholic physicians.

All the resources of medicine — doctors, psychiatrists, nurses, hospitals and healing institutions — play a critical role in the recovery process. It is essential that they realize alcoholics are not the stereotyped image all too many segments of society still label them to be. Every facet of medicine regularly deals with alcoholic patients, though medical personnel often blind themselves to this fact. Selective care is provided for patients that "can't easily be refused" — with their treatment handled under the guise of more respectable and acceptable captions. Eminent physicians and psychiatrists are treating alcoholics and are accomplishing meaningful results, and thus repudiating the myths that have surrounded medicine's relationship to treatment.

Every medical counsellor is in an advantageous position to establish a solid medical-patient relationship. Most patients seek advice and guidance during early stages of their alcoholism, though not recognizing the relationship of their problems — hangovers, nervousness, inability to eat or sleep, upsets in the family and the like — to their drinking. During routine questioning, most physicians gloss over the patient's drinking history because of social attitudes about alcoholism and unwillingness to brand a patient an alcoholic.

More often than not, an alcoholic, seeing a physician or psychiatrist, will by design only appear when sober. Thus they are able to fool or manipulate their doctors. Oh, they might admit to taking a few, might even say, "Forgive me today, I drank too much last night and have a hangover, don't let it influence you." Unless astute, aware and knowledgeable about the illness, doctors can be taken in, though they wonder why their patients don't get well or do as they are told. With the progress made today, with the literature, advice and cooperation available, there is no longer justification for any medical resource to refuse to accept responsibility in an overall approach to the treatment of the alcoholic.

Many an alcoholic seeking a doctor's advice is told, "Lay off the hard stuff." Every doctor has the opportunity to learn that alcohol might be the number one problem, and that a period of abstinence would enable him or her to diagnose better the other ills present. An honest and thorough discussion would save them both discomfort and wasted time, and would assist in effecting recovery. The physician might also learn that a family member's disorders could be related to the problem drinker, and might recognize other symptoms noted in the *Phases of Alcoholism*. The approach to a patient must avoid moralism, preaching and condemnation. The facts to be presented are always the same.

By reaffirming the patient's worth as a person, and by evidencing awareness and understanding, the medical contact strengthens a relationship with the patient. A doctor may counter, "But this takes a lot of my time!" Perhaps so, but if the interview is handled properly once or twice it may initiate immediate therapy and prevent countless other wasted calls while achieving recovery for the patient. Is this not the aim of the practice of medicine?

A doctor's willingness to open-mindedly discuss the personal area of a patient's life in itself may give the patient the encouragement and knowledge necessary to face up to making a decision about his or her illness. A positive attitude is demonstrated and the patient's motivation aided by establishing follow-up appointments. Enough has already been said about the use of labels in this process. Every consideration should be given to the patient's other ills. He or she may be suffering from another serious ailment long unattended. The doctor's ability to view the patient in an unbiased way, without labels and preconceptions, is therefore a key in recognizing symptoms that may well have gone unnoticed previously.

With sound medical practice and care, *most patients do not require inpatient treatment*. However, when it is indicated, it should be provided with the same efficiency and thoroughness as in other illnesses and without camouflage: hospitalize an alcoholic, as an alcoholic, for alcoholism. When everyone concerned with the patient takes this approach, the patient can more readily be led to make it unanimous.

With the patient's knowledge, involve the family and any other collaterals required. Advise the spouse of his or her role and of the need to curtail his or her drinking while the patient attains sobriety. Explain that initial medical assistance is but the first rung on the ladder to recovery, and that the doctor can best serve as a member of a total team. Make the patient understand that medical care can prepare a patient for total recovery or simply allow one to get well enough to go on another binge. Seek the patient's permission to immediately call in other treatment resources and personally make necessary follow-up appointments to an alcoholism agency, a

Alcoholism: Treatable Illness

known and carefully chosen Alcoholics Anonymous sponsor, or, where indicated, to a special treatment center for extended care, while encouraging participation by the spouse and family. Follow up the referral with continuing medical checkups — and warn against the misuse of medications. Medications are discussed separately in the chapter entitled "Convalescence and Recovery." Patients can be returned regularly for vitamins or other therapy as a means of continuing counselling.

Whether it is a physician, a psychiatrist, a nurse, any hospital staff member, or the associates of those resources, empathy is the key. The attitude and therapy reflected and demonstrated on initial and continuing contacts is the difference between success or failure. The language and form of approach taken by any of the resources of medicine is almost identical. Psychiatrists do well to recognize that alcoholism is a multi-ailment illness, physical, emotional, social and spiritual, rather than to emphasize cause and effect. An orderly or receptionist with adverse attitudes can undo and reject all the work of the specialists if allowed to express prejudice or displeasure in their relationship with the alcoholic.

Be forewarned that some alcoholics are seeking an authoritative source, to substantiate that they are not alcoholics. Such an attitude can deter treatment indefinitely. This attitude is adversely bolstered by those doctors who will not let go of a patient or coordinate their efforts with others. One in that category has for several years had a patient (who is never sober) under treatment for depression; another patient, hospitalized seven or eight times in ten months because of drinking, is still being told, "It isn't necessary for you to go to A.A. You aren't really an alcoholic. Your drinking is but a symptom of other serious disorders." At their wit's end, the family doesn't know how to change things.

In another instance, a psychiatrist was called in by the family physician. Concerned by the family's complaints, the doctor checked with the psychiatrist and was greeted with considerable hostility for interfering. This is not to minimize the importance of professional roles; rather it is to question why the best means of treatment are not more generally utilized by all members of organized medicine, rather than by an understanding minority.

Perhaps I seem overly hard on the psychiatric profession. It is certainly not my intent to discredit the meaningful contribution many make in this field. Personally, I owe a great deal to this profession. Exemplified by the late Doctors Harry Tiebout, Karl and William Meninger, Ruth Fox, James Hurley, Julius Guild, Nelson Bradley and many others too numerous to mention, individual psychiatrists have cooperated closely with Alcoholics Anonymous and other available resources. Many have gone the extra mile when others refused to help any longer.

Take the case of an alcoholic who for years was in and out of A.A. groups and alcoholism clinics. He had visited every worthwhile private facility. On the occasion of his last drinking bout, a consultant psychiatrist made it his business to visit the patient several evenings in a row. Long after all patients were bedded down, the doctor talked informally with this alcoholic. Gaining the patient's ear and confidence, he strove to instill motivation and helped the alcoholic regenerate some faith and dignity in himself. Perhaps the way had been paved, and the patient softened up by his own desperation. Nevertheless, this alcoholic, now well recovered and happily sober, still wonders how a man of that doctor's eminence could and would take the time, after hours, to visit with him, a hopeless drunk, with never a belittling word or disparaging label. That psychiatrist understood that the patient was a sick alcoholic, desperately in need of a friend first, and of a doctor.

It has been my experience to work closely with many doctors, psychiatrists, nurses, hospitals and institutions, and to find that once medical resources are oriented to their role, most are more than willing to cooperate. All medical contacts need to be reassured they will not be adversely used and imposed on. One must respect the demands already being made upon the capable members of these professions and recognize that there are channels of communication and procedure which of necessity must be followed. This is especially so in hospitalizing patients.

More and more general hospitals are beginning to include professional counselling for social service needs. Working in harmony with the hospital staff, alcoholism counsellors have been used with most effective results. Where not available, an "on call" list of recovered alcoholic counsellors can fill the same role. Some now provide intervention services for patients who, though hospitalized for other ills, are also found to be serious dependency cases. Of course, too, there are today some very excellent private resources or centers specializing in the care of those dependent upon alcohol or other drugs. Most state and provincial official programs also conduct a spectrum of services.

It is unfortunate that medicine as a whole is often criticized for being unwilling to share in the responsibility for treating alcoholics. While this profession also has its extremists and opportunists, much of the responsibility for achieving the cooperation of medical resources rests with those charged with the obligation of developing educational services, professional orientation and training and community rapport. The support the profession has always rendered the efforts of the programming of which I have been a part justifies this statement.

When a spouse sees a doctor about an alcoholism problem in the home, the doctor should be prepared to suggest the same approach outlined earlier, and to recommend and encourage a counselling session with both the patient and the spouse. The doctor may already know the case well, having treated the alcoholic in the office or at home. If the doctor achieves a "counselling session," an appointment personally arranged with another resource will be especially effective as a strategy offered by him. Most doctors know a few former patients or friends who, as stable recovered alcoholics, are available for help in such situations. As a

Alcoholism: Treatable Illness

medical person the doctor can frankly discuss the medical aspects of the illness, while refraining from emphasizing the "evils of drink." A few well-chosen questions can open up the potential areas of concern. Having both the spouse and the alcoholic in attendance prevents covering up or procrastination.

A friend, who had been drinking extensively, called the other day to advise he was going to see his doctor. Pleased, I suggested it was an opportune time to discuss his and his wife's growing concern over his heavy drinking. He replied, "George, I play golf and drink with my doctor! Now you know I won't level with him, and he won't embarrass me!"

In similar fashion, a female alcoholic, finding it very difficult to establish meaningful and constant sobriety, was referred by her family physician to a psychiatrist. In virtually the same way as my other friend, she told me, "George, I can talk with you about my drinking but all this guy wants to talk about is my sex life! He ignores my drinking, so I will see him to please everybody else and forget it till the next time I have to go."

A doctor who has the humility to be willing to take, or at least try, a different approach might be surprised at the results. He might suggest: "You know alcohol plays a more serious and critical role in many of our ills than we realize. Unfortunately, because of social attitudes about it we tend to ignore or minimize our drinking. Many problems that seem to be emotional disturbances on the surface are attributable to the overuse of alcohol. The manifestations that you and others like you sometimes indicate are symptoms of several kinds of ailments, one of which might be alcoholism. Now to be honest with you and to do justice to your complete treatment, I want you to collaborate with me on a program of sobriety, so we can make a proper decision. If it is alcoholism, many of the symptoms you now show of other serious disorders may all disappear. I can only work with you if we are honest with each other and try every possible avenue of assistance. This is a major one. Alcoholism is an illness, you know, and much more prevalent and serious than most of us realize. Nevertheless it is a decision which, as we learn about it together, you will have to make for yourself."

This generic approach will serve any medical contact in any setting: across a desk in an office, in a hospital or institution, at home, or wherever the patient is seen. The degree of the patient's illness dictates the firmness or decisiveness of the approach. The nature of other ills will also determine the degree of other care required — after the veneer of alcohol is removed. If alcoholism is indicated, even in its earliest stages, the medical practitioner must fit the patient into all the other resources available, and as a doctor, continue his or her role as a member of an all important team.

A student once asked the late Dr. Jellinek if psychiatry alone would enable a patient to recover. His reply is a classic: "If the alcoholic had the means to retain a psychiatrist full-time, and if the psychiatrist was willing to devote all of his energies and time, perhaps to a few patients (even then each would disrupt the other), such a means of recovery might be possible.'' In view of Dr. Jellinek's initiation to this field, beginning during his work with schizophrenics, this presents an interesting and positive viewpoint.

In another instance, Dr. Jellinek was questioned on the best role for a psychiatrist to take in the treatment of alcoholics. He replied that, in his opinion, "Alcoholics should initially be approached with the warmest and simplest of supportive therapy, without undue probing or deep therapy. As most alcoholics achieve sobriety many false impressions disappear and any latent or basic problems become evident. Psychiatry at the proper time could later prevent the alcoholic from relapsing.''

Alcoholics should continue a relationship with their medical contacts, thus ensuring complete and adequate care for all ills as they become evident. Similarly, patients receiving treatment for other ills, where evident, should receive priority treatment for the alcoholism.

When problem drinking has progressed to a point in any patient when it is the number one problem, it is impossible to treat successfully any of the other ills the patient may evidence, physical or mental, without dealing initially with the alcoholism.

Nurses may play an especially significant part, whether in a hospital, in a home visiting service, in industry, in schools, as public health nurses or teachers, in institutions, and in all of their many roles. You will recall my own expressed indebtedness to the nursing profession — hence I am prejudiced! To me, a nurse offers an avenue of help no other member of the medical professions can fill. The average unassuming nurse, friendly, warm and kindly, is a natural confidant. People will talk to nurses when they will not confide in their families, doctor, clergyman or anyone else.

Some of the soundest employee recovery or assistance programs in force today came about as the result of occupational nurses. One in particular in the midwestern plant of an international organization inaugurated programming for alcoholics, in spite of the adverse attitude of an alcoholic superintendent. In later years, that company helped develop and support widespread programming, both within the company and in the communities in which they operated. In another instance, a nurse in a brewery initiated referrals to a clinic, worked closely with Alcoholics Anonymous, and kept track of the patients' activities, group counselling and families.

Nurses attached to health, welfare and rehabilitation agencies may collaborate with other workers who visit homes in line with their duties. Aware and knowledgeable about alcoholism, they may then initiate referrals for both the

Alcoholism: Treatable Illness

spouse and the alcoholic. A nurse in a welfare setting carried on education and intervention programming and personally took her patients to clinics or A.A. As a result of her efforts, the whole department was better oriented and much more effective.

School nurses are regularly in contact with the problem drinking situation, especially with the growing number of teenage problem drinkers. They learn of cases in which problem drinking seriously affects the stability, security and progress of students of all ages. They can provide direction and guidance in such situations, and where necessary, instigate coercive measures to deal with the problem.

A high school nurse, disturbed at the behaviour of a student, visited with him and learned about the alcoholism in the home. She arranged to provide him with tutoring and guidance, and after visiting the home, she called in special help. She got the cooperation of the father's employer and bit by bit she put the whole family back together. Gratified with the results, she made a study in the school and soon found more cases that she could handle alone.

A nurse is less threatening to patients. Her position, uniform and reputation demand subconscious respect; thus she is a key figure in every area of treatment. Nurses make ideal counsellors, receptionists and follow-up workers, and are often more capable than workers from other disciplines. Visiting nurses regularly walk into problem drinking situations involving every aspect of family and community concern. Oriented to the illness, trained and knowledgeable in the procedures to follow, and permitted to deal with alcohol problems, the nurse is of immeasurable value in our fight against alcoholism.

The Teaching Profession

Teachers and guidance counsellors can play a unique collateral role in an overall approach to alcoholism. Essentially, they are in a similar position to the school nurse. Those with feeling soon discern the conflicts and problems that disturb the well-being and learning motivation of their charges.

However, before teachers, individually or collectively, can make a positive contribution, they must be aware, knowledgeable and understanding of the illness with which they are dealing. Unbiased courses about alcoholism should be a part of their academic pattern, extension and refresher courses, their seminars, and the innumerable programs in which they participate.

In all too many instances a teacher's exposure to learning about alcohol problems and alcoholism is the result of hearing a prejudiced presentation in the classroom. Today this need no longer be the case, and more widespread use should be made of the alcoholism resources available.

Teachers cannot avoid knowing about, or neglect corrective action towards, the drinking habits of their students. Nor can they ignore the problem drinking situations of the parents which adversely affect the students' schooling. A knowledgeable approach to this more adult social behaviour is important to the well-being and progress of students. Above all else, teachers through personal example can do much to set and teach acceptable mores. After all, teachers are recognized as acceptable role models whom students watch and imitate. This is a preventive role which should be fitted into an overall approach to this illness.

Business, Industry and Labour

A number of years ago, the personnel services director of a large manufacturing company was preparing to address several hundred members of a medical association. It was mid-morning. As he was being introduced, a fine looking, impeccably dressed man wended his way down the middle aisle, intent on reaching the safety of an empty front chair. Blind to reproving glances and stoutly warding off the restraining hands of shocked associates, he resolutely made his way down that silent gauntlet. Then he fell flat on his face.

The timing was perfect, for the speaker had been standing just a few moments, awaiting the outcome of this momentary drama. Then, forcefully, but with a manner and tone that expressed complete understanding, he said, "Ladies and gentlemen, that is an example of what we are going to talk about!" His topic was "Alcoholism in Industry." Had the real-life drama been so planned, it could not have had more impact or been better staged.

The leadership and positive approach toward alcoholism taken by business, industry, labour and the civil and military authorities has provided a major breakthrough toward achieving the recognition and acceptance of alcoholism as a treatable illness. Acknowledging hard facts and dollar-and-cent values, they have influenced medicine, community programming and personnel education. The efforts of industrial medical directors in such organizations as Allis-Chalmers, Canadian Bell Telephone, the Canadian Labour Congress, E.I. DuPont, Eastman Kodak, Great Northern Railway, International Harvester and many others, have served to prove the merit of the concrete programming initiated.

The services within organizations such as these, encompassing as they do internal medical and intervention programs, widen the horizons of their activities to include other treatment disciplines, with far-reaching results for all concerned. Several well-known labour leaders have stimulated sound and basic policies for the education and treatment of employees. The understanding and cooperation of business, industry and labour are essential to the success of the employee alcoholism programming which has been developed to date.

The occupational physician and nurse, working in close cooperation with management and personnel services, are thus able not only to salvage advanced and serious cases of alcoholism, but to reach early stage problem drinkers with

Alcoholism: Treatable Illness

appropriate prevention strategies. The availability of proper programming, without embarrassing or maligning the employee, attracts voluntary requests for help from the patient or his family.

In a community in which several occupational programs are active, a judge refers alcoholics in his lineup to the personnel counsellors of the companies which employ them. The judge found he could thus establish an immediate and effective program for the rehabilitation of alcoholics appearing before him. These organizations worked hand-in-hand with other related community resources, including Alcoholics Anonymous, alcoholism clinics, and the health and welfare agencies. While we often hear about the costs, we know very little about the savings of such progressive efforts.

The approach to the alcoholic taken by the industry or company with its own medical department may follow the procedure outlined for medical collaterals. Smaller organizations, lacking this service, can work closely with available community resources. A program of recovery for alcoholics in smaller businesses and industry may start with the owner, manager, superintendent or personnel officer.

An effective approach to the alcoholic employee that has gained increasing recognition is the use by business, industry, labour and government of "Employee Assistance Programs." Concern over the fact that alcoholics and other troubled employees were not discovered or helped until the severity of their problems made such help more difficult led to the initial development of "broad brush" employee assistance programs.

Although alcoholism is a major and costly concern, employees often have other problems that cause them to be personally less productive, while having an adverse effect on the performance of their associates. Recognizing this, special programs were designed to help employees with a variety of problems — marital, financial, legal, alcohol and/or medical. A well-documented advantage to this kind of program, *where confidentiality is assured*, is the opportunity it affords for employees to refer themselves to the program, and for those close to them to seek guidance without fear of discovery or embarrassment. This kind of program, based on the premise that everyone has problems once in a while, is less stigmatizing to the individual and is subsequently used by all levels of employees, executives as well as line workers. Most programs work closely with community services and use a wide range of helping resources, so whatever the problem, help is available. Moreover, help is available not only for the employee but also for members of his or her family. A serious problem at home has reflected in the work of more than one employee.

By emphasizing job performance, these "employee assistance programs" encourage the supervisor not to get involved in the cause of an employee's problem, but to deal only with the results upon the employee's job performance and to refer the individual to the recovery services available. It is entirely up to the employee whether or not he or she chooses to use the program; its use is totally confidential.

A well-run program will offer periodic training to acquaint supervisors with the services offered, program benefits, effective ways to utilize the program, and proper employee referral procedures. A supervisor, faced with a troubled employee, might deal with the situation in the following manner: "Jack, we seem to have a problem. I've come to know you as a competent and conscientious worker, but in the last six months your work just isn't up to the quality you've maintained in the past. You call in sick often, and you are late a good deal of the time.

"You may say that it is a personal problem, and that you can handle it yourself. That may well be; however, we all need help with our problems once in a while.

"Now, telling me your problems isn't going to help either of us. I don't have the training to help you. But, Jack, you know our company has a program to help in just such a case as this, 'Employee Assistance Program.' They can help you with your problems, and the services are confidential. I won't be told anything about your problems. If you need any special help or time off, the company and the program can make those arrangements.

"I can't force you to go, Jack. That is entirely up to you. But your work problem is also my problem. If you choose not to go and your job performance doesn't improve, I will have no choice but to proceed according to company policy.

"I hope that you will take advantage of this opportunity, Jack. I've come to depend on the skills and expertise that you can deliver." Certainly this approach is better than the "perform or get out" approach that was once considered the proper response to this and similar situations!

When employees are given the opportunity for professional advice and help, some surprising results have occurred. Early on, the Director of Employee Assistance Consultation for the Hazelden Foundation, a widely known and successful treatment center north of Minneapolis, Minnesota, once said to me, "One of the most interesting results we are finding is that when people come in for help with various problems, a goodly portion of them, when carefully evaluated by our assessment staff, are found to have their problems directly related to alcohol abuse. Their major problem is alcohol, which as we all know, causes a host of other problems." Today Hazelden serves as consultant to E.A.P.'s worldwide.

This is perhaps one of the greatest advantages of Employee Assistance Programs. The fact that people will seek help for many other problems rather than alcohol is a further illustration of the strength of the denial system. Because these people will seek help for other problems, an Employee Assistance Program offers a chance for professionals to intervene much earlier in the progress of the illness and to better determine if the problem really is the abuse of beverage alcohol.

When intervention into serious problems, especially alcoholism, occurs early,

Alcoholism: Treatable Illness

employees, employer and society all benefit. Concrete economic benefits are reaped by the employer and society in general, when skilled, productive employees are salvaged and become an asset to themselves.

Conjunctive with recognition of the employer as a vital collateral in coping with problem-drinking situations, is the manner of dealing with applications from recovering or recovered alcoholics. It is critical to the patient's recovery that he be received well and his hopes not immediately dashed by an inference that he is "a no good drunk." The employer, aware of the practical and productive benefits possible through the employment of recovered alcoholics, should develop a positive basis of dealing with their applications. This is a two-way street. Policy and procedure are the same for management, personnel services and labour. Unions, with the responsibility of referring members to jobs, serve in the role of employer.

New employees always include some alcoholics. Though an individual has been terminated for alcoholism, references may not indicate problem drinking. Sound personnel practices usually ferret out this information eventually, or it may only be suspected that something is wrong. For example, take a man applying for an average position. His application notes he has held excellent positions or has been self-employed. A credit report might show instability, a bankruptcy, the loss of family and other positions, and possibly a period of unaccountable unemployment. If submitted without reasonable explanation, the man is automatically rejected. Several reasons are to be considered, including possible alcoholism. Though the man's abilities are desperately needed, it may be deemed safer not to take a chance.

Conversely, the alcoholic must realize that personnel investigative procedures will enable a potential employer to learn more about one's drinking than he or she knows. A recovered alcoholic should be helped to appreciate the employer's viewpoint and, when seeking a position, should be the first to acknowledge the reasons for his vocational decline. An alcoholic is a pretty safe bet when he personally volunteers: "You will find my work record sound and productive, and my abilities perhaps better than average; however, you may also find my stability questionable. You see, I was a practising alcoholic. I now know my problem and am doing something about it." If circumstances warrant, the alcoholic could add: "I have gone to a clinic and am active in A.A., and if you wish a personal reference, I will grant them permission to tell you how I'm doing."

I remember the case of a man who, during the war years, left an institution and started over again on a labour crew with one of North America's largest organizations. He had once been district superintendent of a banking chain. Family, position, everything was gone when he entered the institution to begin the process of recovery. On his application, he filled in everything, past work history, the whole score, but added the following: "...lost everything due to alcoholism — am starting over and am sober." He became supervisor of all the financial affairs of that organization, with about twenty years of sobriety behind him before his death from a heart attack.

Another alcoholic, once the manager of an organization, applied for a salesman's position. His family had stuck with him and gone to the bottom, too. When this man entered A.A., they were down to apple and orange crates for furniture. In his interview, he stated, "I think I am a good man. If I stay sober in my new-found program of recovery, I will make you the best employee you have. If I don't, you will have lost nothing because you terminate me with drink number one." He became their sales manager.

Every alcoholic, by expressing honestly his own position, clears the deck for himself. If he announces his own problems, no boss can ever accuse him of hiding anything if other employees raise the question, "Do you know what and whom you hired?" At the same time, if the alcoholic, having declared himself and his problem, is rejected, he is fortunate to find that out because as an alcoholic he should never be employed by or work with someone prejudiced against his illness, and he should know it right away.

A recovering alcoholic recently proved this principle to his own satisfaction. A capable, personable and well educated young man, his alcoholism cost him a lucrative business, a lovely family and accepted status in the community. His drinking caused him to have a "dead work period" of two years. After a history of several commission sales positions and a number of relapses, he finally determined he had to start over properly. He took counselling, got into an A.A. group, and went after permanent employment. He became resentful over the attitude of those to whom he applied for work and their apparent rejection. His counsellor admonished him to return to these employers and lay his cards on the table.

The reaction of each was the same. His disclosure explained the blank period and the reasons for which a man of his apparent background was seeking to start over. Every potential employer was understanding, interested and sympathetic to this approach. They realized no guarantee could be given for his continued sobriety — but they were willing to cooperate. The alcoholic is a new man. As he expressed it, "It is as if the whole weight of the world is off my shoulders." His burst of honesty was rewarded with firm offers of three jobs. One employer said, "You'll be right at home here. I haven't had a drink in over a year, and the top man has been sober for nine years!"

Alcoholism rehabilitative services and programs for business, industry and labour together represent one of the most important facets of activity in this field. Much more could and should be said about the role of these collaterals in the treatment of the alcoholic employee. While limitations of this text will not permit the attention this topic deserves, there is a growing library of alcoholism literature, together with excellent consultant resources, available through Alcoholics

Alcoholism: Treatable Illness

Anonymous, The National Council of Alcoholism, The Rutgers Center of Alcohol Studies, the Hazelden Foundation, the Christopher D. Smithers Foundation, and most provincial and state alcoholism agencies.

The Clergy

Clergymen, though sometimes biased by the teaching and precepts of their religions, are important members of the total treatment team. During the early phases of the progression of the illness, the alcoholic, smitten by remorse, may seek pastoral counselling. If rejected by a moralistic blast, antipathy or a self-righteous attitude, the alcoholic's guilt is further increased and may result in the rejection of religion. Remember, the last symptom felt by chronic alcoholics in the desperate final stages of their illness is a vague sense of spiritual need. This conscious or subconscious yearning for help and comfort, or perhaps forgiveness, can be the spark which, if nurtured properly, will achieve recovery.

Having seen the return of many prodigals, and as the result of new awareness, most religious denominations have seriously re-evaluated their positions in dealing with the problems of alcohol. Courses are offered to help orient the clergy to their sphere of responsibility, good examples of which are the North Conway Conference, the Hazelden Clergy Training Program, and pastoral counselling sessions of Rutgers Summer School on Alcohol Studies. Splendid materials on pastoral counselling interpreting the morality of drinking, drunkenness and alcoholism are available. Clergymen and priests should seek every opportunity to make themselves familiar with the medical and social factors of alcoholism, as this illness represents one of the most serious but neglected concerns of the ministry.

As with the doctor, the clergyman's contribution demands honest and sound motivation. The clergyman can say, "I'm glad you came to me, and I do understand your need. I'll do everything I can to help you. The first thing to learn about your kind of drinking is that willpower, morals or religion alone can't help control alcoholism. It is an illness — not a weakness. Moral obligations are involved, but that comes later. First you must appreciate that you are a person who shouldn't drink. An alcoholic is not bad, or immoral, but is a person who drinks compulsively, losing control without knowing how or why — that is the sickness part of it."

The clergyman should then give the alcoholic every opportunity to unburden and be helped to realize the import of the illness and be guided to forgive self. Strengthened and reassured, the alcoholic can better cope decisively with the drinking. The minister might add: "First you need medical attention, and then you are going to need someone who understands this problem from A to Z. These needs I will personally assist you with as soon as you are physically well and comfortable; then, if you wish, we'll tackle your spiritual worries. Now let's go together to a doctor (clinic or center) who will start things off for you."

The clergyman should make the appointment and be willing to accompany the alcoholic to that initial referral. Empathy and friendship will do more than a thousand words and are a great deal better than saying, "Yes, you need help, let's kneel and pray." At that point, the alcoholic may need a drink to keep from falling apart! As stated by the Rev. John C. Ford, S.J., former professor of Moral Theology, Catholic University, Washington, D.C., an eminent authority on this subject, "One must never approach an alcoholic on the basis of what is usually called morality. Anyone who has dealt in an insightful manner with even one alcoholic can vouch for the validity of this statement and practise. On a practical and therapeutic basis, to preach at or to moralize with an alcoholic is the ultimate in counselling futility."

In addition, the clergyman should offer to help the family. "I'll visit your wife, husband or family, help them to understand and get started on a program with you. We'll lick this thing together. Remember, call me at any time." He then goes through the same process with the family. It takes a big person to recognize a limited role. Doing little things with the alcoholic will give him trust and confidence.

Chaplains of hospitals and institutions play a vital and unique part in any recovery program when used as team counsellors. Their training, experience and services are invaluable. Many clergymen have provided exceptional leadership in developing programming on alcoholism. Those conducting church seminars, retreats and missions can reach a large number of alcoholics if their presentation is knowledgeable and understanding, and not moralistic. All church personnel have a particular responsibility to help alcoholics and their families.

Many members of the clergy — both as non-alcoholics and as themselves recovered alcoholics — have served as excellent counsellors, aiding alcoholics in Alcoholics Anonymous to take their fourth and fifth Steps.

The pastor of a large metropolitan congregation was moved to another community. His understanding had attracted a number of A.A. groups to use the facilities of that church. The congregation numbered many reunited and recovered families. The pastor's counselling of alcoholics made his contribution to that church immeasurable.

A newly appointed pastor, on learning that A.A. groups regularly met in one of the church studies, questioned this privilege and took measures to make their continued stay unwelcome. The groups moved, and the church lost some of its leading workers and parishioners.

During a public seminar on alcoholism, one of the panels discussed the spiritual side of recovery. A lady in the audience asked, "Wouldn't a good basic foundation in one's religion save an alcoholic?" One of the panelists, a young priest, replied, "Well, I'm not so sure. I do know that a fine Protestant chaplain brought me, a Catholic priest, recovery, and I later learned that he was helped to his sobriety through the efforts of a friendly rabbi! When people are ill, God or such

Alcoholism: Treatable Illness

'Being' as the individual recognizes is closer than one's religion, but religion may keep that person closer to his God."

There are several precautions the ministry must recognize. An "eager-beaver" pastor in a community lacking alcoholism treatment resources, though able to do many things (including sponsoring an A.A. group), should always keep his own role uppermost in mind and know when to retire from the scene. Similarly, a recovered alcoholic cleric must use diplomacy and tact and not suddenly want to save the world, or else he will lose contact with reality. More importantly, it is necessary for every clergyman to remain a working part of a total team. It is not unusual, even for a recovered person successful in his own struggle and perhaps with others, to wonder suddenly, "Isn't this really a clergyman's job? Why must an agency or A.A. group be used? If I am a good minister of my faith, isn't this supposed to be my calling?" He takes over and plays God to all people in all things. The results are disappointing, the resentments many and deep — and much work must be done all over again.

An aware, knowledgeable and understanding member of the ministry can be an instrument, not only of achieving an alcoholic's sobriety and complete recovery as a whole person, but also of helping the alcoholic and those close to him or her achieve the serenity of spiritual peace. Among some of the finest recoveries from alcoholism are members of the clergy of all denominations, who found in the simplicity, hope and faith of Alcoholics Anonymous their own sobriety. As a result, they bring to the struggle against alcoholism a new and effective tool — an understanding of human weakness, sickness and recovery.

A Case for the Legal Profession

The varied collaterals represented under legal contacts have a significant relationship to the whole spectrum of alcohol-related problems. Dealing primarily with the abuse, misuse and overuse, legally and illegally, of beverage alcohol, they include: judges and magistrates of all courts; attorneys, lawyers, barristers and solicitors (in North America, each of these, while perhaps a specialist, is still a "lawyer"); the police and special protective agencies (city, state, provincial, military, school, transportation, etc.); sheriffs, FBI, RCMP, vice squads; detective bureaus and special investigators, public and private; and local, national and international policing agents. In addition, there are probation and parole officers and correctional and penal institutions of every type directly involved with the application of legal decisions. This text emphasizes their close relationship to an overall approach to the treatment of alcoholism.

To consider the role legal collaterals play, one should appreciate that their function varies with the alcoholics concerned, who, broadly speaking, fit into three divisions. The first of these categories contains those who are repeatedly faced by the police, courts and institutions. At times, legal aid may be required for the families of these tragic end results of alcoholism.

Second, there is a large group of problem alcoholics who have not advanced to the stage of the first — those who are just beginning to get into trouble. Many are still working with intact families; however, they are reaching the fringe area. Without help, their alcoholism and concomitant problems will mushroom rapidly. At this stage legal counsel is very much in the picture. The alcoholic or the family seeks legal aid to keep from going to jail, to handle debts, to forestall a divorce, to save a home and the like.

The third division, though hidden, is by far the largest. It encompasses those alcoholics and their families, associates and collaterals, who, though in trouble, are usually able to keep things covered up — with the aid of legal profession members.

Presenting the case for the affirmative, remarkable results are being achieved by those members of the legal profession who are aware that alcoholics are in need of other than punitive treatment. The willingness to assist by these potential referral agents is impeded by the lack of uniformity of laws and statutes governing their actions. Little has been done to separate or interpret legal differences among offences of deviant drinking, problems of drunkenness, and alcoholism, thus hampering selective care for those who are not criminals, but sick alcoholics. This is not to protest the detention of those drinkers whose antisocial actions necessitate correction and confinement, for the protection of society as a whole and hopefully the rehabilitation of the offender.

Understanding judges, supervisory police personnel, prosecuting attorneys and probation officers, working individually or (preferably) collectively, interrupt the downward path of many alcoholics before they reach the revolving door stage of the arrest/court/confinement process. Such authorities have contributed to the recovery of alcoholics simply by a stay of proceedings to assess the problem at hand and to begin referral procedures for treatment. Correctional institutions find that rehabilitative procedures of reviewing inmate case histories, followed by alcoholism counselling and group therapy prior to release, reduce the endless return of alcoholics for all types of confinement, criminal and non-criminal.

In several major cities where alcoholism is a problem of acute dimensions, individual judges and members of the police have instituted rehabilitative programs. Concerned by the failures of old methods, these pioneers have introduced "home-made" programs to deal constructively and humanely with alcoholics appearing before them. As sporadic and individual as these services may be, they have been functioning successfully, encouraging others to follow their example. It is a criticism of all levels of government that so frequently rebels going against the accepted officialdom of society must shoulder the responsibility of seeking recovery for the alcoholic. Many of these efforts, A.A.-oriented, receive

Alcoholism: Treatable Illness

little outside assistance. Proving what can be done by those interested in constructive action, they are achieving dramatic results.

Earlier in this text, reference was made to the excellent recoveries being achieved through court programs for convicted drinking and driving offenders. This is one of the most effective countermeasures found to date. Properly presented and operated in cooperation with all local resources and facilities, this service is to the courts and the offender what employee assistance programs are to the employed and employables of society. Other types of court rehabilitation and probation programs offer the same hope of reducing the waste in our judicial and correctional systems.

Years ago, a kind and well-disposed judge took the time to see if something could be done. He would pull case after case out of the lineup, see them in his own chambers, call upon the assistance of members of A.A. and, wherever indicated, refer the alcoholic to a clinic or hospital. Though a non-alcoholic, he probably sponsored more people to sobriety and recovery than any A.A. member in his city. His interest had begun the day a former classmate, a dentist, appeared dishevelled, bewildered and very sick in his Monday morning lineup. The judge and the dentist began the first A.A. group in that city more than forty years ago. Many such judges heroically continue to fight the antiquity, waste and costliness of so many of the present systems of treatment and referral in various jurisdictions.

The establishment of special judges and courts with the responsibility of determining sound procedures for all alcoholics and addicts merits consideration in larger cities. As well as providing a special service, such courts relieve others of problems which they are ill-prepared to handle. Their effectiveness is dependent upon the personnel involved and the available cooperation of all other resources.

In such settings, the alcoholic — at the discretion of the special court — may be guided to accept care voluntarily, or he may be put on probation, have his sentence suspended (depending upon the offence charged), have his case adjourned, or be remanded and directed to seek treatment. The related resources of other legal mechanisms and of health, welfare and rehabilitation agencies may be required and applied in a coordinated, positive and effective manner. This overall procedure can work with any of the levels encompassed in the three divisions described. All such services at every level of society must be performed with the dignity and rights of the individual uppermost in mind. Thus, the system can offer protection in matters of personal status, relationships with family, employment and community, and can introduce the alcoholic to therapy without undue embarrassment or resentment.

However, it must be noted that this proposed separate court structure does not attempt to speak to or deal with legal aspects of third party damage caused by drinking. Neither, under our legal system, can the alcoholic remove himself from the ambit of legislation expressly intended to focus on the consequences of his behaviour. So, the alcoholic who drinks and drives would, in most jurisdictions, remain just as liable to criminal prosecution for something like vehicular homicide or criminal negligence causing death, or other appropriate charges. Similarly, if an injured party launches a civil action for damages caused by the alcoholic while he was intoxicated, *and that party proves his case to the standard required in the jurisdiction*, the existence of a separate or special court with special powers would not of itself shift the liability from the alcoholic unless the facts of a particular case so warranted. The author would emphasize that in his opinion, the use, overuse or abuse of alcohol should never be deemed an excuse or a defence against any unacceptable behaviour or criminal act, notwithstanding that members of the legal profession, in defending their clients, often use drunkenness as a defence with respect to the question of criminal intent.

In communities where special services exist and are aided by broad alcohol education, understanding and cooperative police are a valuable ally. Orientation courses on alcoholism as a part of police training effect early and sound referrals for treatment. A community where such training was accomplished found it was not unusual for a squad car to arrive at the clinic with an unpretentious citizen in need of help, for a police officer to request assistance for someone in a hotel or for the officer to take an alcoholic to A.A. Police with this orientation might detain an inebriate for his own protection and then call a counsellor for guidance to treat him, without finding it necessary to lay a charge or make an arrest. As a result of this initial procedure, among many others, a clergyman, a doctor and the president of a company are now recovered alcoholics.

This background will also prevent serious mistakes. It enables a protective agency to use good judgment and to differentiate between apparent intoxication and other ills. A detective, summoned to a hotel to arrest a seemingly intoxicated woman, called a doctor. The woman was found to be in a diabetic coma.

Two factors emerge from the exemplary experience of such members of the legal profession and the protection/enforcement communities. The first has preventive implications. During early arrests and court appearances, proper screening, investigation, direction and therapy would reduce the numbers continuing the progressive path of alcoholism, thus salvaging many alcoholics while they still retain family and most physical, emotional and social assets. Secondly, a humane and sound policy and procedure in dealing with repetitive alcoholic cases utilizing the resources of all legal collaterals controls better the numbers of and costs incurred in connection with those trapped on the treadmill of alcoholism.

Recognizing this responsibility, members of the legal profession in the United States have achieved far-reaching decisions through the courts of appeal, which

Alcoholism: Treatable Illness

have ruled that "a chronic alcoholic is not a criminal." These decisions led to federal legislation in support of this dramatic advance in dealing with chronic alcoholism.

Society is also learning that, even among the homeless men and women with chronic alcoholism, some recoveries may be achieved. Their legal referral to institutions capable of providing indeterminate care and special techniques would be a blessing to the alcoholic and family, and would relieve (if not eventually eliminate) the "revolving door" process. The enormity of the economic and social burden this minority group represents repudiates any presumed social and technological advances claimed. It costs many thousands of dollars a year to maintain an offender in a correctional institution.

Over and above the alcoholic problems dealt with openly by legal, protective agents of the community, there are myriads of legal involvements which make no headlines and add up to no official statistics or costs, but which represent a fantastic portion of the alcoholism problem. These hidden cases comprise a cross-section of society: a wife seeking legal advice to protect her own and the children's interests from an alcoholic husband; the businessman with a damaging alcoholic partner; the corporation board trying to sever the contract of an alcoholic executive; the relative seeking legal controls for the protection of children from alcoholic parents; the impaired driver striving to hold a licence. The list is long.

An attorney, who dealt with almost twenty separation and divorce cases involving alcohol in the space of a few months, decided there must be a way of salvaging these marriages. He discussed the situation with several associates and visited an alcoholism clinic. An orientation course was developed for his interested group, and as a result of their new understanding and approach, this group of lawyer-counsellors helped to initiate treatment for the alcoholic partner and saved almost seventy-five percent of their clients' marriages.

Where the well-being and even safety of children is at stake, to allow alcoholism to progress to a hopeless state is itself unethical and criminal. False pride or embarrassment and reluctance to take steps — all hamper positive and intelligent action.

A psychiatrist, a doctor and a lawyer met outside an exclusive home wondering what to do. All were concerned with the individual inside. Their friend, a businessman, was winding up a bender. He had beaten his wife, chased the children with a knife and inflicted considerable damage to the home. As king of his castle he couldn't be touched until he came outside. No one wanted to arrest or commit him. He desperately needed care, for the protection of the family and himself.

Such cases have prompted some socio-medical-legal studies by committees representing these several interests in an effort to establish an acceptable basis of enforced care for like sufferers. All too often, the only recourse is a mental commitment or "common drunk" warrant. In most instances, families are reticent to use these procedures. At best, they provide only custodial and/or protective custody.

Fortunately, increasing attention is being paid by legislators to issues relating to domestic violence and other problems associated with alcohol and drug dependencies. In many jurisdictions there are mechanisms in place which are designed to protect innocent individuals from abusive dependent family members. The procedural mechanisms by which the protection is afforded can sometimes be the death-knell of the family in any event, and this is often appropriate where continuing violent and antisocial behaviour is evident. But there is a real question, in cases where the violence is clearly linked to alcoholism, as to whether the legal and social mechanisms and procedures which often accompany the separation of the abuser from the abused also take into account the possibility that the family and the alcoholic are suffering from an illness and might all be saved. Separation must be effected quickly and quietly when violence is involved; but we must eliminate the presumption that separation must of necessity be permanent in cases where alcoholism is involved, and that the violent perpetrator is violent by nature and should be treated accordingly.

An objective assessment by the law societies of their own responsibilities and roles would reveal a tremendous potential for remedial action, not only for the alcoholics among their clientele, but for the actions of their membership. A growing number of bar associations, recognizing the growing number of dependent drinkers within their own ranks, have instituted counselling, treatment and stress management programs. The profession is becoming more aware of its responsibilities, not only to society, but to its own impaired members. Every lawyer is a vital cog in a total recovery program, both for other members, and for clients. Attracting more participants to the team is the real issue. Effective referrals by legal collaterals of alcoholics requiring treatment is possible with every type of dependency patient. This beginning intervention can lead to eventual recovery of a client as well as to meaningful solutions to family and other problems.

Agencies as Collaterals

A plant superintendent, responsible for the work of several departments, was reputed to have a chronic ulcer condition. His wife also worked, giving them an above average income. Because of the man's chronic condition, excessive absenteeism was excused. One of their youngsters, a problem at school, had been in a number of difficulties; another had run away from home. The plant where the man worked inaugurated an all-out employee assistance program. A personnel service officer, concerned because two shifts were shut down following another ulcer bout by the superintendent, took it upon himself to investigate. He and the occupational nurse found the superintendent and his wife were both alcoholics. The home was run down, the lights cut off, and both were in a drunken stupor. With the assistance of management, several agencies, the local clinic, and Alcoholics Anonymous, the couple achieved sobriety and recovery.

A guidance clinic and the agencies involved with the children had not investigated the alcoholism. The judge and probation officer who had supervised the boy had not been concerned with the parents. The years of absenteeism blamed on the ulcers left much to be desired. This case must have represented a fantastic loss to many people, personally, professionally and economically.

Though community agencies have the greatest number of contacts with problem-drinking situations, the experience of alcoholism programs indicates that both public and private health, welfare and rehabilitative agencies and institutions refer the least number of alcoholic patients to treatment. Two reasons probably predominate for their poor use of specialized alcoholism facilities.

Firstly, these agencies reflect a lack of orientation to alcoholism and its relationship to other ills and disorders of society. Few workers have received any schooling or training in the recognition or care of alcoholics. Until this neglected factor in their education is rectified, the responsibility for such awareness rests with trained alcoholism specialists or alcohologists. The failure to incorporate education on alcoholism into the mainstreams of academic life remains a critical omission.

Secondly, agency workers have the same innate attitudes and prejudices as others, in spite of their social service background. Abetted by a natural wish to protect agency and personal prerogatives, they tackle only their own sphere of interest — and therefore, the treatment of the whole person is neglected or ignored, and one of the agency's most serious concerns also remains unresolved. This should not and need not be so. Many alcoholics and their families regularly cross the paths of all community resources: family service, courts, guidance clinics, welfare and employment bureaus — every operating agency.

Workers may be restricted by existing regulations from openly doing anything about drinking problems. The defence is also made that demands on their services preclude taking the time to study outside problems. "Anyway, there is not much you can do for an alcoholic!" This negative attitude is happily becoming obsolete.

If properly oriented to alcoholism, agency counsellors can coordinate their services with those of alcoholism agencies and Alcoholics Anonymous on a reciprocal basis with mutual benefit. Many such situations, regularly and properly handled through normal community resources, with adequate guidance, would open the door to effective earlier patient referrals. Understandably, the alcoholism facilities involved likewise have a responsibility for intercommunication and interaction. They must be able and willing to accept the suggested referrals. It is damaging indeed to find an alcoholism resource incapable of coping with the referrals developed or an Alcoholics Anonymous group unwilling to cooperate.

To further these interests, a growing number of schools on alcohol studies are providing specific orientation and training to the social services. Well established schools with sound programs are available throughout North America. In addition, specialized literature to meet the needs of each discipline and type of agency service is being published.

Changes in attitude by agency personnel, together with the implied hope and confidence their objective approach suggests, will brush off on both workers and patients; thus, community action is born. This growing ripple of awareness, knowledge and understanding will in itself have both direct and indirect results. All workers will become more willing to make referrals of patients to treatment, and patients will more readily recognize a developing dependency as well as more willingly accept the help offered.

Agencies as collaterals must learn to recognize and acknowledge the importance of their role in dealing with the alcoholic. This is particularly so in the continued care and follow-up of many alcoholics and their families, who, having recovered from the illness alcoholism, urgently require many of the services available through the resources of other community agencies.

Governments, together with dry and wet vested interests, are also agencies. Working cooperatively, they can play a vital role in promoting effective services and in establishing more meaningful and acceptable controls.

The drys and wets could both support education and research and bring pressure to bear to force appropriate authorities to define clearly the problems of alcohol, drunkenness and alcoholism. By removing pressures for or against drinking per se, their correlated efforts could put emphasis on the misuse and dependent use of alcohol, which after all is the major source of conflict for both groups.

Governments, as senior agencies, can play many sound roles. As employers, they can initiate positive referral procedures for their employees, as a personnel function of civil service; initiate and demand proper acceptance and treatment of alcoholic patients in their institutions; establish adequate treatment coverage within employee insurance and other benefits, and develop meaningful policies within health, welfare, rehabilitation and other governmental services.

Such action on the part of senior governments would have a tremendous impact on lesser governments and every public and private agency, while giving impetus and encouragement to all facets of programming.

Anyone Can Be a Collateral

A butcher, concerned by the drinking of one of his best customers, was instrumental in that alcoholic's recovery. For years, he had procured the liquor,

Alcoholism: Treatable Illness

delivered it, and added it to the grocery and meat bill! Being a heavy dependent drinker himself he went along, until things got out of hand; then he sought advice and help for his customer. After some years of sobriety, the patient returned the favour. One day, there stood Mr. Butcher, wanting to know how the recovery process worked! So the referral source became a referral patient — and is also now sober. After a clinic has been operating for a sufficient time — and if they have an effective treatment program — an increasing number of patient referrals will come from former recovered patients. Some will even be referred by unsuccessful patients!

Friends of alcoholics may sometimes play a more objective and effective role than the family or such key collaterals as the doctor, employer or minister. Recovered alcoholics, as friends of practising alcoholics, are often expected to work miracles. It's quite a switch from the distrust and disparagement once received. Initially, a sober alcoholic must adapt himself to being watched, first with suspicion and disbelief, then with amazement, and eventually with fawning praise from well-meaning family and associates — not all of whom may be sober themselves all the time. Once their sobriety is accepted, recovered alcoholics are often asked to drop in and see other alcoholics about their drinking. Of course, they are to go in unannounced and unsupported!

This rarely works. An introductory approach should be well established by the spouse, with the invitation agreed upon by the patient. Nevertheless, when all else has failed, an outside friend may sometimes help.

Such an experience opened my eyes. Jim, a doctor concerned by the drinking of a fellow psychiatrist, requested help. He told me our mutual friend Bill had just been suspended, and was sick and alone in a hotel apartment. His wife had taken the children and left. Bill refused to see Jim or anyone else. Would I try to see him? I agreed. After all, what was there to lose?

I barged in on Bill's apartment. He didn't answer the bell, but the door was unlocked so I went in. Bill was in bed, awake, sick, and fairly lucid (later I learned that the door was unlocked because he was awaiting a fresh supply). Defensively belligerent, he asked, "What do you want? Are you here to gloat over the remains? It's none of your business what I do." There was no turning back, so I retorted, "Bill, it's my business all right, and I'm not getting out till you hear me through. So you might as well listen, and I'll be done that much sooner.

"I'd be a devil of a friend if I just stood by while you throw away your whole life! If I were delirious with fever and you knew it, as sick as you are, as a friend you'd stand by and get me some kind of help. Well, you're just as sick or worse, but because of your pigheadedness and assumed knowledge you miss the simplicity of this illness — so shut off the rationalizations and get this through your skull. You're sick from an illness called alcoholism."

Though Bill did not seem to be listening, I continued, "As far as I'm concerned we'll be friends whether you get sober or keep drinking. What you do is not always your own business. I'm here because Jim and I and a lot of other people know you're sick and need help. You can't tell me you're happy this way. You're too clever and too fine a man to pour yourself down a sewer — but if that's the way you want it, chum, so be it.

"Your wife couldn't take it any more! She couldn't watch you destroy everything you both hold dear and kill her respect and affection for you. Your associates at the hospital want you, but not the way you are. This way, you're a danger and a discredit to yourself and everybody about you. You know it, too — that's why you're trying to stay drunk, to blot out thinking about it.

"Well, go ahead. But remorse will eat holes in you. As an intelligent person, you can't honestly tell me you like what you are now. All your reservations you can use for a chaser. Your cause is that bottle at this point, and the effect we both know. It starts there. The image that keeps you from seeking help — the drunk you are every time you drink.

"We've been over all this many times before. Haven't you paid a big enough initiation fee yet? You still have a choice." There was no reaction from Bill. He simply turned his head away, so I made ready to leave.

"Well, Bill, think it over. If I can help, call me or anyone you want, but someone. As your friend, I wish I could help." I left.

Five weeks later Bill phoned. "George, I'm OK," he said. "I admitted myself into Hazelden. I'm sober. I'm at the airport and I'm going after Jean. Hold your fire till you hear from me. I'm too choked up to say much yet but you'll understand, I know. Thank God for friends!" — and he hung up.

Bill joined an A.A. group in his wife's home town, loved it there and stayed. Seems the group and the local institution needed a doctor who understood. Oh yes, and his last letter told me they have a new daughter — conceived and born in sobriety.

Anyone can be a referral source: friends, a harassed banker concerned with a customer's loan, an insurance agent concerned with a client's protection, a landlord concerned with a tenant, a neighbour concerned by what he sees and knows. There are more avenues and resources than we could ever discuss. The only point to make is this: if some alcoholic patient needs help, find a way to get through, but first know what resources are available to help and know something about the illness.

Sometimes it helps just to approach an alcoholic and be forthright enough to say, "Everything I have tried to say or do has failed us both. I'm afraid I've been trying to play God, so we'll have to let someone else try. However, I'll be standing by and hoping and praying." Then, step aside. Heartbreaking and hard, yes, but sometimes best. Often this very act is the turning point and the alcoholic gets the message.

In almost every instance an alcoholic is seeking a way out. He or she may not

Alcoholism: Treatable Illness

immediately accept the truth but a seed is sown. Learning all the facts, presenting them properly, is the soundest possible means for any collateral to intervene and to assist the still practising alcoholic to recovery. Anyone who does otherwise must be prepared to see the alcoholic gradually deteriorate and become progressively worse.

The most insidious aspect of this illness is that the alcoholic is usually the last to realize the progression of his or her alcoholism, because those close to an alcoholic defer and retard possible recovery by doing nothing positive about it. This is the real tragedy of alcoholism, as we know it today.

Cooperation during the initial approach, the treatment period and throughout the personal growth of aftercare — with the alcoholic patient, spouse, other family members and the collaterals — is the key to effective and happy recoveries. Learning to *talk with* and *not at* the alcoholic is the demonstrated difference between empathetic acceptance and rejection.

As with most illnesses, the main criterion for measuring the effectiveness of any treatment therapy proposed is the number of lives saved. Every public health service for all of society's ills has faced this cold and hard fact, regardless of the humane implications.

After A.A. had been operative for only several years, it was estimated that perhaps fifty percent of the first contacts for help made sobriety at once. Another fifty percent of those who relapsed one, two or three times then achieved lasting sobriety — and another twenty-five to fifty percent of the remainder might eventually obtain sobriety.

Treatment centers strove to achieve like results, and did. It is my experience and I can safely report the following:

Those who enter and/or are treated alone, do achieve still 50-55% lasting sobriety.

When the spouse and other family members are also involved in treatment the percentage of recoveries achieving lasting sobriety increases by 10-15%.

When other collaterals, such as the employer, family physician and like others are involved, a further increase in recovery rates can be anticipated of another 10-15% bringing total recoveries to 70-85%!

These significant results speak for themselves and demonstrate the importance of involving all key figures close to and associated with the alcoholic patient in treatment for the recovery of the whole person, as a member of a whole family and a whole community.

Notes

1. *The Journal* Vol. 10 No. 1, Addiction Research Foundation. Toronto, January 1, 1981.

21. Convalescence and Recovery

The recovering alcoholic faces a period of convalescence as he or she learns to live without the crutch of alcohol. For some, this can be an easy process, but for others it is arduous and painful. This is not too different from any other convalescence. To be relieved of a dependence upon alcohol, the patient must of necessity unlearn many habits which have almost become second nature.

Rechannelling Resources

In guiding the alcoholic to learn and establish new patterns to live by, one must teach him or her to rechannel energies and resources and to substitute new habits for old adverse ones. Gregarious persons, most can be guided to use their therapy or an A.A. group to socialize, instead of a bar or a tavern. If thirsty, one should take a drink — but of a beverage suitable to one's limitations. Substituting sound and safe habits expedites the learning and unlearning process without setting up a barrier against every want or wish.

Having accepted their illness, alcoholics are usually stimulated to rekindle the flame of self-advancement. Often accused of being immature, they will now understand that once dependency on alcohol set in, learning or growing stopped. Now, with the alcohol eliminated, they can overcome this shortcoming. This will provide them with sound reasons and ways for overcoming childish reactions, resentments, intolerance and self-centeredness. The alcoholic may compare drinking bouts to a child stamping its foot in resentment or showing anger or frustration by smashing things.

Some alcoholics stop drinking and remain abstinent from alcohol, but unfortunately never learn to enjoy the full scope of sobriety. Remaining bitter, unforgiving and aloof, some cases never achieve peace of mind and so miss out on the relief of sharing their problems with others. Isn't this, too, like non-alcoholics with other illnesses?

When the innate capabilities and energies which most alcoholics possess are brought into focus and positive use during an honest experiment in sobriety, remarkably successful results are achieved. To accuse the alcoholic of lacking courage, intelligence or motivation is usually to seek to excuse our own inability to

Alcoholism: Treatable Illness

find and call upon these qualities. The alcoholic should be aided to learn self-control and self-discipline and to assume a growing share of responsibility. During this inventory process, the alcoholic should be encouraged to recap assets as well as liabilities. Both alcoholism agencies and Alcoholics Anonymous groups may overstress all the bad points of the alcoholic without balancing the ledger. If the alcoholic is to be guided to work at defects, he or she should be encouraged to appreciate and helped to recognize the compensating gratification of improvement and progress, thereby reducing fears and strengthening resolutions to improve further.

Though spouse, family and other collaterals may lack faith in the alcoholic's recovery, they must appreciate the importance of trust and encourage the shouldering of responsibilities. One way to call out the best in alcoholics is to have them anticipate the need to be strong for self, spouse and family, and through continued example to build up trust. Normally, most alcoholics will measure up to major problems but will be thrown by small things, including the attitudes and resentments of others. Recognizing the alcoholic's deep sensitivity, one must take every care to ''accentuate the positive and eliminate the negative.'' A basic goal of treatment is the enforcement and continuous reinforcement in the patient's mind of an understanding acceptance of alcoholism as a treatable illness, by providing all the supportive medical assistance and guidance possible during the early period of recovery. The alcoholic must be helped to recognize that to stop drinking is only the first step to total recovery and complete and rewarding sobriety.

As the alcoholic gains insight, he or she should be reassured and not be deemed hopeless and weak-willed, but rather a very human person, with the same mind, heart, body and soul as before, with but one major adjustment — learning to live without needing to drink beverage alcohol. If the alcoholic can be taught to seek immediate guidance before taking that first drink, he or she is on the road to recovery.

Many alcoholics, having been brought to the point of doing something about their problem, may visit a clinic or an A.A. office only once or twice, and then drop all formal contacts for further help. Unknown to anyone, they may have been studying and trying to resolve their problems for a long time before. A very few orientation sessions enable them to resolve a decision and to accept their alcoholism without further reservations. They may then move to A.A. and other relationships of their own choice or reestablish themselves in church groups, youth activities and the like. Some continue on in A.A. groups until these other relationships take over. There are many such cases who never look back, and who maintain a very effective and happy state of sobriety. The treatment agency (A.A. or a clinic) has played its role by providing the patient with understanding and the patient does the rest.

Other cases may take a much longer period, requiring intensive care and every resource of several facilities. Some alcoholics do require psychiatric care, and regrettably some won't recover. Many alcoholics, burdened by other problems too long unattended and no longer capable of absorbing a recovery process, continue on to their own tragic end. Is this not often the case with any illness? Do or can all cardiac or cancer patients necessarily follow the doctor's advice? Do all diabetics and epileptics maintain the regimen of treatment demanded of them?

In the treatment of alcoholism it is vitally necessary to impress both the patient and the counsellor with the importance of recognizing alcoholism as a progressive and permanent illness. When an alcoholic stops drinking, it is easy to assume the illness no longer exists, and it's not uncommon for friends and relatives alike to say, "You've been sober for a long time now. Surely you can now take one drink!" Should the alcoholic be inclined to agree and drink again, then everyone will say, "Why did you do it?" The word "cure" must be eliminated from the alcoholic's language. When he or she stops drinking, the dependency is only arrested and, like any allergy sufferer, reingestion of any alcohol beverage immediately reactivates the illness and makes it worse than ever.

Every effort should be made to rechannel the alcoholic's sober energies into accepting the illness and not just admitting it. Some patients will retain reservations about their drinking for a long time. Therapy must be directed to motivating a relinquishing of such reservations. Continuing participation with the treatment resources, particularly an Alcoholics Anonymous group, will achieve this goal.

Recovery of the Whole Person

In the analogy comparing alcoholism to a three-legged stool, the several elements embodied in this illness — physical, emotional, social and spiritual — were interpreted. Recovery of the alcoholic as a whole person demands continuing and equal attention to each factor. If any one facet is left untreated, the others are bound to be adversely affected. The very nature of alcoholism requires a total recovery of the patient as a "whole" person, if the alcoholic is to enjoy rewarding, continuous and happy sobriety. While an interpretation of treatment techniques has not been detailed, every physiological and psychological aspect should receive thorough care. There is a growing and ever-improving flow of professional and scientific information focusing on this type of care and attention.

The alcoholic's social problems can be met by rechannelling energies and resources into many positive and fruitful vocational and avocational interests; into mutually beneficial activities with members of the family; sound relationships with old and new friends, and other such pursuits. A continuing recovery contact is essential. The most positive and effective long-range therapy is participation in an A.A. group of personal choice, which will also include much of the above, and Al-Anon for the spouse.

Alcoholism: Treatable Illness

A prerequisite to whole recovery is the rekindling and nurturing of the inner person's needs — the spiritual side of recovery. There is a regrettable and undesirable trend among counsellors of all social science disciplines to neglect and even ignore the importance of a patient's spiritual well-being. While this is not limited only to the treatment of this illness, it is catastrophic to the alcoholic. Professed agnosticism or atheism by a counsellor is harmful and may be interpreted as rejection by the patient. Workers are known to make light of and even ridicule alcoholics for a new-found dependence on a "Higher Power." Some profess that Alcoholics Anonymous involves too much "God stuff," and that patients would be well-advised to develop practical insight and dependence upon themselves. Other counsellors, emphasizing a neo-Freudian philosophy, interpret alcoholism to patient and spouse as an expression of sexual problems. This creates new blocks and disturbs them both. While important to some patients, this approach should not supersede spiritual needs.

Most patients are more amenable to and have a deeper appreciation of spiritual convictions following recovery. Treatment centers aware of this facet of recovery act on it by including pastoral counselling for their patients. Even those who profess to be agnostics come to accept and are heartened by a relationship with some form of Higher Power, as they individually understand it. Some younger alcoholics today — especially those in their mid to late teens — may deliberately avoid A.A. because of what they see as the "God" aspect, even if they believe that A.A. might otherwise help them.

Regrettably, some young adults are quite cynical. Incredibly well-informed, this generation of young people is regularly exposed (in reality and in the media) to death, violence, starvation, drug abuse, AIDS, the spectre of nuclear holocaust, and to ill-advised activists concerned about real or fancied religious slights. Some of these will take the view that any Higher Power worthy of the name wouldn't inflict so much suffering on so many innocents — or "especially me!" Most alcoholics in the latter stages of their illness are prone to ask: "Why me?" Despite these obstacles, in my own experience I am always amazed and very gratified to see an ever-increasing number of young adults subscribing to this basic precept in the A.A. program.

In the early years of Alcoholics Anonymous, church leaders questioned the spiritual concept of A.A., feeling it might be detrimental to, or in competition with, their religions. As they saw the transformation taking place among recovered alcoholics of their congregations, their opinions changed. They found sober alcoholics evidenced a total personality change; they developed sound religious convictions and returned to or sought religious affiliation. Most alcoholics feel the precious gift of their sobriety is brought about and given depth and meaning through spiritual aid. For this reason, it is possible to understand the sense of conviction and rejection an alcoholic feels when his spiritual leanings are questioned. During treatment, the alcoholic's spiritual concern should be relieved and his or her beliefs strengthened and encouraged.

These thoughts may seem contradictory to the alcoholic's initial resentment over the "hell and damnation" approach to his illness. Not so. Much of the alcoholic's resentment is based on remorse, guilt and fear of reprisal. Reaffirming and regenerating his beliefs relieve these obstacles to recovery. The alcoholic is always gratified to learn a new meaning for his Deity and to understand the Higher Power as warm, forgiving and benevolent. Those who cannot subscribe to this concept in treatment should never try to work with an alcoholic.

Until the alcoholic appreciates dependency as an illness over which one has no control when trying to drink as others do, a moral issue is not really involved. However, once one is aware of the full portent of alcoholism as an illness, as a recovering alcoholic he or she will be imbued with the moral obligation to do something about it and to utilize every tool available, to achieve and then to maintain sobriety. With the return of judgment and reasoning ability, the alcoholic now has a moral responsibility to control his or her illness by total abstinence from beverage alcohol.

Though more and more patients are seeking help at an earlier stage, there are those who on initial contact may require emergency care for personal needs: medical care, meals, a bed, notification of wife and employer and the like. The counsellor involved may find it desirable and necessary, on the first interview, to undertake to satisfy these needs. This can be the case even when the patient is normally well able to handle all personal requirements. The patient's aloneness, confusion and disintegration may demand this positive assistance. Such help is not babying the alcoholic, nor is it fostering self-pity and further dependency — provided that it is administered in a positive way as a necessary part of the total continuing treatment process. In many instances, recognition of such needs will instill motivation and insure the patient's continuance in treatment.

Every patient must be advised that an all-out and joint effort is needed to successfully treat the illness. Immediate and regular contacts should be required and maintained in any source of counselling. The alcoholic cannot be told, "Be back in two weeks and we'll see you then"; nor can he be given a supply of pills with the admonition, "Now don't drink, and return in two weeks." The disturbed patient cannot be advised, "Get sober, make up with your family, find your things, see your boss and save your job, then call me for an appointment." These cliches sound stupid; nevertheless, they are regrettably tried and used every day.

I remember asking a patient how he was doing. He answered, "Fine. The first few days they had me seeing the nurse, the doctor, two or three counsellors, and I was talking to or having coffee with someone all the time. I sat in on a day group;

Alcoholism: Treatable Illness

took my wife to an evening group, was introduced to a member from A.A. and went to meetings with him. I never stopped. I didn't have time to get a drink, and I'm sober at last!'' This is in contrast to the experience of a wife who called the other evening to see if I would use my influence to get her alcoholic husband an appointment at the clinic, as the earliest date he could make was ten days away. In some instances, Alcoholics Anonymous members can be lax in this regard also. A pat reply of some is, "If he wants help, let him call himself," or "There's a meeting next Thursday at eight p.m. — tell him to see me there."

It should be explained to the patient that recovery is a step-by-step process, and that it takes persistence by all concerned, especially the alcoholic. He or she must appreciate that before any other problem can be resolved, absolute abstinence is necessary, and that each case is a little different and must be treated accordingly. Above all else, the alcoholic, if he or she is to recover as a whole person, must be helped to realize recovery must be achieved for self alone, and that sobriety is more important than spouse, family, job or material possessions. It is more precious than the demands of others, because without sobriety all of these may be lost. Through sobriety, they will all be automatically retained or regained.

Dangers to Sobriety

Every alcoholic should learn to accept alcoholism as an illness which may only be arrested — never cured. This is not a contradictory statement. Experienced alcohologists confirm complete recovery demands continued abstinence from the agent alcohol, which — though not necessarily the cause — triggers the illness. To believe otherwise is to harbour reservations dangerous to permanent sobriety.

In every other respect, a recovered alcoholic may regain and enjoy a full, healthy and contented life. In fact, as a result of the insight gained through treatment, he or she can be the architect of a happier, more mature, stable and fruitful life. He or she demonstrates the necessary fortitude and intelligence to overcome a precarious and wretched existence. Primarily this is true for those who accomplish recovery of the whole person, learning to treat each disorder that originally helped bring about the illness and later maintained the state of alcoholism.

To set these ills and problems aside is a serious detriment to complete recovery. The physical and emotional disorders once anaesthetized by alcohol, not dissipated through sobriety, must be dealt with as they arise. The alcoholic who merely abstains from beverage alcohol without improving his or her "whole self" does not enjoy or share the full fruits of sobriety. In spite of this lack, Alcoholics Anonymous achieves the miracle of sobriety with many such patients on the basis of admission, faith and example. Nevertheless, when called upon, the skills of medicine, psychiatry, the social sciences and the clergy, together with A.A., may play their most meaningful role in the after-care and follow-up care of alcoholics.

During early stages of recovery many alcoholics experience a "honeymoon glow" as a result of improved feelings and the increased recognition received. With returning self-esteem and everything righting itself again, overconfidence can develop which can bring about feelings of complacency and false security. Those closest to the alcoholic, on recognizing any danger signals that may preface a return to drinking should help guide the patient to deal with the symptoms promptly. The recovered alcoholic shows good judgment in following a routine of regular medical checkups as in convalescing from any other sickness. If the alcoholic lacks other continuing recovery contacts or is still holding on to old reservations — which have not been dealt with honestly and thoroughly — this neglect can pose a serious danger to sobriety.

The family and other collaterals may create conflicts: the spouse who resents and won't accept a mate's inability to drink as others do, or friends or business associates who belittle the alcoholic's not joining them in a drink or two — these impose pressures which are a constant threat.

Recovering alcoholics must resolutely determine what is most important. The choice is always theirs. When the alcoholic learns to make honest and definite decisions about the use of beverage alcohol with family and associates, he or she is declaring or making a very strong statement and strengthening both personal stature and recovery.

Can Alcoholics Drink Again?

The alcoholism treatment world is still involved in the old hassle between some minority elements who feel alcoholics can be taught to return to social drinking and the majority of alcohologists who from long and hard experience believe permanent abstinence to be the only means of total and assured recovery. A few hopefuls suggest the alcoholic, when completely "cured" physically and psychologically, should perforce be enabled to return to a controlled drinking state. This opinion reflects the ultimate goal of psychiatry and analysis: that perfect state of physical and mental health permits no plausible reason for any ill to exist, much less alcoholism. Be that as it may, it doesn't work with the alcoholic. I have seen too many alcoholics fail, for me to be willing to chance it or recommend it to anyone else.

This subject recalls two tragic alcoholic examples. Both were brilliant scholars and recognized medical specialists. Each had enjoyed sobriety for two or more years through the joint efforts of an alcoholism clinic and Alcoholics Anonymous. Like many with that degree of training, they were dyed-in-the-wool diagnosticians and therefore carried some reservations and wondered if they really had tried everything. Accepting the simplicity of the illness alcoholism and applying the

Alcoholism: Treatable Illness

simplicity of the recovery process is hard for many such alcoholics. Each had a relapse which should have been dealt with promptly and easily. However, they were recommended to and took psychiatric care for lengthy periods. Each was assured that with the insight gained, men of their position and capabilities should be able to return to social drinking. They tried hard — too hard. Each died tragically in the midst of an alcoholic bout.

Is it not sounder and simpler, as a part of treatment, to impress on the alcoholic's mind the waste, danger and utter uselessness of needing a drink to live a complete life? These men, in the prime of life, as specialists in their fields with much to contribute to the medical needs of those who do desperately require their skills, could have been told, "Of course you may drink — but as an alcoholic you should not, and may no longer do so with safety. While sober, it is your own choice and responsible decision." Why is it necessary to further confuse the alcoholic, once recovered, by re-instilling this negative attitude and negative approach to treatment?

A new and serious source of concern is the growing number of *allegedly non-alcoholic beverages*: wines, champagnes, and near-beers. Advertised to be free of any alcohol content, they are not always so. Most if not all of these beverages do indeed contain measurable amounts of alcohol. Though these beverages contain perhaps only a small percentage or minute amount, in my opinion it is a very dangerous experiment to try or to foster the use of these so-called safe substitutes.

Most certainly, too, the taste and appearance of these beverages remain the same. More seriously, they beguile the user into a false sense of security, and may suggest "*I am cured.*" This leads to the unwarranted assumption that one can resume drinking the "real thing" comfortably and safely. It has long been known that *alcoholics are never cured* — their illness is only arrested as long as they abstain totally from *any* alcohol.

Again, I must ask: why is it so important socially or philosophically for alcoholics to be able to drink beverage alcohol as others do? What is the need for this push toward the social use of alcohol, particularly in instances where the push originates with the beverage alcohol industry? Isn't this merely another marketing strategy to sell more product — and be damned with the results?

Each of the efforts to re-involve alcoholics in the use of beverage alcohol culminates in serious and unnecessary tragedy, with greater losses and costs to society as a whole. It is tragic to see a spouse or someone close hold reservations and wonder if the alcoholic is not really only a heavy drinker who may now drink socially again. Influenced by their own feelings of the importance of social drinking, directly or indirectly, they may be instrumental in bringing about the alcoholic's relapse into the illness alcoholism and his untimely end.

It is certainly the experience of Alcoholics Anonymous that once alcoholics understand their illness, realize that they are alcoholics, and again enjoy the well-being of sobriety, they can never again safely take another drink and enjoy it. Alcoholics who take this warning on faith alone save themselves and those close to them needless suffering and anxiety.

Relapses

The resources of medicine would never be overloaded if all patients recovered from every illness without a relapse. Unfortunately the illness alcoholism, too, has its share of relapses. The patient, family and those closely related to the recovery process of the alcoholic should be intelligently informed that a relapse may occur. Their awareness and preparedness will enable them to use the experience as a regrettable but positive step in treatment and total recovery, directed to the acceptance of one's self as an alcoholic. To do otherwise is to anticipate failure.

Sound counselling and good sponsorship will avert the alcoholic's need to test just once more. However, many alcoholics still holding fast to the reservation that "If all else is okay I should be able to drink again" may need a last convincing experience to clear out such cobwebs once and for all. Some may try several times. This is an individual fight which each alcoholic faces. Those who progress early from recognizing, to admitting, and to accepting their alcoholism have much less difficulty in this area of recovery. A relapse may also reinforce the need to take more immediate and positive measures with other problems.

Alcoholics who begin recovery at an early stage and are less damaged can have this asset working for or against them, depending upon the manner in which they are counselled through to recovery. Some alcoholics will use their illness as an excuse to continue drinking, announcing, "Remember, I'm a sick person." They may seek and even demand the attention and care they received during recovery. This new excuse for dependency must be corrected.

Patients concerned with financial, domestic and other worries or pressures, and with the urgency of coping with the practical demands of these problems, may break off treatment too soon. Remorseful and guilty over past failures, and driven by the need to recoup everything as quickly as possible, they may telescope needed treatment. Without having acquired sound guards to protect recovery, they can easily regress and slip back into old routines of alcohol dependency. Alcoholics must constantly be reminded about "doing first things first." Alcoholics Anonymous bolsters this need by suggesting that alcoholics face their problems only "24 hours at a time" and "easy does it."

The alcoholic and his or her spouse, collaterals and counsellors alike should remember that the illness and its related problems usually were developed over a long period of time. Therefore, recovery will not be achieved overnight. It will take time to change the subconscious and defensive habits the alcoholic has learned. After years of sobriety, while sitting at home reading and to all intents and purposes completely relaxed, I was jolted out of my reverie by the doorbell. Without thinking, I quickly put a glass of ginger ale under the skirt of my chair. Though laughable, this exemplifies and warns of the depth of old defensive mechanisms. Constructive change demands patience, tolerance and continuing effort by the patient and those about him, to unlearn adverse habits and traits and to replace them with positive steps to recovery. Following the original moment of truth, the admission, the alcoholic must ask himself every now and then, "What do I want and where do I want to go with my life? What am I willing to put into my recovery?" One can maintain one's sense of values by making this comparison. In one hand a glass of beverage alcohol; in the other, also within grasp, potential recovery, bringing with it self-respect, happiness and freedom from enslavement, augmented by renewed belief and faith in self and by regained physical, social, emotional and spiritual wellbeing. Are these precious possessions not worth more than the imagined satisfaction of one drink? This decisive moment of truth is faced and refaced as the alcoholic again and again decides to attain and know these benefits realistically or to have them become a mirage in an empty glass. This period of repeated temptation will pass, along with dreams of being drunk, the desire for a cold beer on a hot day or a long tall one with the old crowd, and all the other mirages.

Should the alcoholic relapse, every effort must be made to rekindle motivation and renew hope, both for the patient and those closest to him. A relapse can cause everyone to forget that alcoholism is an illness. It is surprising how quickly old moralisms reappear! It must be stressed that the initial period of sobriety was sound progress, and the alcoholic is not a hopeless case, but one who now warrants a renewal of effort and faith. This approach reassures the patient, the family, the boss, and even those A.A. or other associates who may wonder, "Has he really hit bottom yet? Is she ready, does she want to quit?" Some alcoholics are sicker than others and require just a little more effort and counselling.

A relapse can provide an opportunity to deal positively with defects in the alcoholic's recovery routine, and will emphasize the need to deal honestly and objectively with other obstacles to the achievement of complete sobriety. It is important for alcoholics to know those about them understand and do want to help. A relapse may evidence the need for personal adjustment — resolution of a family conflict, vocational concerns, a change of associates and contact with therapy groups more suitable and acceptable to the alcoholic's needs. In some instances the alcoholic may need to learn that he or she cannot immediately "become president" again, but must accept and work through the state of life the drinking created and so find one's true identity. Such adjustments require careful guidance and supervision. Problems will not be evidenced all at one time but will arise throughout the early and even later period of sobriety. The relapse is often simply an escape from such problems.

Sometimes, too, the family may expect more of the alcoholic than he or she can give. Take the case of an executive of a family company. His drinking brought him to a state of mere existence in a suite on the ground floor of their lovely home. While awaiting committal to an institution, he fell and was hospitalized for his injuries. The doctor first feared for his life and then for his sanity. It took months of care before he was home. His wife taught him to read again by going over his favourite sports and comic paper sections. He relearned to walk and eventually played a few holes of golf daily. It took two years for him to regain physical health. Considerable emotional disturbance remained.

He had an A.A. contact throughout, from whom he grasped hope and the faith to recover. At the end of two years' sobriety, his family felt it was time he reassumed the management of the company. Though doing an excellent job of public relations with old accounts and dealers, when faced with this major responsibility, he escaped by getting drunk. Only then did everyone agree to listen to the doctor and wife. She had understood all of this for some time but, because she was dependent on income from the family and company and had two daughters to raise and educate, she allowed herself to go along with their demands. Now she took a stand. They moved to another city and opened a small gift shop. They were happy and progressively successful — and he remained sober. There is an anticlimax to this case. Several years later, this man evidenced recurring ill health which, without medical examination, was attributed to a carryover of his alcoholism. Following his sudden death, an autopsy revealed a brain tumour.

As indicated by the above experience, alcoholics may suffer serious physical and emotional damage from their drinking which, if unrecognized and unattended, can bring about an involuntary relapse. Wrong attitudes to alcoholism cure forestall adequate investigation and treatment of many alcoholics.

An alcoholic, sober about ten years, suffered considerable pain which was labelled psychosomatic. He relapsed into alcoholism, to which he added pills. Rejected by his physician and even some A.A.s, he was taken in hand by a recovered alcoholic friend who could not believe this man did not want sobriety. He nursed him along until he could get him under the care of an understanding specialist in a reputable midwestern university hospital. A thorough examination revealed a cyst pressing on the patient's brain. Simple surgery relieved the pressure and pain and the need to drink or use pills. He picked up his sobriety and has never looked back.

In the mid-forties in a veterans' hospital, the well-disposed efforts of the director and the female supervisor of social services, in cooperation with members

Alcoholism: Treatable Illness

of Alcoholics Anonymous and a local center, initiated programming for alcoholics. After orienting key personnel and achieving the cooperation of the superintendent, she went to work. Her charges included alcoholic patient-residents of the home who had been there since the first world war, all of whom regularly left their monthly cheques in neighbourhood taverns. Prior to this new regime of treatment, case files were closed after review by those concerned with the usual, "Oh, one of those drunks." After the program was in operation for a sound period, something marvellous happened. Patients began to leave the Veterans Center and become sober, self-sustaining members of society again, after being hospitalized all those years. Along with alcoholism, most were found to be suffering from other medical problems, none of which had really ever been treated. How many of these had once been considered hopeless relapses?

Alcoholics find it easier to accept physical disorders than emotional ones. Many back away from needed psychotherapy, being reticent to deal with emotional problems. This can be overcome and relapses prevented through sound initial counselling procedures.

There is still much to be learned about the effects of continued and excessive use of alcohol. Physical damage and emotional disorders are sometimes evidenced in those alcoholics who regress and then relapse seemingly for no apparent reason, even after years of abstinence. Here again, continued follow-up care and a physician's and counsellor's awareness may provide preventive assistance, as in the examples cited. These problems are not unique to the alcoholic, but are distributed among other members of the family, whose continued care is essential to the continued sobriety of the alcoholic. Every resource and skill of all the healing sciences is required to find more positive answers to alleviating the problem of relapsing alcoholic patients.

There are alcoholics who seem unable to maintain sobriety. In a number of these cases the alcoholism, though a major problem, is secondary to other serious disorders. Enforced abstinence, by providing a sufficient opportunity to deal with other disorders, enables a few to attain intermittent but improved periods of sobriety. There are also those cases in which the illness has progressed to such a point as to cause severe deterioration. These patients, though perhaps wanting sobriety, can no longer of their own volition remain abstinent from alcohol.

Alcoholics Anonymous, recognizing this inability on the part of some to sustain recovery, warns:

Rarely have we seen a person fail who has thoroughly followed our path. *Those who do not recover are people who cannot or will not completely give themselves to this simple program, usually men and women who are constitutionally incapable of being honest with themselves.* There are such unfortunates. They are not at fault; they seem to have been born that way. They are naturally incapable of grasping and developing a manner of living which demands rigorous honesty. Their chances are less than average. There are those, too, who suffer from grave emotional and mental disorders, but many of them do recover if they have the capacity to be honest.[1]

Even among these apparently hopeless cases the combined skills and resources of a total team — Alcoholics Anonymous, medicine, psychiatry and the social sciences — are achieving recoveries.

A relapse may represent nothing more than a lack of care, insight and understanding. Many alcoholics have received medical attention and have gone out into their new world only to find that no one cares. It is not unusual for a potential group member to visit a large A.A. group for weeks and never have anyone say hello, or to go to a doctor with a serious complaint and be told, "Just don't drink." The alcoholic, as human as anyone else, suffers all the pressures and physical, emotional and other ills as everyone else. Unfortunately, the alcoholism may prevent the patient from receiving quite the same quality of treatment.

Every time an alcoholic admits to another person, "I am an alcoholic," he or she strengthens sobriety. Like the diabetic taking a positive approach to that ailment, this is an indication of both an intellectual and emotional acceptance of one's illness, without reservations or bitterness. Be warned that alcoholics, their families, and all their collaterals are among the first to forget that alcoholism is an illness once all conflict, pain and symptoms of the illness are dissipated.

Relapses may be prevented by applying, on a day-by-day basis, the measures outlined earlier. Two points should be re-emphasized. The first is simply to repeat that one's alcoholism may serve to hide serious physical and emotional problems, most of which will dissipate as sobriety progresses. However, if such problems do not eliminate themselves they should be dealt with. Let me give you an example.

After six months of sobriety a patient told his counsellor he was happily sober, his family was reunited, and he was enjoying life to the full. However, he knew periods of irritability and did not always feel physically well. His counsellor suggested, "Have you had another physical checkup? Now that the 'coating' of alcoholism is gone, perhaps something else is wrong. You were pickled for so long, how could anybody really diagnose your other problems? Besides, let's face it, when you were drinking or hung over, not too many people were anxious to bother with the other problems." The patient did see his doctor, told him all about his alcoholism, and what he had done about it. The doctor discovered he was also a diabetic and put him under proper treatment; now he is completely well.

Secondly, alcoholics must learn better living habits. This involves the full cooperation of the spouse and family. Few alcoholics ever eat breakfast. Learning to eat this and other meals regularly is a sound insurance premium alcoholics can pay to attain permanent sobriety. If eating toast still causes gags, one can learn to establish better eating habits by drinking eggnogs and the like. Other good living practices are mandatory: getting adequate and proper rest; spending time with family; learning to discuss and work out the family budget and plans; respecting the needs of others — all part of the alcoholic's new approach to life, and all positive measures to prevent trouble. Should "shakes" suddenly reappear, he or she should try orange juice with honey or sugar; if thirsty, a Coke, malted or hot chocolate may help; if jumpy, eating will relieve the need for a drink. Often the simple signs of hunger are mistaken as a need or craving for a drink.

It is always well to caution a recovering alcoholic that he or she will not be met with a brass band at a clinic or an A.A. group, or in any place that one seeks sobriety, just as he or she did not receive such treatment at a favourite bar. The flags that fly and the horns that blow will have to be created for one's self, and so one must expect life as usual as a normal part of recovery. However, if alcoholics will make as much effort to stay sober as they sometimes did to get or find a drink, few need relapse.

Medications

The "therapeutic" use of potentially addictive medications is a source of continuing dispute in the treatment of the alcoholic, and with medicine in general. This is particularly true in recent years with the advent of several new generations of tranquillizers, muscle relaxants and anti-depressants that have often been prescribed repeatedly and for long periods of time for everything from whiplash to post-partum depression. No area of discussion can raise more arguments, cause more discord and create greater impediments to recovery than medication. I take the blunt view: the use and over-prescribing of medications is but a poor substitute for sound treatment.

Because alcoholism is deeply tied to the type of personality that can develop any addiction, those alcoholics who substitute another chemical or pill will, with apparent ease, end up with a dual addiction. The alcoholic's dependency on alcohol, if unduly exposed, is transferred to drugs, sedatives, tranquillizers and any mood-changing or comfort-giving medication. Even elixirs, cough syrups or alcohol-loaded tonics can be dangerous to the alcoholic. A medication that provides too great a feeling of well-being or comfort is a harmful substitute, the use of which may lead to disastrous results.

The police picked up a man sitting on the curb, dazed, unable to walk steadily, or to say much about himself. After being detained for several hours, he was revealed as an alcoholic patient attending a clinic. He had been given two sedative pills and allowed to go home. The medication had reacted suddenly and violently. He had another dozen in his possession to carry him over the weekend.

Experience proves that the quality of a doctor's or counsellor's rapport with an alcoholic patient is more important than the medication involved. Many noteworthy physicians have emphasized this factor in treatment. Others suggest that supportive medications even of the Antabuse or Tempasil type may not be all they are touted to be. Medications should never be administered as a means to avoid giving the time, energy and expertise of counselling that all patients, especially alcoholics, require.

This problem and danger to sobriety is magnified by the publicity accompanying the release of each new wonder drug. The continued education of some physicians is frequently limited to the perusal of these glowing cure-alls, which don't work alike for all patients and rarely work safely with alcoholics. Medications are but one supportive tool, nothing more. The early raves about the potential of L.S.D., followed by the tragic aftermath of its use, are a repetition of the adverse reaction found even with such splendid medications as sulpha, penicillin and erythromycin. These, though exceptionally useful, have their allergic reactions with some patients. There is also the example of valium, which has profound therapeutic effects when properly prescribed and monitored, but which is a highly addictive and insidious time-bomb when improperly used. Some people are even allergic to the vitamins that help other patients.

An alcoholic, close to DTs, was given a massive injection of vitamin B12 and immediately went into convulsions. On recuperating, he was found to be completely allergic to particular vitamins.

Innumerable alcoholics have relapsed following years of sobriety as the result of using sedation or tranquillizers innocently prescribed for tension, heart disorder and like ailments. Based on years of observation, the Fellowship of Alcoholics Anonymous has formed firm opinions on potentially addictive medications. Having a sound appreciation of this danger, they endeavour to instill in their membership a healthy fear and respect for potentially addictive medications. While their protective approach is the basis of some professional disagreement, nevertheless they are to be commended for standing by their opinion.

There is disagreement within the professions about various medications. The use of various substances is debated pro and con by those propounding one or the other as being absolutely safe for everyone, with the fears of other "experts" being groundless. Conversely, there are those who argue that all potentially addictive medications are worse than alcohol! Those professionals who have worked closely with alcoholics for years support the latter attitude. Drugs should be administered only in a completely controlled setting, preferably a hospital.

An alcoholic patient who would not accept her alcoholism was under the care of a psychiatrist. Prior to seeing him she had visited several other doctors and held a number of open prescriptions. She would use any of her medications on top of alcohol. It might be added that the doctor did not believe her to be an alcoholic, and was only convinced when forced to see her at home at the end of a three-day drinking bout.

The patient moved to another city. Just prior to moving, she was inebriated for about ten days. Feeling she needed something, she called the doctor. He arranged for the husband to pick up a rather large quantity of sedatives to help her through the move to her new locale, and to tide her over until she could contact someone there. She was still drinking during this period. A week later, she was found dead. The combination of the overuse of both alcohol and sedatives had taken its toll. Patients cannot be held accountable for the number of pills taken while drinking excessively. There are thousands and thousands of similar cases everywhere about us — individuals improperly, unethically and illegally treated with pills.

The free and easy prescribing of medications to those incapable of properly handling them continues to be a serious problem. For some reason, perhaps because of present public acceptance of pills in general, they are handed out frequently by counsellors without medical supervision or authority, and in quantities that should be considered illegal. To give any medication to an alcoholic who is still drinking, or to one who is hung over, can have serious consequences. In this condition the alcoholic has no personal judgment or control over the manner or quantity in which the medication is to be used, and so is easily susceptible to an involuntary overdose. Those who are alone at home or in a room without supervision are particularly prone to this danger. Time after time, alcoholics have been known to get into more trouble with medication added to their alcohol than they would have otherwise.

A female alcoholic, under the care of a physician and a psychiatrist for depression during menopause, while attending an alcoholism clinic had in her possession enough varied pills to knock out the proverbial horse. Emotionally upset over a drinking relapse, she returned to the clinic and was given supplies of three additional medications by a counsellor. No questions were raised as to the medications she had on hand, no check made with any of the doctors as to whether these were safe. These were simply additional medications that would "help her to feel better."

The free and easy giving out of pills will attract to treatment centers non-alcoholic addicts seeking another source of supply. Such addicts and the alcoholic alike may have in their possession other prescriptions from other sources. It is not unusual for the alcoholic or addict to blame the alcoholism clinic or doctor for the medication that is producing the negative effect — and thereby protect his own alternate sources of supply. Many alcoholism agencies are unjustly accused by patients and A.A. members alike for supplying medications procured elsewhere. It is imperative that alcoholic patients never be given an open or refillable prescription.

Often doctors, having an inadequate knowledge of alcoholism, with all sincerity of purpose, will freely give an alcoholic medication. The physician innocently starts him or her off on a new dependency; sometimes the doctor doesn't believe the patient's revelation of his alcoholism and doesn't accept the patient's reluctance to use medications. Some female alcoholics seeking aid for female problems also become dual addicts. Often nervous disorders, bad backs, menopause and other stated ills are but a coverup for the alcoholism which is hidden by the patient as well as the family. There are also disinterested physicians who prescribe medication simply to be rid of the patient. They often handle help requests on the phone without seeing or examining the individual's condition and refer these "nuisances" to pharmacists for medication.

There is no question but that some medications are necessary and useful instruments in the treatment of alcoholism. When handled under supervision and administered in keeping with the demands and needs of the individual case, they can perform a vital service for some. Nevertheless, they should never be prescribed without the full realization of the alcoholic's circumstances. They should never be given to the patient or the family to be used surreptitiously to work a miracle cure; nor should they be given under an open prescription or without the authority and supervision of a qualified physician. Where required in massive dosages for an extremely serious case, they are more properly administered in a hospital setting.

There is no simple solution to this problem. The use of medications in the treatment of the alcoholic requires much more intensive study. There is much research and practical experience to support the view that the simultaneous use of alcohol and even so-called mild tranquillizers may compound the adverse reaction of either or both. A positive position on the use of medication suggests the following: *the use of potentially addictive medications with the alcoholic must be handled with extreme care — every precaution must be taken against the overuse of any medication, and the use of non-therapeutic drugs (whether supervised or not) must be entirely avoided.*

Notes

1. *Alcoholics Anonymous*, Chapter V — 'How It Works.' Reprinted with permission of the Directors of A.A. World Services, Inc.

22. Alcoholics Anonymous

The Fellowship of Alcoholics Anonymous has been acclaimed as the greatest sociological phenomenon of our time.

Though much has been said and written about A.A., as it is more commonly known, sound information about how it works is perhaps not as well known as it might or should be. The alcoholic, when referred to Alcoholics Anonymous, invariably reacts, "I don't think I'm bad enough yet for that." Collateral counsellors (doctor, clergyman, employer, agency worker and others), unless they are well aware of the workings of the Fellowship, are too prone to assume the same attitude. Many seem to base an alcoholic's need for A.A. on his pocketbook or status. It is not uncommon for some to say, "Well, of course, he or she has a little problem with alcohol but professional care alone should help — I'm sure they don't need A.A." If this is the reaction of all too many contacts, how then is the patient to feel? Remember, the patient will reflect the attitude of everyone around him or her.

Anyone concerned with treating alcoholics should be thoroughly aware of, understand, and closely cooperate with the services of Alcoholics Anonymous and the Al-Anon Family Groups.[1] Almost 50% of the referrals to A.A. are today received from private and public treatment resources.

All too often the information we pick up about A.A. is attained through hearsay or as we acquire it on a personal and local level. If our knowledge is received from a member or source with a limited or biased appreciation of A.A.'s service, then we end up with an incomplete and/or biased understanding of the Fellowship. As it is, most people are still confused. Is it a religious movement? Is it a reform group only for skid row inhabitants? As with any organization, Alcoholics Anonymous has its share of well-meaning but eccentric members who make their personal interpretation of A.A. loudly known. Regrettably, those members receiving the most benefits and best able to describe the movement are much more reserved and properly anonymous.

As Alcoholics Anonymous provides by far the most effective and continuing form of therapy for any alcoholic, regardless of vocation, education or social status, let us review the Fellowship in a thorough fashion.

Alcoholics Anonymous by and large represents a cross-section of our total society. Its membership includes both men and women alike, of every known profession, educational background and skill, and of every colour, race and creed. And contrary to some negative first impressions, there is a group of members to suit any individual need.

Alcoholics Anonymous defines itself as follows:

Alcoholics Anonymous is a fellowship of men and women who share their experience, strength and hope with each other that they may solve their common problem and help others to recover from alcoholism.

The only requirement for membership is a desire to stop drinking. There are no dues or fees for A.A. membership; they are self-supporting through their own contributions. A.A. is not allied with any sect, denomination, politics, organization or institution; does not wish to engage in any controversy, neither endorses nor opposes any causes. Their primary purpose is to stay sober and help other alcoholics to achieve sobriety.[2]

Alcoholics Anonymous is essentially a relationship of partners, each of whom is dependent on the others for support in a continuing program of permanent sobriety. Though some few members may merely indicate an abstinence from drinking and show no other character improvement, this is not representative of the full meaning of sobriety or the whole way of life that A.A. strives to impart. A clearer perspective may be had by thoroughly studying several basic A.A. books: *Alcoholics Anonymous*, the *Twelve Steps and Twelve Traditions* and *Alcoholics Anonymous Comes of Age*. These and other books, together with pamphlets and materials directed to specific groups and needs, are all available through the official publications division of Alcoholics Anonymous, or through local A.A. groups.[3]

Historical Data

The story of the inception of Alcoholics Anonymous is a fascinating one. A portion of A.A.'s history is taken from official materials.[4]

A.A. had its beginnings in June of 1935 at Akron, Ohio, as the outcome of a meeting between Bill W., a New York stockbroker, and Dr. Bob S., an Akron surgeon. Both had been hopeless alcoholics.[5]

Prior to that time, Bill and Dr. Bob had each been in contact with the Oxford Group, a mostly nonalcoholic fellowship that emphasized universal spiritual values in daily living. In that period, the Oxford Groups in America were headed by the noted Episcopal clergyman, Dr. Samuel Shoemaker. Under this spiritual influence and with the help of an old time friend, "Ebby," Bill had sobered and had then maintained his recovery by working with other alcoholics, though none of these had actually recovered. Meanwhile, Dr. Bob's Oxford

Alcoholism: Treatable Illness

Group membership at Akron had not helped him enough to achieve sobriety. When Dr. Bob and Bill finally met, the effect on the doctor was immediate. This time he found himself face to face with a fellow sufferer who had made good. Bill emphasized that alcoholism was a malady of mind, emotions and body. This all-important fact he had learned from Dr. William D. Silkworth of Towns Hospital in New York, where he had often been a patient. Though a physician, Dr. Bob had not known alcoholism to be a disease. Responding to Bill's convincing ideas, he soon sobered, never to drink again. The founding spark of A.A. had been struck.

Both men immediately set to work with alcoholics at Akron's City Hospital where one patient quickly achieved complete sobriety. Though the name Alcoholics Anonymous had not yet been coined, these three men actually comprised the nucleus of the first A.A. group. In the fall of 1935, a second group of alcoholics slowly took place in New York. A third appeared at Cleveland in 1939. It had taken over four years to produce 100 sober alcoholics in the three founding groups.

Early in 1939 the Fellowship published its basic textbook, *Alcoholics Anonymous*. The text, authored by Bill, explained A.A.'s philosophy and methods, the core of which was the now well-known Twelve Steps of recovery. The book was also reinforced by case histories of some thirty recovered members. From this point, A.A.'s growth was rapid.

Also in 1939, the Cleveland Plain Dealer carried a series of articles about A.A., supported by warm editorials. The Cleveland group of only twenty members was deluged by countless pleas for help. Alcoholics sober only a few weeks were set to work on brand new cases. This was a new departure, and the results were fantastic. A few months later Cleveland's membership had expanded to 500. For the first time, it was shown that sobriety could be mass produced.[6]

Meanwhile at New York Dr. Bob and Bill had in 1938 organized an overall trusteeship for the budding society. Friends of Mr. John D. Rockefeller, Jr., became board members alongside a contingent of A.A.s. This board was named the Alcoholic Foundation. However, all efforts to raise large amounts of money failed because Mr. Rockefeller had wisely concluded that great sums might spoil the infant society. Nevertheless the Foundation managed to open a tiny office in New York to handle inquiries and to distribute the A.A. book — an enterprise which, by the way, had been mostly financed by the A.A.s themselves.

The book and the new office were quickly put to use. An article about A.A. was carried by *Liberty* magazine in the fall of 1939, resulting in some 800 urgent calls for help. In 1940 Mr. Rockefeller gave a dinner for many of his prominent

New York friends to publicize A.A. This brought yet another flood of pleas. Each inquiry received a personal letter and a small pamphlet. Attention was also drawn to the book, *Alcoholics Anonymous*, which soon moved into brisk circulation. Aided by mail from New York, and by A.A. travellers from already established centers, many new groups came alive. At the year end, the membership stood at 2,000.

Then in March, 1941, the *Saturday Evening Post* featured an excellent article about A.A. (by Jack Alexander) and the response was enormous. By the close of that year, the membership had jumped to 6,000 and the number of groups multiplied in proportion. Spreading across the U.S. and Canada, the Fellowship mushroomed.

By 1950, 100,000 recovered alcoholics could be found world-wide. Spectacular though this was, the period 1940-1950 was nonetheless one of great uncertainty. The crucial question was whether all those mercurial alcoholics could live and work together in groups. Could they hold together and function effectively — this was the unsolved problem. Corresponding with thousands of groups about their problems became a chief occupation of the New York headquarters.

By 1946, however, it had already become possible to draw sound conclusions about the kinds of attitude, practice and function that would best suit A.A.s purpose. Those principles, which had emerged from strenuous group experience, were codified by Bill in what are today the Twelve Traditions of Alcoholics Anonymous. By 1950 the earlier chaos had largely disappeared. A successful formula for A.A. unity and functioning had been achieved and put into practice. [See *Fact File*, section 3.]

During this hectic ten-year period, Dr. Bob devoted himself to the question of hospital care for alcoholics, and to their indoctrination with A.A. principles. Large numbers of alcoholics flocked to Akron to receive hospital care at St. Thomas, a Catholic hospital. Dr. Bob became a member of its staff. Subsequently he and the remarkable Sister M. Ignatia, also of the staff, cared for and brought A.A. to some 5,000 sufferers. After Dr. Bob's death in 1950, Sister Ignatia continued the work at Cleveland's Charity Hospital, where she was assisted by the local groups and where 10,000 more sufferers first found A.A. This set a fine example of hospitalization wherein A.A. could cooperate with both medicine and religion.

In the same year of 1950, A.A. held its first international convention at Cleveland, and there Dr. Bob made his last appearance and keyed his final talk to the need of keeping A.A. simple. Together with all present, he saw the Twelve Traditions of Alcoholics Anonymous enthusiastically adopted for the

Alcoholism : Treatable Illness

permanent use of the A.A. Fellowship throughout the world.

The following year, 1951, witnessed still another significant event. The New York office had greatly expanded its activities, and these now consisted of public relations, advice to new groups, services to hospitals and prisons, loners and internationalists and cooperation with other agencies in the alcoholism field. The headquarters was also publishing standard A.A. books and pamphlets, and it supervised their translation into other tongues. An international magazine, "The A.A. Grapevine," achieved a large circulation. These and many other activities had become indispensable for A.A. as a whole.

Nevertheless, these vital services were still in the hands of an isolated board of trustees, whose only links to the Fellowship were Bill and Dr. Bob, and they were perishable. Therefore, it had become absolutely necessary to link A.A.'s world trusteeship (now the General Service Board of Alcoholics Anonymous) with the Fellowship that it served. Delegates from all states and provinces of the U.S. and Canada were immediately called in. Thus composed, this body for world service first met in 1951. Despite earlier misgivings, the gathering was a great success. For the first time, the remote trusteeship became directly accountable to A.A. as a whole. The A.A. General Service Conference had been created, and A.A.'s overall functioning was thereby assured for the future.

A second international convention was held in St. Louis in 1955 to celebrate the movement's 20th anniversary. The General Service Conference had by then completely proven its worth. Here on behalf of A.A.'s old timers, Bill turned the future and custody of A.A. over to the Conference and its trustees. At this moment, the Fellowship went on its own; A.A. had come of age.

During the past decades, A.A. has become truly global and has revealed that A.A.'s way of life can transcend most barriers of race, creed and language.

Had it not been for A.A.'s early friends, the movement might never have come into being. And without its host of well-wishers who have since given of their time and effort — particularly those friends of medicine, religion and of world communications — A.A. could never have grown and prospered. The Fellowship here records its constant gratitude.

Alcoholics Anonymous celebrated its 25th anniversary in July 1960 at the international convention held in Long Beach, California. The 30th anniversary and international convention was held in Toronto, Canada, in July of 1965. The 35th anniversary and international convention was held in Miami Beach, Florida, on July 3 - 5, 1970. The 40th anniversary and international convention was held in Denver, Colorado, on July 3, 1975. The 45th anniversary and international convention was held in New Orleans, Louisiana, in July 1980. The 50th anniversary and international convention was held in Montreal in 1985. The 55th anniversary and international convention was slated to be held in Seattle, Washington, in July of 1990.

230

Membership

Late in 1989 there were over 1,500,000 members in approximately 45,000 groups in over 100 countries throughout the world. Comprising both men and women, the membership is representative of every race and creed, and every social, professional and economic walk of life. Currently it would appear that A.A. is again evidencing a marked upsurge in membership.

It is virtually impossible to estimate accurately the total numbers of individuals who have found lasting recovery through the A.A. Fellowship. An impressively large number, having found personal sobriety, become relatively inactive, hence are no longer counted as acknowledged group members. This is compounded as the Fellowship grows by the very informality of organizational structure which is unique in itself. The membership (including active and nonactive members) probably is two or even more times greater than those acknowledged in recorded groups. This group registry is a numerical record only; no name listing is maintained, thus respecting the anonymity of individual members. Group secretaries simply submit the information that there are X number of people in that group, from which the membership total is estimated.

As the A.A. fellowship is known, at least by name, by most people everywhere, and is as available as the local phone book, it is the most practical means available whereby progress and continuing follow-up may be maintained for alcoholic patients.

Organizational Structure

Organizationally, A.A. is a very loosely knit structure. Members associate themselves with a "home group." A few may attend more than one group; where no group exists, individual members carry on as "loners." There are many kinds of groups: closed, open, family, home and discussion. The group usually has a secretary and/or a group representative. To better describe the group representation, communication and service supervision, we draw the following from a Fellowship pamphlet on A.A. Service Structure:

1. Each local group designates a General Service Representative (G.S.R.) who serves as a link to A.A. Worldwide Service Agencies.

2. At area assemblies, group representatives select an area committee and designate a delegate (and alternate) to the Annual Conference.

3. At the Conference Meeting, which meets yearly at G.S.O. in New York, delegates from all A.A. areas in U.S. and Canada meet with the Board of Trustees and General Service Staff (also members of the conference).

4. A board of Trustees, responsive to Conference advisory actions is entrusted with integrity and continuity of A.A. service agencies.[7]

In Alcoholics Anonymous there are no leaders as such. Members filling a position of service carry the role of "trusted servants."

Alcoholism: Treatable Illness

The program of Alcoholics Anonymous is presented as three Legacies, namely Recovery, Unity and Service. A quote from the A.A. publication, *Partners in A.A.*, interprets these three Legacies:

The First Legacy is expressed in the 'Twelve Suggested Steps' for PERSONAL Recovery.

The Second Legacy has been defined in the 'Twelve Traditions' for GROUP Survival.

The Third Legacy is the structure for assuring continuity of A.A. SERVICE to alcoholics world-wide. Since 1950, this structure has been in the form of the General Service Conference of A.A. through which [each] group and others in [that] area share responsibility for the future of the movement.

Alcoholics Anonymous at Work

The philosophy and principles, as incorporated in the Twelve Suggested Steps of Recovery of the First Legacy, are the heart of the A.A. program. These steps are:

1. We admitted we were powerless over alcohol — that our lives had become unmanageable.

2. Came to believe that a power greater than ourselves could restore us to sanity.

3. Made a decision to turn our will and our lives over to the care of God as *we understood Him.*

4. Made a searching and fearless moral inventory of ourselves.

5. Admitted to God, to ourselves and to another human being the exact nature of our wrongs.

6. Were entirely ready to have God remove all these defects of character.

7. Humbly asked Him to remove our shortcomings.

8. Made a list of all persons we had harmed and became willing to make amends to them all.

9. Made direct amends to such people wherever possible, except when to do so would injure them or others.

10. Continued to take personal inventory and when we were wrong promptly admitted it.

11. Sought through prayer and meditation to improve our conscious contact with God as *we understood Him*, praying only for knowledge of His will for us and the power to carry that out.

12. Having had a spiritual awakening as the result of these steps, we tried to carry this message to alcoholics, and to practice these principles in all our affairs.[8]

The Twelve Steps do work for many if not most alcoholics. Those who do apply them in their total form and who do learn to live the "Way of Life" embodied within all of the Steps, will achieve recovery and sobriety. In fact, these principles have been applied by many with problems other than that of alcoholism, with gratifying success.

The precepts which members of Alcoholics Anonymous exercise with all related services and their philosophy on outside issues are defined in their Twelve Traditions. These traditions reflect A.A.'s past relationships with others, and the trial and error experience of thousands of groups in many countries, over a period of more than five decades. They are the basis of the informal but stable structure that has enabled the Fellowship to carry the A.A. message convincingly to the many thousands of alcoholics who have sought their help. The traditions apply equally among members and their groups, and with the outside world. These Twelve Traditions are:

1. Our common welfare should come first; personal recovery depends upon A.A. unity.

2. For our group purpose there is but one ultimate authority — a loving God as He may express Himself in our group conscience. Our leaders are but trusted servants; they do not govern.

3. The only requirement for A.A. membership is a desire to stop drinking.

4. Each group should be autonomous except in matters affecting other groups or A.A. as a whole.

5. Each group has but one primary purpose — to carry its message to the alcoholic who still suffers.

6. An A.A. group ought never endorse, finance or lend the A.A. name to any related facility or outside enterprise, lest problems of money, property and prestige divert us from our primary purpose.

7. Every A.A. group ought to be fully self-supporting, declining outside contributions.

8. Alcoholics Anonymous should remain forever nonprofessional, but our service centers may employ special workers.

9. A.A., as such, ought never be organized, but we may create service boards or committees directly responsible to those they serve.

10. Alcoholics Anonymous has no opinion on outside issues; hence the A.A. name ought never be drawn into public controversy.

11. Our public relations policy is based on attraction rather than promotion; we need always maintain personal anonymity at the level of press, radio and films.

12. Anonymity is the spiritual foundation of all our traditions, ever reminding us to place principles before personalities.

It is important to realize the full portent of these Traditions, as one is confronted at times by extremists who presume to authoritatively represent Alcoholics Anonymous as a movement per se.

Alcoholism: Treatable Illness

While the Fellowship has always sincerely urged to the membership the concept of cooperation and the non-involvement of A.A. on outside issues, A.A. is no different from any other association of people. It has its share of minority members whose irresponsible actions detract from the effective role Alcoholics Anonymous plays. A few opportunists have used such individual provocations for unjust and all-encompassing destructive criticism of the movement, by allowing the adverse actions of a few mavericks to reflect upon the really fine accomplishments of the Fellowship as a whole.

The Fellowship is well aware that cultists help cause controversy and confusion. They repel potential members desperately in need of help and are responsible for retarding cooperative programming with other treatment resources. Though non-alcoholic neophytes, both lay and professional, do create similar problems, the recovered alcoholic in Alcoholics Anonymous has a further responsibility. The A.A. member in any position of service is accountable for measuring up to the precepts suggested by the Traditions of Alcoholics Anonymous and has the obligation to show, by personal example, a respect and appreciation of the efforts of others on behalf of the alcoholic.

Potential new members, treatment resources, collaterals and the public are often confused by the individualism of members and groups, as each A.A. group operates as a separate entity and with complete autonomy. While the traditions are not binding on any group or individual, they do recommend the course to be taken by members in working with others to provide continuing and progressive service to those alcoholics who still suffer.

An eminent psychiatrist and a good friend of A.A., in a talk to an anniversary gathering of Alcoholics Anonymous Home Groups, expressed these thoughts. Taking as the topic of his discourse "A.A. — Remedy or Disease," the doctor interpreted the A.A. Twelve Steps of Recovery as he saw them. He paid high tribute to the accomplishments of most members of Alcoholics Anonymous. However, he warned against the extremists and cultists who practice only the first of the Twelve Steps without choosing to apply the finer principles of all of the other Steps to their lives. He was concerned by those who were content with joining A.A. and who, though they stayed abstinent from alcohol, never learned to live the way of life that A.A. can provide. Perhaps the enigma of Alcoholics Anonymous to many "outsiders" is that A.A. does work — often under seemingly hopeless circumstances — and sometimes, too, in spite of some of its own members! The fact that all of these people, who represent so many types and problems, get along as well as they do is in itself a miracle.

In the beginning, Alcoholics Anonymous primarily attracted members who had suffered severely. Older in age and defensive about their new-found recovery process, they rebuffed many who seemed too young or unhurt to qualify as alcoholics. As the Fellowship grew and became stable, A.A. began to draw more and more young people and those much less damaged by their alcoholism. As such members entered A.A., the older leaders' influence lessened. However, as A.A. continued its dramatic expansion, a need for some form of intercommunication and cooperative direction became apparent, necessitating a service structure to meet these demands. A few self-righteous ones came out of retirement to reassert seniority. Unable to let go or appreciate the progressive changes in the whole alcoholism field, they seriously affected the outlook of the followers who continued to expound their attitudes and narrow viewpoints. Representations of this small core sometimes disillusion and repel alcoholics requesting help from A.A., while disenchanting "counsellors" seeking to work cooperatively with A.A.

The vice-president and personnel manager of an organization called an A.A. central office requesting information for an old friend and key employee. He was told there was nothing he could do. If the man wanted help, he could call the A.A. office for himself!

A clergyman, who had worked closely with A.A. for years in one parish, called the office in his new locale. Wishing to meet a few recovered alcoholics whom he might use as contacts and sponsors for members of his congregation, he was told this was against A.A.'s tradition of anonymity, and that he should send his parishioners to such and such an open meeting, on such a night at such a time.

The supervisor of a welfare agency, concerned with the problem drinking situations she encountered, visited an A.A. office. After being impolitely briefed on her inadequacies as an alcoholism counsellor, she resolutely sought a few personal contacts by attending open A.A. meetings. Though "the Fellowship" of Alcoholics Anonymous advocates, "Let's be friendly with our friends," such adverse experiences lose both friends and patients. In the long run, it is the sick alcoholic who continues to suffer, and is pushed away from treatment and A.A.

Much of this injudicious conflict stems from myths propounded by an ill-advised minority who claim: "Only an alcoholic knows when another is ready for help. Only a 'true' alcoholic deserves help," and the like. These pompous declarations deter the development of sound public relations with outside resources, whose support A.A. has long needed and endeavoured to attract. Happily these problems are resolving themselves.

More and more alcoholics are finding recovery through alcoholism treatment centers and are being referred for help through the many counselling sources discussed earlier. As many as 50% of all new referrals to A.A. today come via treatment centers. These alcoholics seeking help today are much more representative of the problem drinking population — in terms of percentages, fewer and fewer are from skid row. These patients are usually referred to Alcoholics Anonymous for aftercare. The growing number of such referrals is developing an A.A. membership which is more stable and better informed about the illness alcoholism than its predecessors.

During earlier days, some "old timers" felt threatened by the ever expanding influx of "high bottom" members who still retained more personal assets, family and economic, social and vocational positions. Contrary to the principles of recovery, such unwarranted fears helped to maintain the stereotyped image of the alcoholic as the derelict and misfit of old.

While the confusion and discord which these few defensive isolationist members created may have caused some to drop away from A.A., the more stable and sober members simply sought greater peace and anonymity in other open, closed or home-type groups. It is in this latter setting that the vast majority of A.A. members worked, grew and prospered. These sounder, less critical and more cooperative members continue to build up the reputation of Alcoholics Anonymous as living, totally recovered examples of what the Fellowship can do and is truly accomplishing.

Much if not all the credit for improved attitudes within the Fellowship of A.A. is due to the exemplary efforts of the late co-founder Bill W. and to Dr. John L. Norris, formerly the Medical Director of Eastman Kodak and the non-alcoholic Chairman of the Board of Trustees of A.A., and to the instigation of an effective public information program by A.A. public service officers. "Dr. Jack," as he was belovedly known, laboured world-wide to orient A.A. members, the professions and society per se about alcoholism and the role of A.A.

Smaller "closed" groups are in fact a return to the original form of A.A. meeting and sponsorship, held in homes or private settings where members met in an anonymous, protected and warmer environment. As each group became too large to rotate meetings within its circle of homes, new groups were formed. To many, these are still the most effective therapy medium, as they try to achieve the total well-being of both the alcoholic and those closest to him or her. As the membership grew, central meeting places, clubs and other types of structured assemblies came about. Each type of setting fills the needs of the varied membership, and for the most part each group does recognize and respect the others' prerogatives.

It must ever be borne in mind that many of those individuals who from time to time were controversial have rendered contributions to other alcoholics and to Alcoholics Anonymous that are immeasurable. These members worked arduously to establish A.A. itself and devoted their very lives to helping others to sobriety. While they are often criticized for their inability to keep apace or to accept change, nothing can ever be taken from the service they rendered or the accomplishments they achieved. Nor is this a contradiction of any impersonal evaluation of A.A. itself, not at all. It is a clear cut realization that alcoholics are, after all, human beings too — perhaps more so than most other people! As such, they manifest the same individuality of thought and action, the same contrariness and perversity as all of us. Therefore they, too, include some bad with the good.

There are two sides to this coin. Few counsellors in this field know of or realize the hardship and struggles early A.A. members endured. Not too many years ago alcoholics were rejected by all. Doctors and hospitals could not or would not treat them; the clergy threw up their hands in despair; health agencies and institutions ignored them; families disowned them; of necessity, they were their own doctors and counsellors in every phase of their illness. The bitterness of this rejection is still vivid in the minds of many who suffered the indignities of their fellow men during their illness.

Many early A.A. members vividly recall a cure as being a jail sentence — hard work and fresh air and a straitjacket in D.T.s. To ask for a glass of water was to have it thrown in one's face by an ignorant orderly. A job, when one was offered, took the form of a shovel or a broom. A bed, perhaps even from one's own family, was a pad on a basement floor. The reasons for bitterness are long and many. Small wonder that distrust and resentment still hold forth in some "old timers" and their disciples.

Now, finally, in winning their battle to have alcoholism recognized as a treatable illness, these A.A. members see themselves set aside, ignored and considered dedicated eccentrics. They quite properly resent the label of "second class citizen" from professional workers, knowing A.A. must play a role in the continued care of alcoholics where other services leave off. Perhaps alcoholics are supersensitive, but they do know when a counsellor or worker is sincere or honest. They sense empathy and antipathy both, and they soon spot the phonies. After all, they have been learning to defend themselves and exist in a hostile world ever since the onset of their illness.

It's true that in Alcoholics Anonymous members strive for position and recognition, just as people do in every setting. But for the membership, alcohol is thicker than blood. As "bottle gangs" protect each other on skid row, as fellow sufferers hide and save face together in the upper strata, so too do recovered alcoholics find sobriety, security and strength together. Some fear new methods, seeing them as potentially abusive rather than beneficial and fearing that their dignity will be lost in the recovery process if a simplicity of recovery is replaced with a complexity of labels. This is not greatly different from the distrust that still sometimes exists between general practitioners and psychiatrists, or between social workers and psychologists, and between administrators and medical or social science personnel. Most people — including professionals — have some fear of change and progress.

My own recovery from alcoholism was the end result of a team effort including the finest of medical care, a knowledgeable chaplain, the faith of a devoted sister, and the diligent support of understanding friends. For me, prayer and the grace of God melded these efforts into eventual sobriety. Still, I remember only too well the complexity of relationships existing among all concerned. I can recall back in 1938 being told I was not an alcoholic and that I should "lay off the hard stuff"; in 1939 I was told I was too young and too unhurt by the ravages of alcohol to be a "true alcoholic" or to be ready for help. Granted, I was then only twenty-eight years of age, still possessing family, job and most of the material things of life. Notwithstanding, I knew I had a problem and sought medical and other aid. No one faced me with my true condition, though I was often hurt by those who took every opportunity to ridicule my alcoholism.

Introducing the New Member

In referring an alcoholic to the Fellowship of Alcoholics Anonymous it is well to point out that he or she will not necessarily like the same people or places, or agree with the same things said or done. It is therefore sound practice to suggest that the alcoholic participate in several types of meetings. In this way, one can be induced to seek out an A.A. setting in which each feels comfortable and at home. Wherever possible, it is well to ask the patient's permission to have members of A.A. call at home to initiate the potential new member into the routine of their particular group and program. This serves a double purpose. It acquaints the new person with the Fellowship generally and with a member or two personally.

An alcoholic's first introduction is the most critical A.A. contact. Initial reception and reaction can be a start on the road to sobriety and a fuller, better life — or it can be a return to the disastrous insecurity of continued dependency. The new man or woman is the most important person in attendance at any meeting, and all those present have a responsibility to help that new member determine a better choice.

Important to a new patient's introduction is the old-fashioned idea of a sponsor. Nothing works quite so well for an alcoholic as to have some one person upon whom to lean, and as a guide through the initial contacts and steps. As the alcoholic's recovery progresses, he or she may change sponsors to find another A.A. member particularly compatible to his or her likes and needs. *Sound sponsorship is not only one of the best means of introducing a patient to Alcoholics Anonymous, but is also one of the preventatives used to help the patient avoid a relapse*. Many effective treatment resources try wherever possible to introduce patients to individual recovered alcoholics active in A.A. before their departure. This insures an effective aftercare and follow-up program and a sound introduction to Alcoholics Anonymous groups. Groups vary. Some are affable, have greeting committees, arrange sponsorship, and go all out to attract and hold a new member. Small groups encourage greater individual participation. Large groups may offer the reticent person a chance to listen and be anonymous. Most larger communities have groups suitable to any alcoholic's wants and needs. As a worker in this field, I have had occasion to see all these forces in action; somehow, they all do work, though certainly some achieve more success than others.

Alcoholics Anonymous has two factors at work that serve to keep individual members under control. Firstly, every individual member has hanging over his or her head a personal "Sword of Damocles" — the knowledge of what that first drink can do: trigger a return to pathological drinking.

Secondly, though one or two (or even several) A.A.s can get off-base, even become controversial to everyone about them, eventually their group will correct and resolve the issue. The whole group will not stay irresponsible indefinitely.

Alcoholics Anonymous does provide almost miraculous recovery for many presumed "hopeless cases." Because of the respect and acceptance it has acquired through the recovery of those who had no other source of referral or recourse, the Fellowship sometimes finds it difficult to live up to the responsibility of the reputation it enjoys. As a result, A.A. has been set apart and relegated to a special position of esteem — sometimes, in the case of new members or groups, before complete maturity and stability has been attained in all activities or within all of the groups and membership. New groups in smaller cities and rural areas suffer some of the same growing pains today that those in older established areas suffered years ago. Nevertheless, the movement as a whole is recognized and respected world-wide.

Though the relationship of Alcoholics Anonymous to outside organizations in the field of alcohol studies is widely known and respected, a few thoughts are pertinent here. The Fellowship of Alcoholics Anonymous reflects an ideology that is completely distinct from any other treatment resource. While the whole program of recovery in Alcoholics Anonymous is based on the simple set of Twelve suggested "Steps of Recovery" and its relationship with others is guided by the conservative set of Twelve "Traditions," the precepts contained in both Legacies are representative of deep and positive principles from the best in theology, medicine and the social sciences. The ideology of A.A. speaks for itself. It has made the field of alcoholism respectable and acceptable to the patient, spouse, family and collaterals, the professions and the general public. Above all, the Fellowship of

Alcoholism: Treatable Illness

Alcoholics Anonymous has convinced others to accept alcoholism as a treatable illness and stimulated action to finally cope with society's most neglected medical, legal, social and spiritual ailment. No other body can lay claim to achieving this goal.

Another element important to the effectiveness of the A.A. recovery is to be found in a precept vital to their existence: *the membership must ever be governed by principles over personalities*. There is a profound and positive maxim to be found in their Tradition of Anonymity, which is not merely a safeguarding of name; rather, it is a selfless gesture of giving, so as not to take undue credit for the precious gift of recovery.

In seeking out a possible reason for success that may be attributed to the Fellowship, one may conclude that at least part of the secret is encompassed within those innate qualities which A.A. re-instills: hope is regenerated; human dignity (the attribute by which all persons really live) is rekindled; and a grateful sense of humility and faith is reborn.

While seeking a way to sum up A.A. at work, I find no better grouping of thoughts than those expressed by the deceased co-founder of Alcoholics Anonymous, Dr. Bob, in his last talk presented to the International Conference of Alcoholics Anonymous at Cleveland, Ohio, in July 1950, which in part reads:

". . . there are two or three things that flashed into my mind on which it would be fitting to lay a little emphasis; one is the simplicity of our Program. Let's not louse it all up with Freudian complexes and things that are interesting to the scientific mind but have very little do with our actual A.A. work. Our 12 steps, when simmered down to the last, resolve themselves into the words 'love and service'. We understand what love is and we understand what service is. So let's bear those two things in mind.

" . . . Let us also remember to guard that erring member, the tongue, and if we must use it, let's use it with kindness and consideration and tolerance.

"And one more thing; none of us would be here today if somebody hadn't taken time to explain things to us, to give us a little pat on the back, to take us to a meeting or two, to have done numerous little kind and thoughtful acts in our behalf. So let us never get the degree of smug complacency so that we're not willing to extend, or attempt to extend, that help which has been so beneficial to us, to our less fortunate brothers . . . "

Perhaps all of these principles and facets of recovery that are Alcoholics Anonymous are reflected best of all in the simple prayer used by their membership, in meditation, in time of personal need, and collectively when the chairman of most meetings calls the group to order and says: "Shall we open (or close) our meeting in the usual manner?" In unison, the hearts of all present ring out:

GOD grant me the SERENITY
To accept the things I cannot change,
COURAGE to change the things I can,
And WISDOM to know the difference.

Al-Anon Family Groups

During the initial years of development from 1935 to 1940 the membership of Alcoholics Anonymous was composed almost entirely of men. Those wives who were still hopefully hanging on to their husbands were quite naturally drawn together. As the men struggled to grasp sobriety in their new Fellowship of Alcoholics Anonymous, the wives — while cooperating as best they could — learned at the same time to sustain each other by discussing and seeking solutions to their own common problems.

In so doing, they founded an auxiliary which was to become the Al-Anon Family Group movement and which is now as appealing, active and widespread as A.A. Sharing and aiding throughout those initial years was the late beloved and inimitable first lady of Al-Anon, Lois, wife of Bill W., the late co-founder of A.A.

Following publication of Jack Alexander's article in *The Saturday Evening Post* in 1941, A.A. experienced a dramatic expansion. The article, by introducing the work of the fledgling membership of Alcoholics Anonymous to the public at large, called attention to the remarkable success being achieved through A.A. and offered a practical ray of hope to the suffering alcoholic. New members flocked in, and new groups developed and spread. At the end of the war the informal auxiliaries also began to grow; by 1950 there were perhaps fifty wives' groups. A central contact clearing-house service of volunteers was initiated early in 1952 in New York to register and assist both the activated groups and those requesting aid to form new ones.

Between 1954 and 1955, the original Clearing House Committee was incorporated as a nonprofit body, to be known as The Al-Anon Family Group Headquarters, Inc., with offices in New York. By the end of 1955, 660 groups had been listed, and the number grew to over 1,500 by 1960. By 1990, there were approximately 20,000 Al-Anon Family Groups worldwide (including Alateen) in over seventy countries with approximately 275,000 members.

Similar to Alcoholics Anonymous, Al-Anon is self-sustaining and neither seeks nor accepts contributions. While they follow the "Twelve Steps" of the A.A. program in seeking recovery from the effects of alcoholism in their own lives, they have adapted the "Twelve Traditions" to their special needs and principles. These are:

241

Alcoholism: Treatable Illness

1. Our common welfare should come first; personal progress for the greatest number depends upon unity.

2. For our group purpose there is but one authority — a loving God as He may express Himself in our group conscience. Our leaders are but trusted servants — they do not govern.

3. The relatives of alcoholics, when gathered together for mutual aid, may call themselves an Al-Anon Family Group, provided that, as a group, they have no other affiliation. The only requirement for membership is that there be a problem of alcoholism in a relative or friend.

4. Each group should be autonomous, except in matters affecting another group or Al-Anon and A.A. as a whole.

5. Each Al-Anon Family Group has but one purpose: to help families of alcoholics. We do this by practicing the Twelve Steps of A.A. ourselves, by encouraging and understanding our alcoholic relatives, and by welcoming and giving comfort to families of alcoholics.

6. Our Family Groups ought never to endorse, finance, or lend our name to any outside enterprise, lest problems of money, property, and prestige divert us from our primary spiritual aim. Although a separate entity, we should always cooperate with Alcoholics Anonymous.

7. Every group ought to be fully self-supporting, declining outside contributions.

8. Al-Anon Twelfth Step work should remain forever non-professional, but our service centers may employ special workers.

9. Our groups, as such, ought never be organized; but we may create service centers or committees directly responsible to those they serve.

10. The Al-Anon Family Groups have no opinion on outside issues; hence our name ought never be drawn into public controversy.

11. Our public relations policy is based on attraction rather than promotion; we need always maintain personal anonymity at the level of press, radio, T.V. and films. We need guard with special care the anonymity of all A.A. members.

12. Anonymity is the spiritual foundation of all our Traditions, ever reminding us to place principles above personalities.

As A.A. attracted women members, family groups also attracted non-alcoholic male spouses, as well as parents, brothers and sisters, and even friends of alcoholics. All recognized a need to understand alcoholism. This applies as well to the children of alcoholics, out of whose need grew the Alateen groups.

The membership of Al-Anon is best described by quoting in full the introduction to one of their official publications, *"Living with an Alcoholic with the Help of Al-Anon"*:

> The Al-Anon Family Groups are a fellowship of wives, husbands, relatives and friends of members of Alcoholics Anonymous and of problem drinkers

generally. Members of Al-Anon are banded together to solve their common problems of fear, insecurity, lack of understanding of the alcoholic, and of the warped family relationships associated with alcoholism.

The message of the Al-Anon Family Groups is a story of hope. It is the story of men and women who once felt helpless and powerless to deal with the alcoholism of their loved ones. Today these men and women no longer feel lost or lonely. They have learned that there are simple things they can do directly to help themselves and indirectly to help their alcoholic partners.

Many who are now members of Family Groups have already seen their loved ones achieve sobriety, but they have found that life with a sober alcoholic can present special problems of adjustment. Others still have active problem drinkers in their homes. All of them need the fellowship which Al-Anon affords.[9]

The working program of Al-Anon Family Groups may be interpreted by quoting two excerpts from one of their official publications. These excerpts, which precede and follow their applications of the A.A. Twelve Steps of Recovery, are:

. . . base their lives squarely upon the Twelve Steps of Alcoholics Anonymous. Although these steps were originally designed for alcoholics, it has been found that they offer a solution for most of the problems of daily living.

and

The only change necessary to make these A.A. steps completely applicable to ourselves is the substitution of "others" for the word "alcoholics" in the last step. Notice that even the phrase, "We admitted we were powerless over alcohol," is appropriate to the partner of the alcoholic, too. For certainly we nonalcoholics were powerless to help our husbands, wives or friends to control alcohol. To us, as to them, alcohol was an over-powering problem.[10]

It is noteworthy to emphasize that Al-Anon provides a resource of continued assistance for those close to an alcoholic *whether or not the alcoholic patient stops drinking.* Having seen the effectiveness of Al-Anon therapy with the spouses and children of many alcoholics, one may appreciate better the important contribution a Family Group makes in assisting those who must live with the tragedy of this illness in their homes.

The growth of Al-Anon was not without its problems. There are many A.A. members who still resent Al-Anon activities as prying into their affairs and who look upon these groups as gossip circles. Certainly this can happen. However, whenever groups are organized in accordance with the precepts and structure suggested by their headquarters — and when they follow the principles of their traditions — such issues are not a problem. Al-Anon members are urged to tell their story, not that of the alcoholic. Each group, like A.A., is autonomous and follows many divergent patterns in running its own meetings and affairs.

Alcoholism: Treatable Illness

Al-Anon's services are supervised by an annually elected board of trustees. Similar to Alcoholics Anonymous, delegates from the U.S. and Canada are elected on an area basis, meeting annually with their board of trustees and headquarters staff. Though there is an emotionally close kinship to Alcoholics Anonymous, Al-Anon never was, and is not today in any way related organizationally to the A.A. Fellowship.

The Al-Anon Family Groups hold no opinion on outside issues. The group is not a religious, temperance, social service, employment or welfare agency. It does not prescribe treatment for the alcoholic, nor improperly endanger the anonymity of the alcoholic. While Al-Anon members may feel that Alcoholics Anonymous offers a solution to the recovery and sobriety of the alcoholic, they also recognize and utilize the resources and facilities of such professional agencies as are available to them.

In many instances much of the credit for the initial care and sponsorship provided to women alcoholics as early members of Alcoholics Anonymous came about through the assistance of wives and Al-Anon members. The knowledge and principles which they had learned both for their personal benefit, and to enable them to play a more functional role for their recovering spouses, provided them with the awareness and understanding necessary to cope with the special problems of women alcoholics.

In the early days, it was not easy for problem-drinking women to hurdle deep-rooted fears and prejudices directed to them in their illness, nor for them to overcome their own fears and embarrassment. At the same time, A.A. men were often reluctant to get involved with potential women members for a variety of reasons. In a small or new community this can pose awkward and difficult problems for female alcoholics requiring A.A. therapy. Well-oriented wives of A.A. members and Al-Anon groups can bridge the gap for new female alcoholic members by providing personal and social contact. In this way they are accepted and have the opportunity to learn what programming is all about. Al-Anon women members help educate the non-alcoholic husband to acquire and accept his responsibility in assisting and cooperating with the recovery of the alcoholic wife.

The spouse or family of an alcoholic may be reticent about seeing a public agency, but might be willing to talk to another person with the same problem. Here again, the principle of team work among all collateral and counsellor referral sources, the doctor, the priest or minister, the social service worker and others can be brought to play an effective role. The Al-Anon member, as a vital component of the recovery team, becomes able and willing to cooperate.

As with A.A., while most alcoholism counsellors and agencies are generally aware of the resources of Al-Anon, they are not as familiar with these Family

Groups as they should be. For this reason, most counsellors and workers in the field do not use this resource as much as they should in providing help and follow-up support for non-alcoholic family members. Al-Anon Family Groups are available in most communities. Where they don't exist the Al-Anon Headquarters will, on request, assist in their development.

Anyone related to problem drinking situations — spouse, family members, doctors, clergymen and alcoholism agency personnel — should procure and study the Al-Anon Family Group publications. Again, as with A.A. materials, these are available in several languages. This will enable those concerned with alcoholics to derive mutual and reciprocal benefits. In communities where Al-Anon Family Groups do not exist, any of the previously mentioned collaterals, with direction, can stimulate the development of this splendid service for alcoholics and those closest to them.

Alateen

As the effectiveness of Al-Anon Family Groups spread, young adults were exposed to the benefits these provided. Children accompanying their parents both to A.A. and to Al-Anon Group meetings learned to understand and accept the various facets of the illness and how to cope with them better.

Some children of alcoholics, still embarrassed and distrustful, and not easily relating to adults, are more willing to seek and accept advice and understanding from their own contemporaries — and thus Alateen came into being about 1957. Alateen Groups, sponsored by the Al-Anon Family Groups, number about 3,000 by 1990. Their precepts and principles being similar, their services are guided by the Al-Anon Family Groups Headquarters. Alateen is in no way officially related to Alcoholics Anonymous; however, it may and does use both A.A. and Al-Anon members as advisors and counsellors.

Young adults, by learning a new image for the alcoholic, may thus come to appreciate that their fathers or mothers, though respectable business persons or professionals (or as others in responsible positions), can be alcoholics. This knowledge and understanding, when associated with a sound Alateen group, provides a therapeutic tool to deal better with young people's problems. More importantly, it may be an instrument by which the alcoholic parent is finally reached.

Alateens are beginning to play a particularly important role in those communities where alcohol education is emphasized both at community and academic levels. Again the many collateral counsellors and alcoholism agency workers can draw upon this excellent resource to deal with individual problem drinking situations. Many alcoholic parents have been drawn into treatment through the aid of concerned, interested and aware young adults.

These groups, growing at an amazing rate, incorporate young people generally between the ages of twelve and twenty and are divided into appropriate age levels. Alateen groups are a vital and recognized service for the related non-alcoholic. Literature and direction pertinent to their structure and activities is available through the Al-Anon Family Groups Headquarters, Inc.

Notes

1. Though it is important for the alcoholic patient, the spouse, family and all collaterals to be fully aware of the many strengths of this splendid Fellowship, this section concerns itself primarily with the relationship of Alcoholics Anonymous to the patient and those closest to him. A second book, *Practical Alcoholism Programming*, deals more directly with the relationship of A.A. to workers in the field and counsellors per se.

2. *A.A. Grapevine*, "The Preamble" — with permission.

3. A new book now in process of completion takes up the history from *Alcoholics Anonymous Comes of Age* to its current status.

4. *A.A. Fact File — Historical Data*. Reprinted with permission of the Directors of A.A. World Services, Inc.

5. Both Bill W. and Dr. Bob S. are now deceased: Bill on Jan. 4, 1971, and Dr. Bob on Nov. 16, 1950.

6. It was also in 1939 that the first A.A. Group came to Dayton, Ohio. It was founded by the late Roy Shroyer, who became known to the author.

7. *Partners in A.A.* — reprinted with permission of the Directors of A.A. World Services, Inc.

8. *Twelve Steps and Twelve Traditions* — Reprinted with permission of the Directors of A.A. World Services, Inc.

9. *Living With An Alcoholic*. Quoted with permission of the publishers, Al-Anon Family Group Headquarters, Inc., 1966, a world clearing-house for serving the families of Alcoholics Anonymous, and other problem drinkers. P.O. Box 182, Madison Square Station, New York, New York 10159.

10. *Living With An Alcoholic*. Quoted with permission of the publishers, Al-Anon Family Group Headquarters, Inc., 1966, a world clearing-house for serving the families of Alcoholics Anonymous, and other problem drinkers. P.O. Box 182, Madison Square Station, New York, New York 10159.

23. *An Honorable Approach*

Three factors seriously impede an enlightened and positive approach to alcoholism: the ignorance which exists about alcoholics and their illness; our apparent inability, even unwillingness, to appreciate that anyone who uses beverage alcohol is a potential alcoholic, and existing general apathy to the misuse of alcohol beverages. The latter is intensified by society's acceptance of the deviant behaviour related to much of our so-called social drinking.

That alcoholism is an illness — a treatable illness — with greater potential for recovery than can be assured in most ailments, is being substantiated in every aware and intelligent community by an ever-increasing number of recoveries. It is not the purpose of this book to provide a manual on all the dynamics of therapy necessary to treating the alcoholic. It is its purpose to point up the need for an ever-improving and more imaginative and courageous approach than has been taken to date. It is emphasized that awareness, knowledge, understanding and acceptance will achieve a much more productive climate of operation; and that empathy toward the alcoholic as a person will continue to undo the ignorance, prejudice and emotionalism of the past.

Alcoholics, their families and their collaterals can be taught to rise above embarrassment and stigma to seek the help they need and to instigate effectively coercive measures with those alcoholics too sick to ask for help of their own volition. Family and collaterals close to the alcoholic can and should be guided to seek the advice and help they so urgently require.

While some people may drink beverage alcohol, as most should enjoy all of life's pleasures (in moderation), others involuntarily lose control and are the last to know why. Initially, it is not too important whether they drink because they are sick, or are sick because they drink. It is important that those who need and want understanding care do find it.

In my experience I have seen many alcoholics, as different from one another as people are everywhere, but who are very much alike in their illness and misery. There were once-intelligent, sensitive faces which alcoholism stripped of light and beat into immobile masks; there were the dull and blankly lost faces of those who

Alcoholism: Treatable Illness

had tried but failed to break the cycle of their alcoholic dependency. Each in turn required assistance; sick first, alcoholic incidentally. Some had other ills in common, malnutrition and deficiency diseases. Others were heir to illnesses of their own. Alcoholics are sick, not alone in their uncontrolled craving or dependence upon alcohol, but in the physical, mental, social and spiritual damage they suffer. These aspects of alcoholism make the illness a medical, legal, social and spiritual problem of immeasurable proportions — and as such, a private and public health problem and social responsibility demanding every priority. Solving this problem will bring about a general strengthening of our society.

Alcoholism is no single disease like tuberculosis or typhoid, each caused by an identifiable organism; it does not always take a recognizable course, though it does have typical symptoms and stages of progression. No single effective treatment can be prescribed for all patients. There are as many types of problem drinkers and alcoholisms as there are people. As human beings, sensitive to the agonies of others, we must understand that men and women who are uncontrollably and repeatedly seduced by alcohol cannot be held solely accountable for the misery and misfortune they heap upon themselves, their families and those associated with them. They are sick people in need of treatment. Assuredly, if the sinners are really to stand up and be counted, it is we, the so-called well ones, who permit their illness to go unattended.

As noted earlier in this text, the writer is a recovered alcoholic. I say this neither with chip on shoulder, nor with any false halo, but as a simple statement of fact. In spite of unrealistic claims to the contrary, science has certainly not as yet found a satisfactory pill or process to enable the alcoholic to return safely to social drinking. Therefore, though I may drink whenever I might wish to do so, a return to sane reasoning, coupled with the sounder judgment achieved over the years through sobriety, certainly suggests that *as an alcoholic I should not drink*. In light, too, of my own and others' experiences, I know that I shall die an alcoholic. However, I now have the choice and decision whether at the time of my demise, I am a sober alcoholic, or a practising "wet" one! These thoughts were better stated by an anonymous philosopher who in effect defined misery as "an abject submission to life," and happiness as "an enlightened acceptance of life."

Alcoholics, with the help of those about them and the guidance of aware, knowledgeable and understanding professional or lay associates, can achieve an enlightened acceptance of life.

As one of the lucky ones who learned in time as a young man that my illness, though incurable, could be arrested by treatment, I resolved in the late 30's and early 40's (when the road to recovery was neither pleasant nor gratifying) that there must be a way to help the "younger" alcoholic; to recognize and treat the female alcoholic as a sick person rather than as a sinful person; and to try to reach earlier those many more fortunate alcoholics still working, still with their families about them, and still enjoying the good things of life. This text is dedicated to their needs.

Alcoholism is an illness of the lonely. The alcoholic has been the most ignored and rejected of all the world's sick ones. I know of no more miserable existence than that of the alcoholic; alone, bewildered, frustrated, rejected by all and still idealistic, sensitive and needing the support of others. With all this generation has to offer, perhaps the greatest and most lasting contribution it may make is that it sought and found at least the beginning of a solution to alcoholism.

While western nations are generous in providing both private and public funds to the socially and economically handicapped peoples of the world, they have at home a problem which they have ignored and neglected beyond any other. It is an oversight that must be remedied before it steals more minds and bodies than can be replaced.

Many nations have recognized and responded to this internal peril more realistically than we have. They are publicly manifesting their concern and establishing national controls and services to combat the problems involved. The English-speaking nations choose to delay and to tamper with fate. Bacchus will eventually demand his due, and in the process humanity must suffer. This, all alcoholics learn.

Nor are prohibition, bigotry and ignorance the answer. We can no more close beverage alcohol outlets because we have alcoholism than we can close candy stores because we have diabetics. Most people drink and will continue to do so. Like death and taxes, this is a part of our way of life we cannot change. Therefore, we must learn to live with it properly. Temperance and moderation in its truest sense is the only solution, but achieving this is another matter entirely. We make a beginning as we become willing to be knowledgeable about the illness alcoholism.

Surely, too, we are as capable to deal with and as interested in the humanities as we are in technological advances. While it is gratifying to enjoy the ''highest living standards in the world,'' it is also important to recognize and to maintain that dignity and those ideals which brought North Americans to their present stature.

As discussed in a second book — *Practical Alcoholism Programming* — when public and professional recognition, response and acceptance through their expressed opinions demand concerted action, then and only then will control and eventual prevention become a reality. This will be as dramatic and effective as the movement a scant few decades ago to prevent polio. Today we see full-scale movements at work to combat cancer, heart disease and the hidden killer AIDS. Such total efforts will eventually succeed because they are based on an emotional demand to attain progressively successful results.

Alcoholism: Treatable Illness

The effect of alcohol on those who abuse it is recorded in earliest history. Measures of every extreme have been tried to control it, but always as a moral or social evil, and rarely as the manifestation of an illness in itself. Those who would still offer punitive judgment as the only answer might recall before pronouncing judgment that every person's Higher Power awaits his or her death. Sometimes we're lucky enough to be given some borrowed time to try again. How can we then take it upon ourselves to judge and condemn each other, especially if we believe in the essential dignity of every person?

If we believe these precepts, we must recognize alcoholics as people like ourselves and accept them as human beings deserving of our attention and care. By positive action we can respond to their needs. With such recognition, acceptance and response, we achieve an honorable approach to society's primary alcohol problem: alcoholism.

Appendix

Progressive Warning Symptoms

THE TWENTY QUESTION TEST [1]

Test yourself and answer these questions as honestly as you can about your personal use of beverage alcohol.

1. Do you lose time from work due to drinking?
2. Is drinking making your home life unhappy?
3. Do you drink because you are shy with other people?
4. Is drinking affecting your reputation?
5. Have you ever felt remorse after drinking?
6. Has your drinking caused financial difficulties?
7. When drinking, do you turn to lower companions and inferior places?
8. Does your drinking affect your family's welfare?
9. Has your ambition decreased since drinking?
10. Do you crave a drink at a definite time daily?
11. Do you want a drink the next morning?
12. Does drinking cause you difficulty in sleeping?
13. Has your efficiency decreased since drinking?
14. Is drinking jeopardizing your job or business?
15. Do you drink to escape from worries or trouble?
16. Do you drink alone?
17. Have you had memory losses because of drinking?
18. Has your physician ever treated you for drinking?
19. Do you drink to build up your self-confidence?
20. Have you ever been hospitalized because of drinking?

If you have answered "yes" to any one of the questions, there is a definite warning that you may be an alcoholic.

If you have answered "yes" to any two, the chances are that you are an alcoholic.

If you have answered "yes" to any three or more, you are definitely an alcoholic.

Are You An Alcoholic?

The Twenty Question test and a review of the symptoms experienced by the developing alcoholic may lead you, or someone close to you, to a personal decision.

Alcoholism: Treatable Illness

Being aware of the warning symptoms of alcoholism may enable the drinker to seek recovery as early as the first phase. Once into the second phase, the illness is confirmed. If not arrested, it will definitely progress into the third phase. Once the illness has reached the crucial phase, the alcoholic patient cannot stop alone. He or she, having lost control, is now drinking compulsively and must seek help to find recovery.

The symptoms do not follow in the same order for all drinkers. Both excessive and alcoholic drinkers may indicate similar symptoms; *the paramount difference is the involuntary loss of control in the amount, time, method and location of the drinking — in other words, the loss of the ability to drink according to intent.*

Pre-alcoholic and Premonitory Phase

1. You Drink Socially

You drink now and then with no particular pattern, purely for sociability, perhaps excessively on occasion. Most drinkers rarely go beyond this point.

2. Your Drinking is More Important to You

Needing a drink, you may sneak and gulp a few extra; you seek the extra support or comfort of alcohol. You become preoccupied with and dependent upon your drink rather than with the sociability involved. If you are disturbed by your kind of drinking or begin to drink more heavily to hide your discomfort, you are potentially an alcoholic.

3. Early Blackouts

Being more dependent on alcohol beverages, you may change to heavier drinking groups, get "high" on allowable occasions, though certain you can quit whenever you wish. Then you experience a frightening loss of memory, a major warning signal — the blackout.

Crucial Phase

4. Involuntary Loss of Control

While you may still control when you drink, once started you cannot control how much you drink. Your drinking behaviour indicates a change for the worse; it is noticeable to others; it is grandiose or extravagant. You now recognize a difference in your kind of drinking.

5. You Rationalize or Alibi Your Drinking

Feeling guilty and remorseful, you seek out or "trump up" reasons and excuses for your drinking; you become defensive; you project the blame on everyone and everything but your drinking, and you go underground. Your family, job and social relationships suffer; being worried, you may seek medical help.

6. Regular Pick-Up Drink

Perhaps you have already found the medicine in a morning drink, or one at a set time in the day, which you impatiently anticipate and wait for. Your need is now very apparent, even to you. This regular medicine brings you back to life, eases your conscience, provides false courage to face the day or problems at hand. This is no longer pleasurable or social drinking. Your dependence causes marked changes in your pattern of drinking — you drink alone, isolating yourself from your society.

Chronic Phase

7. Bender Drinking

At Point 4, you experienced involuntary loss of control of the amount you drink. Now your illness has progressed to the point that you experience an involuntary loss of control over when and how long you drink. This is the onset of the final phase. You are alcoholic. Your fears, guilt and remorse cause you to feel yourself a failure; your home and job are in jeopardy; you bitterly berate yourself; you hate what you have become and hide in the oblivion of a bender. You drink for intoxication and stay that way until your system gives out. Family, job, friends, personal care, food and shelter seem unimportant. Your drinking is completely out of control.

8. Alcohol Deterioration

Continued drinking is now your means of overcoming the effects of drinking. Your life is a nightmare revolving about alcohol. Remorse, resentment, self-abasement, aggression, defensiveness, all become intensified. You feel continuing anxieties, nameless fears; you may even consider suicide. Poor personal care brings about physical deterioration — the shakes, gags, sweats and the like. It takes less alcohol to knock you out; you guard your supply, as your need is obsessive. Drinking companions and places of drinking change and standards no longer matter. You are trapped.

9. Admission and Recovery

You may have admitted your problem earlier, but now you admit defeat. No longer do your alibis hold water. You are sick and tired of being sick and tired. Your drinking is different.

If your illness has progressed to this point, you need help. Perhaps the pleas and advice of others, or your own desperate needs, get through to you. Had you been able to quit, to do it alone, you would have done so long before now. Because you could not, don't know how to, or are even afraid to, you reject help. Voluntarily, or with the help of others, you must make a decision. Help is available. Why not seek it?

Notes

1. Taken from questions prepared by Dr. Robert B. Seliger for use at Johns Hopkins University Hospital, Baltimore, Md., and edited for use in this manuscript by the author, J. George Strachan.

Self-Help Resources

As a result of the success of the Fellowship of Alcoholics Anonymous, followed by the Al-Anon/Alateen Family Groups, a number of 'self-help' organizations quickly came into being, each suggesting measures by which to better cope with other dependencies and addictions — all modelled after and in large part using the Twelve Steps of Recovery developed by Alcoholics Anonymous. These organizations are:

Adult Children of Alcoholics
Central Services Board
P.O. Box 35623
Los Angeles, CA 90035
(213) 464-4423

Al-Anon/Alateen Family Group
Headquarters, Inc.
Madison Square Station
New York, New York 10010
(212) 683-1771

Alcoholics Anonymous World
Services, Inc.
468 Park Avenue South
New York, New York 10016
(212) 686-1100

Narcotics Anonymous
World Service Office
16155 Wyandotte Street
Van Nuys, CA 91406
(818) 780-3951

Nat'l Assoc. For
Children of Alcoholics
31706 Coast Highway, No. 201
South Laguna, CA 92677
(714) 499-3889

National Clearinghouse For
Alcohol Information
P.O. Box 1908
Rockville, Maryland 20850
(301) 468-2600

Debtors Anonymous
P.O. Box 20322
New York, N.Y. 10025-9992

National Council on
Alcoholism
12 West 21st Street
New York, New York 10010
(212) 206-6770

Emotions Anonymous
P.O. Box 4245
St. Paul, MN 55104

Overeaters Anonymous
World Service Office
2190 190th Street
Torrance, CA 90504
(213) 320-7941

Gamblers Anonymous
P.O. Box 17173
Los Angeles, CA 90017

Canadian Center on Substance Abuse
350 Sparks Street
Ottawa, Ontario
Canada K1R 7S8
(613) 235-4048

Alcoholics Anonymous and the Al-Anon Family Group are available and listed in every telephone book of every community in Canada and the United States. In addition to these major centers of contact, every province in Canada and every state in the United States, including Alaska and Hawaii, support and operate programs about which information is available locally.

Index